PROXIMITY TO
POWER

PROXIMITY TO
POWER

Rethinking Race and Place
in Alexandria, Virginia

Krystyn R. Moon

THE UNIVERSITY OF NORTH CAROLINA PRESS

Chapel Hill

Designed by Jamison Cockerham
Set in Arno, Scala Sans, and Utopia
by Jamie McKee, MacKey Composition

Cover art: "Photograph Showing New Accession of Records,"
NAID 175539855, Records of the National Archives and Records
Administration, RG 64, NARA, College Park, MD.

Manufactured in the United States of America

LIBRARY OF CONGRESS CATALOGING-IN-PUBLICATION DATA

Names: Moon, Krystyn R., 1974– author.
Title: Proximity to power : rethinking race and place in
    Alexandria, Virginia / Krystyn R. Moon.
Description: Chapel Hill : The University of North Carolina Press,
    2025. | Includes bibliographical references and index.
Identifiers: LCCN 2024045139 | ISBN 9781469686066 (cloth) | ISBN 9781469686073
    (paperback) | ISBN 9781469686080 (epub) | ISBN 9781469687735 (pdf)
Subjects: LCSH: African Americans—Virginia—Alexandria—Social conditions. |
    African Americans—Virginia—Alexandria—Social life and customs. |
    Federal-city relations—Virginia—Alexandria. | Alexandria (Va.)—Race
    relations. | Alexandria (Va.)—History. | Washington (D.C.)—History. | BISAC:
    HISTORY / United States / General | SOCIAL SCIENCE / Sociology / Urban
Classification: LCC E185.93.V8 M76 2025 |
    DDC 305.896/0730755296—dc23/eng/20241029
LC record available at https://lccn.loc.gov/2024045139

For product safety concerns under the European Union's General Product
Safety Regulation (EU GPSR), please contact gpsr@mare-nostrum.co.uk
or write to the University of North Carolina Press and Mare Nostrum
Group B.V., Mauritskade 21D, 1091 GC Amsterdam, The Netherlands.

CONTENTS

ILLUSTRATIONS

ACKNOWLEDGMENTS

Serendipity can lead us down a path that we do not expect to take. That is where the decision to write this book starts. On a hot August morning over a decade ago, I walked into city archaeologist Pamela Cressey's office to discuss an article that I was writing. Midway through our conversation Dr. Cressey looked at me and said that she was also working on a project. "I think that you might be able to help," she said (or something to that effect). I have been researching Alexandria's history ever since and have grown to appreciate my adopted home.

None of this research would have happened without the generosity and support of the many Alexandrians whom I have met along the way in writing this book. I am an outsider, sometimes in every possible way, and yet people have shared their stories and answered my probing questions. We chatted together in coffee shops and church basements, in cemeteries and parks, and in conference rooms, museums, archives, and libraries. What I found is that Alexandrians *love* their city.

Past and present residents of the Fort and Seminary neighborhoods were the first Alexandrians to teach me about our history, the good and the bad. Thank you. There have been other new arrivals and long-time residents who have shared stories along the way. I am particularly grateful for Lynnwood Campbell Jr., Dr. Michael Casey, Gwen Day-Fuller, McArthur Myers, Lillian Patterson, Ira Robinson, and Reverend Elliot Waters. Alexandria's historic preservation, history, and archaeological staff along with archivists and librarians have been instrumental to this project too: Eleanor Breen, Francine Bromberg, Gretchen Bulova, Jackie Cohan, George Combs, Al Cox, Pamela Cressey, Audrey Davis, Garrett Fesler, Jeffrey Harmon, Barbara Magid,

Catherine Miliaras, Valerie Myers, Emma Richardson, Benjamin Skolnik, Patricia Walker, and many more. Among these individuals, I especially want to recognize Audrey Davis, the director of African American History, and Eleanor Breen, the city archaeologist, for their friendship and support, including research advice. Jackie Cohan, the city archivist, has humored my many, many record requests to her department. My colleagues at the University of Mary Washington, Sue Fernsebner and Mary Beth Mathews as well as Catherine Cartwright, an independent scholar, also spent time working through earlier versions of the chapters here.

Archivists and librarians from throughout the United States provided access to critical collections related to this project. The University of Mary Washington's library assisted me in finding numerous reports, newspapers, and books either in our collections or through interlibrary loan. National Archives I and II contain a wealth of materials on Alexandria's relationship with the federal government, and there is more to discover. Yearbooks, school catalogs, and correspondence at both Howard University's and DC public schools' archives also illuminate the educational connections between Washington and Alexandria. Additionally, Ronald E. Butchart, now emeritus at the University of Georgia, shared his research on teachers working in the US South during the Civil War and Reconstruction. The Library of Virginia, University of Virginia, Duke University, and the University of Wyoming also housed relevant manuscript collections.

Of course, none of this research would have happened without the support of my family. To Howard, August, and Parker: 사랑해요.

ABBREVIATIONS

ACCESS   Action Coordinating Committee to
End Segregation in the Suburbs

ARHA   Alexandria Redevelopment and Housing Authority

ASALH   Association for the Study of African
American Life and History

ASPBH   Alexandria Society for the Preservation
of Black Heritage

BAR   Board of Architectural Review (Alexandria)

DPC   Departmental Progressive Club

FHA   Federal Housing Administration

HUD   Department of Housing and Urban Development

NAACP   National Association for the
Advancement of Colored People

NEA   National Endowment for the Arts

O&HD   Old and Historic District

USHA   US Housing Authority

VA   Department of Veterans Affairs

PROXIMITY TO
POWER

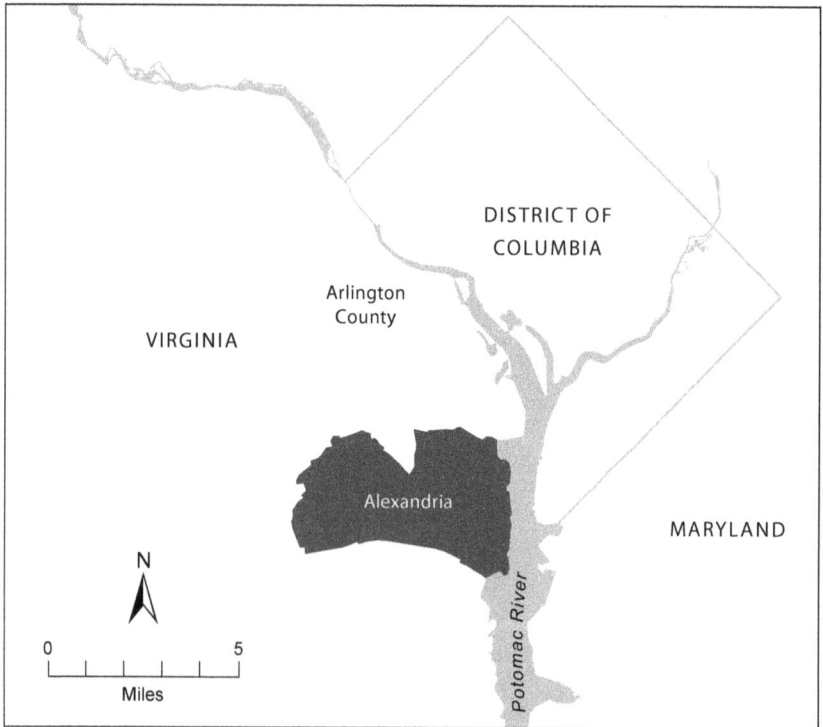

Map 0.1. Contemporary map of Alexandria, Virginia, in relation to Washington, DC.
Map by Elisa Luckabaugh, 2023.

Introduction

Alexandria, Virginia, a Southern city located in the shadow of the nation's capital, has been a microcosm of the struggle for racial equality taking place across the country since the American Civil War. Its proximity to Washington, DC, however, makes it a place where federal policy and local politics interact in unusually intimate ways. Like much of suburban northern Virginia, Alexandria is home to innumerable civil servants, military personnel, and contractors who have historically shaped and continue to shape the federal government. At the same time, Alexandria was (and is) a city on its own terms; it not only predated the establishment of the District of Columbia but was also part of the federal city for a short period of time. It is this synergism that makes Alexandria's history, especially that of its African American residents, distinct from the rest of northern Virginia and, arguably, the nation.

The experiences of Lynnwood Campbell Jr., a local civil rights activist and longtime resident, provide useful examples of the unique relationship between Alexandria and the nation's capital. Born at Freedmen's Hospital in Washington, DC (the only hospital that served Alexandria's Black residents), after World War II, Campbell spent most of his childhood in a partially segregated, mixed income neighborhood. He explained, "On one side of the street there was a city councilman, a white city councilman, there were white families, black families. On Princess Street, there were the white projects; on Oronoco Street, the families were half black, half white." Despite his neighborhood's heterogeneity, Campbell learned early in his life about segregation through the public and parochial school systems, both of which had refused to desegregate after the US Supreme Court's ruling in *Brown v. Board of Education* (1954). Campbell's parents, frustrated by the lack of opportunities for their son, sent him to high school in the District of Columbia, a common practice among Alexandria's middle-class families. Upon high school graduation, Campbell attended Howard University, one of the most prestigious Black universities in the country.

In addition to providing alternative educational opportunities, proximity to the District of Columbia impacted Campbell's career choices and housing options. Like many young men in the 1960s, he joined the US Army during the Vietnam conflict; in the army, he held a position as a finance officer because of his accounting background. After his stint in the military, Campbell returned to his previous employer, Price Waterhouse, before becoming a career civil servant, finding a position with the Federal Home Loan Bank in the US Treasury Department. Campbell had hoped to live near his family in Alexandria, but the local housing market was expensive. Since the beginning of the twentieth century, the expansion of the federal government along with discriminatory housing policies had put pressure on the metropolitan area's housing stock. After moving several times, Campbell finally returned to Alexandria. He remarked, "I don't know anything else. I don't. I've been here pretty much the whole time."[1]

In addition to retelling his own story, Campbell emphasized his family's deep roots, a corrective to other histories of Alexandria that have until recently ignored African Americans. He noted, "My great grandmother was an ex-slave. Her owner purchased her freedom, she lived right around the corner. . . . So I'm a fourth generation. I guess my brother's grandchildren make six generations. We've all been here."[2] His free ancestors most likely lived in Alexandria when the city was still part of the District of Columbia (1790–1846) and had become the site of heated debates over slavery and freedom. Although unsaid by Campbell, his family reflected later waves of Black migration in the early twentieth century too. His maternal ancestors, who had migrated from nearby Fairfax County at the turn of the twentieth century, worked for a local streetcar line, which transported commuters from northern Virginia to downtown Washington in segregated cars.[3] By World War II, some of his paternal ancestors arrived in response to wartime mobilization. They were not alone. Thousands of Black and white families moved to Alexandria to work for the federal government in the 1930s and 1940s.[4]

Through the telling of his and his family's story, Lynnwood Campbell Jr. verbalized the overlooked history of African Americans in Alexandria, people who have lived in the suburbs of the nation's capital for over two centuries. Like other communities, local customs combined with legislation informed how residents navigated race relations; however, proximity to the District of Columbia also impacted people's day-to-day lives by providing alternative resources that potentially subverted the status quo. Of course, Washington, DC, never functioned as a raceless utopia where African Americans found unequivocal freedom and equality. Nevertheless, the nation's capital was where politicians, activists, and residents debated the present and future, including the creation and implementation of discriminatory policies and ways to correct them. These debates, however, contrasted with Virginia's politics where African Americans have historically had limited political clout unless supported by federal intervention. As such, Black residents leveraged the power dynamics among local, state, and federal governments to create a more inclusive and equitable Alexandria.

RETHINKING RACE, INCLUDING ALEXANDRIA

The flow of power between these localities reveals that Alexandria often operated outside of traditional discussions of race relations. Part of this phenomenon can be traced to its social, economic, and political structure during the early republican and antebellum periods, which historians have well documented.[5] Established in 1749, Alexandria was absorbed into the District of Columbia when Thomas Jefferson, James Madison, and Alexander Hamilton agreed to move the nation's capital farther south. The original capital included lands relinquished from both Maryland and Virginia, bifurcated by the northernmost navigable portion of the Potomac River. Free Black mathematician Benjamin Banneker laid the first boundary stone of the diamond-shaped District of Columbia in 1791, just south of Alexandria along the river. In 1801, Virginia formally ceded Alexandria to the federal government as part of the new nation's capital.

Throughout the early nineteenth century, the District of Columbia maintained a sizable free Black population, but most of these residents lived in Alexandria. Virginia laws technically governed social and economic relationships in the District on the Virginia side of the Potomac River, but locals rarely enforced them. The laxity of enforcement drew free African Americans, who hoped to find acceptance and stability, from other parts of the region.[6] As a result, two neighborhoods emerged on the periphery of Alexandria's business district and white residential neighborhoods. The first was the Bottoms, later known as the DIP; it was in a low-lying area to the south of the city's commercial corridor and was Alexandria's oldest free enclave. The second, named in honor of a successful slave revolution, Hayti [pronounced Hay-Tie] appeared west of the Bottoms on lands that Quakers either rented or sold to free families. These neighborhoods were economically heterogeneous, with Alexandria's poorest and wealthiest living side by side. With support from white abolitionists, Alexandria's free African Americans built churches, established fraternal organizations, and sent their children to school.[7]

At the same time, the nation's debate over slavery played out in Alexandria in unique ways. During the early nineteenth century, the District of Columbia hosted numerous pro- and antislavery activists and politicians, all of whom wanted to craft federal legislation that aligned with their beliefs. The presence of these political actors bolstered pro- and antislavery debates on the local level, which divided Alexandria's residents. Quakers had migrated to the city from Pennsylvania in the eighteenth century and brought their abolitionist views. A handful of Quakers also manumitted men and women, circulated antislavery literature, and offered education to free Black children.[8] By the 1820s, Alexandria was also home to the region's domestic slave trade, with firms such as Armfield and Franklin transporting enslaved men, women, and children to cities and towns in the Deep South. Slave trading was big business in Alexandria, DC.[9]

In 1846, white businessowners and politicians, fearful that antislavery debates percolating in the halls of the US Congress would shut down local slave trading, lobbied for Alexandria's retrocession to Virginia. Their politicking was successful, and the federal government retroceded Alexandria later that year. Around the same time, abolitionists in Washington, DC, attained one of their goals. The Compromise of 1850 banned the domestic slave trade in the District of Columbia. Washington's slave traders, however, did not have to go far to remain in business. They merely moved across the Potomac River to Alexandria.[10]

After retrocession, some free African Americans found residency in Virginia, with its more rigid Black-white divide, unpalatable. Virginia law forbade African American educational access and congregating, which in turn closed the city's schools, churches, and fraternal organizations that had been established when Alexandria was part of the District of Columbia. This new

4

racial order frustrated an unknown number of free families who decided to migrate north to states with more moderate racial attitudes.[11] Nevertheless, despite the problems that free Black residents faced after retrocession, natural reproduction and manumissions combined with internal migration meant that the number of free people in Alexandria still trumped the number of enslaved men and women, as reflected in the 1860 US Census.[12]

While the experiences of African Americans in Alexandria prior to 1860 are well documented, what happened during and after the Civil War is not. Current regional studies have focused primarily on African American history in the District of Columbia or Virginia, with little recognition of the crosspollination between the two jurisdictions. Several studies have focused on African American history in Washington, DC, many of which focus on the unique relationship between federal authorities and residents.[13] Additionally, civil rights scholarship tends to concentrate on the Northern cities to which African Americans migrated, or on the Southern localities made famous by well-known civil rights leaders or notorious segregationist practices. Virginia's refusal to desegregate its public school system after *Brown v. Board of Education* (1954) has been the subject of several popular and academic histories.[14] Alexandria's struggles with school integration were even memorialized in the Walt Disney film, *Remember the Titans* (2000).

As many scholars have documented, post–Civil War Washington, DC, became known not only for its unique segregationist practices but also for the distinctiveness of its Black community, with its powerful coterie of civil servants, doctors, lawyers, teachers, and professors. Like Harlem, Washington was a veritable who's who of Black political, intellectual, and cultural life. Anna J. Cooper, Charles Houston, Carter G. Woodson, Mary McLeod Bethune, Duke Ellington, and Alain Locke, to name a few, all lived at one time in the nation's capital.[15] The District of Columbia, however, was also a Southern city, and Black Washingtonians had to carefully traverse its complicated segregated landscape. Federal employment was open to African Americans, but few were able to find high-paying positions, especially after the election of President Woodrow Wilson in 1912, a Virginian.[16] Public transportation, museums, and libraries were technically not segregated, but public schools, recreational facilities, and restaurants were. Miscegenation laws also did not affect couples. As a result, the Lovings, whose federal lawsuit, *Loving v. Virginia* (1967), led to the US Supreme Court's decision that miscegenation laws were unconstitutional, traveled from Virginia to Washington, DC, to marry.

Meanwhile, by the end of the nineteenth century, Virginia fully incorporated the dictates of Jim Crow segregation, which impacted every aspect of people's lives. In the late 1870s and early 1880s, the state experienced a brief stint of interracial political collaboration led by the Readjuster Party, but conservatives took control of Virginia's political life for the next eighty years, playing to white fears of Black domination.[17] There were few to no opportunities for African Americans to unravel the state's segregationist practices, and Black elites often responded by negotiating with white powerbrokers for community improvements on a case-by-case basis.[18] Histories of Jim Crow Virginia, however, mostly avoid the more northern sections of the state. Cities, such as Richmond and Norfolk or Southside, a rural area near the North Carolina border with a large Black population, tend to be central to analyses of Jim Crow Virginia.[19]

Because of its location near the District of Columbia, I argue that Alexandria has operated as a transitional zone where Black residents tapped into resources outside of Virginia to subvert local racial hierarchies. Rather than viewing the government as either a benign or a malevolent force, the experiences of Alexandria's Black community point to the negotiated nature of power relations. Here, negotiated power played out not only among distinct governmental apparatuses (local, state, and federal) but also among individuals who were incorporated into the federal apparatus through political affiliation, employment, or family, friends, and neighbors. Undeniably, the federal government has affected race relations in the United States through the passage of legislation, interpretation and enforcement of regulations, and execution of court rulings. Alexandria's physical closeness to Washington, however, has meant that its residents engaged the District of Columbia in a much more intimate fashion. The federal government often functioned as their employer, or as the employer of their friends, neighbors, or family members. Black Alexandrians also traveled to DC to go to school, to shop, and to socialize. Sometimes, they met with fellow civil rights activists or even went to the White House or the US Capitol to lobby. With their own power base, Black Washingtonians provided support to Alexandrians through their institutions, opportunities, and advocacy organizations. African Americans on both sides of the Potomac River were tied to each other in one other critical way: through their families. Kinship networks that developed during the antebellum period ensured the persistence of deep social and emotional connections among Black Alexandrians and Black Washingtonians.

Ultimately, this elaborate web of historical actors demonstrates the importance of studying liminal spaces to better understand the role that location plays in the social construction of race relations in the past and, by extension, in the present.

To explore Alexandria's relationship with the District of Columbia, *Proximity to Power* analyzes the history of the city's African American residents from the Civil War through the end of the twentieth century. Employment, education, transportation, and housing, all of which were impacted by de jure and de facto forms of discrimination, are integral to understanding everyday life during this period. Additionally, the ways in which residents and politicians have articulated the city's history will be critical to understanding the contradictory ways in which our usable past is (or is not) publicly discussed. For some Virginians, Alexandria reflects the idea that there are many Virginias that can be divided by region, race, political affiliation, and so on. At the same time, Alexandria is part of the District of Columbia's many Washingtons and can be similarly categorized. Alexandria's liminality means that the city straddles multiple identities as a city in Virginia and as a suburb of the nation's capital.

For African American residents like Campbell, living in the vicinity of Washington influenced their everyday lives in multiple, contradictory ways. For instance, the US Supreme Court's ruling in *Plessy v. Ferguson* (1896) justified the segregation of public schools in Virginia and elsewhere. *Brown v. Board of Education* (1954) ended the practice of school segregation, but Virginia, like other Southern states, resisted the court's ruling for over a decade. Campbell's parents, who wanted the best education possible for their son, joined generations of Alexandrians who sent their children to Washington to attend federally funded public schools and, later, Howard University. Although also segregated, Washington's large concentration of Black professionals supported a rigorous school curriculum. By the late nineteenth century, Washington's M Street High School was one of the most prestigious educational institutions in the country.[20]

State politics affected Alexandria too; however, Black residents created a unique set of strategies to navigate race relations by looking to the federal government, and not to Richmond, for support. Furthermore, Black Washingtonians often aligned themselves with friends and family across the Potomac River and protested government-sanctioned discrimination in Virginia. When the Virginia General Assembly segregated Alexandria's streetcars in 1902, African Americans organized a mass meeting in Washington to rally against the new law and lobbied the US Congress for federal legislation to end race-based discrimination in interstate transportation.[21]

The dynamics of local and federal politics, combined with the region's economy, ensured that Alexandria maintained a racially mixed population of longtime and highly mobile residents. The expansion of the civil service in the

Progressive Era and later wartime mobilizations brought additional people to the area, with some choosing to settle permanently while others returned home or moved elsewhere. Federal employment, along with government contracting and service industries, created a robust job market across educational and occupational sectors. Through the 1940s, segregationist practices limited job opportunities, often relegating African Americans to low-paying positions with little-to-no upward mobility. However, in relation to the rest of the job market, federal employment was seen as relatively secure, and by the 1920s, offered a pension. The appeal of federal employment only increased when President Franklin Delano Roosevelt's administration began the slow process of desegregating the civil service and government contractors, starting with the defense industries in 1941.[22]

Moving to Alexandria and deciding to stay, either temporarily or for the long term, was also predicated on the accessibility and affordability of the housing market. The Civil War brought thousands of African Americans to Alexandria, many of whom used the money that they had earned working for the Union army to purchase homes and land for the very first time. Unfortunately, that changed with early twentieth-century segregationist practices—from racially restrictive covenants to discriminatory land use zoning ordinances—and it became difficult, if not impossible, to rent or purchase in certain neighborhoods. After World War II, civil rights leaders A. Melvin Miller and Lt. Col. Marion I. Johnson fought housing discrimination, speaking out publicly and relying on their personal and professional connections to change local policies and practices. They were part of the Secret Seven, an underground civil rights organization that focused on improving the everyday lives of Black Alexandrians. Most of the Secret Seven worked for the federal government or held leadership positions in the local community. Miller was a lawyer at the US Department of Housing and Urban Development (HUD), while Johnson was an officer in the US Army.[23]

By the Cold War, Alexandria's population included immigrants and refugees who wanted to participate in the region's strong job market or lobby the federal government on behalf of fellow exiles or families and friends left behind. Andrew Friedman, one of the few historians to recognize the relationship between northern Virginia and Washington, explains how American activities overseas led to large numbers of refugees from Southeast and Western Asia settling in the area. The effect of these demographic changes on local race relations, however, is outside of Friedman's work.[24] In the 1970s and 1980s, housing continued to be challenging, with immigrants and refugees competing mostly with Black residents for places to live in low- to middle-income neighborhoods. Salvadorans, for example, relied on low-cost, privately held housing because they lacked federal recognition as refugees. And, because many Salvadorans were undocumented, they also did not have access to other federally funded programs.[25] In contrast, Ethiopians, who had fled Mengistu Haile Mariam's communist regime in the 1970s and 1980s, obtained refugee status. They settled in similar neighborhoods after their sponsorships ended but were more likely to move out. Demographer Elizabeth Chacko notes that the arrival of Ethiopian refugees to northern Virginia complicated local notions of Blackness in the late twentieth century.[26]

How has Alexandria recognized its unique and complicated history with its residents and the broader public? Until recently, official histories ignored the contributions of African Americans, such as Lynnwood Campbell Jr., A. Melvin Miller, and Lt. Col. Marion I. Johnson, and instead emphasized the city's connections either to the Founding Fathers or to the Confederacy. Inspired by the Mount Vernon Ladies' Association and other historic preservation organizations, white Alexandrians celebrated their connections to George Washington, conflating the city's history with civic myths about the origin of the nation.[27] Certain white city boosters also praised the contributions of Robert E. Lee, who grew up in Alexandria, and promoted the Cult of the Confederacy through parades, memorials, exhibits, and, by the 1950s, street names.[28] Through the 1980s, the footer of the city's official letterhead read, "Home Town of George Washington and Robert E. Lee."[29]

By the 1960s, the Black Power Movement brought new attention to how history was taught, researched, and celebrated, laying the foundation for more inclusive narratives. A wave of Black historical mindedness swept through major metropolitan centers, including Chicago, Detroit, and Washington, DC. Operating on shoestring budgets, Black neighborhoods and civic organizations produced their own public histories and exhibits and, eventually, museums and memorials.[30] Driven by Black students, Alexandria experienced similar challenges to its treatment of African American history in its public school curriculum by the late 1960s. Over the next few years, Alexandria's public schools incorporated Black Studies into its course offerings, and adult programs on African American history appeared for the first time.

Black historical mindedness laid the foundation for activism in the 1970s through the 1990s, but it focused primarily on local history, with a limited acknowledgment of the role that the District of Columbia played in Alexandria's past. Of course, there were exceptions. Low- to middle-income Black families argued for a new conceptualization of historic preservation, one that mitigated the forces of gentrification caused by the federal government's expansion in the region. They wanted the city government to prioritize the protection of people over buildings and to recognize how white historic preservation had pushed Black residents out of older neighborhoods. Investigations by the National Endowment for the Arts (NEA) and HUD provided evidence of the relationship between historic preservation and gentrification that Black residents had spoken to. Meanwhile, the newly established Alexandria Society for the Preservation of Black Heritage (ASPBH) fought for the preservation of the Alfred Street Baptist Church (ca. 1803), Alexandria's oldest Black congregation that was founded when the city was part of the District of Columbia. The Society won, but only after city officials gave special consideration to the congregation's needs for a larger church building and parking.[31]

Despite dramatic changes in Alexandria's overall treatment of African American history, there were still major problems. It was primarily residents who drove the recognition of Black history, with city officials reacting on an ad hoc basis. Furthermore, while interpretations of the past began to include Black voices, white officials still tried to appease all residents without infringing on anyone's identity politics. By the beginning of the twenty-first century, there had still been no attempt to reconceptualize Alexandria's history, in toto, so that it would provide a more critical and constructive interpretation of past, including its complicated relationship with Washington, DC.

The long history of advocacy and agency by Black Alexandrians through their relationship with the District of Columbia helps us understand the intricacies of power relations in and among a variety of historical actors in the nineteenth and twentieth centuries. The push and pull of Black and white residents on both sides of the Potomac River meant that Alexandria's African American community had access to resources and connections that were unavailable elsewhere. Without question, racial inequalities persisted throughout this period, but they played out in distinct ways that did not necessarily align with other parts of Virginia or the United States.

CHAPTERS

To explore African American history in Alexandria and the influence Washington, DC, has had on it, this book will work thematically and chronologically from the Civil War to the end of the twentieth century. *Proximity to Power* is not a comprehensive analysis of the history of Alexandria's African American community; instead, it emphasizes the importance of Alexandria's physical proximity to the District of Columbia in hopes of understanding the synergism between these localities. In chapter 1, our story begins with a discussion of African American history during the Civil War and Reconstruction. Alexandria's role as a safe haven meant that thousands of self-emancipated refugees arrived in the city from Maryland's and Virginia's hinterlands. The Union army, which needed people in a variety of support positions, provided jobs, housing, and schools. After the war, some African Americans returned home or migrated farther north; many others chose to stay, making Alexandria their adopted home. Chapter 2 focuses on the ways in which Black Alexandrians, in response to the codification of Jim Crow segregation in Virginia, used new transportation technologies to access Washington's job and educational opportunities. By the late nineteenth century, African Americans regularly commuted to the District of Columbia where they found jobs in the civil service or government contracting. Local business owners, both Black and white, provided employment too. At the same time, Washington's educational offerings, which contrasted significantly to Virginia's, appealed to Alexandrians who could afford to send their children to schools across the Potomac River. By the 1890s, the influence of Washington's educational institutions was readily apparent: almost all of Alexandria's teachers, lawyers, and doctors had taken classes at or had graduated from Howard University.

Chapter 3 explores the impact of local practices and federal policies on Alexandria's housing market from the 1910s through the 1960s. In addition to discriminatory zoning ordinances and racially restrictive covenants, Alexandria used federally funded public housing programs and urban renewal projects to reimagine the city's physical landscape, pushing African Americans into hyper-segregated neighborhoods or out of Alexandria completely. In response, residents protested individually and collectively, demanding equal access to the region's housing market. The Fair Housing Act (1968) and similar local ordinances started the process of breaking down racist structures that limited housing options, but it did not end them entirely. In chapter 4, we see how African Americans continued to struggle to find affordable housing by looking at racial and ethnic tensions in Arlandria, a neighborhood in the northernmost part of the city. By the early 1980s, a booming housing market tied to President Ronald Reagan's defense spending and simultaneous cuts to social services made finding affordable places to live in northern Virginia difficult for low-income residents. Cold War politics also facilitated the arrival of large numbers of immigrants and refugees from Central and South America, Asia, and Africa, putting additional pressures on Alexandria's housing market, social services, and infrastructure in ways unseen before. Finally, new arrivals demanded that they be included in conversations about the present and future of the city too.

The final chapter explores the tensions among federal and local authorities and residents over African American public history, historic preservation, museums, and memorialization at the end of the twentieth century. As a result of the Black Power Movement, activists demanded that city leaders create more inclusive narratives about its past, moving beyond histories built upon the legacies of Alexandria's most well-known residents, George Washington and Robert E. Lee. New interpretations appeared for the first time, providing a much-needed corrective, especially to its interpretation of the period when Alexandria was part of the District of Columbia. City officials, however, responded to calls for Black history on a case-by-case basis and refused to engage in the articulation of a more holistic interpretation of the past that might be critical of certain white individuals or groups. Furthermore, gentrification, caused by white historic preservation combined with overall population growth, continued to impact the city and put undue pressure on lower-to-middle-income Black residents.

To understand race relations in Alexandria, it is necessary to look not only at the local milieu but also at the city's relationship with one of the most powerful cities in the country and—by the twentieth century—the world. Washington's significance as a center of African American culture and society along with its international prominence brought material and ideological changes to Alexandria and its Black residents, both past and present. While the creativity and ingenuity of Black Alexandrians should not be underestimated, it is their agency—the use of the resources available to them to better their lives and the lives of their friends and families—that is central to this book.

CHAPTER ONE

Community

In a letter to William Syphax, one of Washington's few Black civil servants and a member of a prominent northern Virginia family, Judge John Underwood described the dramatic changes that African Americans had effected in Alexandria during the Civil War.[1] Within the first months of fighting, enslaved men and women recognized Union-controlled Alexandria as a safe haven, and 8,000 to 10,000 refugees made the city their home. Jobs were plentiful, and as part of the war effort, African Americans found opportunities with the federal government. These new arrivals impressed Underwood with their hard work and investment in the community. "They have, within three years, built over a thousand dwelling-houses, and provided quite comfortable furniture for them." Refugees built these homes on lands either rented or purchased, reportedly worth over $50,000. At the same time, they had completed the construction of three churches, two out of brick and one out of wood. The Freedmen's Bureau also assisted in the erection of two schoolhouses, which it later deeded to the city's Black residents. In only a few years, Underwood remarked, African Americans had transformed the city in ways that had been unimaginable only a decade earlier.[2]

None of these changes, however, came easily. Underwood, a white Radical Republican who moved to Alexandria during the Civil War, worked for the federal government, at first in the US Treasury Department and later as a US District Court judge. He, along with Alexandria's Black residents and other white Radical Republicans, worried about the persistence of racism during and after the war. As in other regions of the American South, Alexandria's Confederate sympathizers challenged changes in their status and, whenever possible, attempted to undermine African American freedom. These white men and women hoped that Alexandria's social and economic structures would continue to reflect antebellum values that placed white people at the top of a racial hierarchy. At the same time, white Union supporters did not always respect Alexandria's Black residents and often refused to recognize them as equals. When law or custom seemed threatened, African Americans faced intimidation and violence from Confederate and Union supporters alike.

Many Civil War and Reconstruction historians have looked at the ways in which African Americans turned to the federal government in the 1860s to navigate local race relations, with mixed results.[3] Central to their fight for freedom and racial equality was full citizenship, including the right to vote and to hold political office. Both men and women expected local, state, and federal authorities to recognize their rights to own land, marry, access social services, testify in court, and make contracts. Finally, African Americans used all possible resources to assert the sanctity of their families and bring loved ones together. Washington's military and political leaders, however, held an array of opinions on the status of African Americans and used their positions to align national policies with their beliefs. White allies in positions of power, such as Underwood, supported African American demands for freedom and equality, but many others did not.

The size and duration of the federal government's presence in Alexandria during the war made the interactions among Black residents, military personnel, and civil servants distinctive in comparison to other Union-held areas of the South. Because of its proximity to Washington, the Union army arrived within hours of Virginia's secession, and the city remained in Union territory for the entire war. The city's location made it strategic for the military's deployment of soldiers and supplies heading to the front. The Defenses of Washington, a ring of sixty-eight forts and ninety-three batteries around the nation's capital, also protected Alexandria from possible Confederate incursions.[4] Surrounded by forts and the Potomac River, with thousands of Union soldiers and civil servants present, Alexandria became a place where African Americans fled to in hopes of finding safety, reuniting with family and friends, and contributing to the war effort. Of course, some African Americans merely stopped in Alexandria before traveling to Washington, DC, or points farther north. Others, however, chose to stay, not only expanding preexisting Black neighborhoods but also establishing new ones. Within these neighborhoods, a close network of family and friends provided emotional and physical support and established a new sense of community.

The connections created between federal officials and Black residents did not disappear when the war ended in the spring of 1865. As in other jurisdictions, the staff at the local Freedmen's Bureau office helped Alexandrians write employment contracts, reunite with family, access medical treatment, celebrate marriages, construct schools, and arrange long-term care for disabled and elderly individuals. Additionally, improved communication and transportation technologies established during the war facilitated the increased movement of information and people across the Potomac River. When certain situations arose, Black Alexandrians contacted federal officials in the District of Columbia whom they hoped would intercede on their behalf. The freedom to send a telegram to federal officials, with the expectation of receiving a response, or to travel to the nation's capital in less than an hour to meet with them, was particularly liberating.

For Black Alexandrians during the 1860s, the navigation of federal and local racial attitudes and practices set the foundation for future connections with Washington. Throughout this period, both old and new Black residents tapped into whatever resources were available to improve their situation, leveraging support when and where they found it. Living among a sizable number of pro-Confederates who refused to see them as equals, African Americans turned to the Union military and civilian personnel, some of whom held abolitionist views, for assistance. However, even white pro-Unionists disagreed about what African American freedom and equality should look like. Thus, Black Alexandrians tried to make the most of their relationships with federal officials to protect their newly won freedom and bolster their rights during the American Civil War and Reconstruction.

THE CIVIL WAR

African Americans in Alexandria maintained a complex relationship with the federal government as they navigated their day-to-day lives during the Civil War. The Union military needed laborers to support the war effort, but its own racial baggage and lack of experience undermined its interactions with free and enslaved residents. To compound matters, large numbers of refugees came to Alexandria during the war, drawn by employment opportunities and the safety of being behind Union lines. Alexandria's Black population surged

Figure 1.1. Alexandria slave jail, interior view, ca. 1861–1869.
LC-DIG-cwpb-01472 and LC-DIG-cwpb-01471, Prints and
Photographs Division, Library of Congress, Washington, DC.

during the war from 2,801 (1,415 free and 1,386 enslaved) in 1860 to 7,653 by May 1865.[5] The sizable number of self-emancipated refugees entering Alexandria required the mobilization of humanitarian aid, which the Union military was unprepared to do. Instead, abolitionist and religious organizations from the North provided food and clothing and advocated among federal officials for safer housing and worker protections. By the end of the war, longtime Black residents and new arrivals had created an elaborate network among military personnel, civil servants, and abolitionist and religious organizations to protect their newly won freedom and articulate their rights as citizens.

During the antebellum period, Alexandria's role in slave trading had been central to Northern perceptions of the city. Thus, one of the first acts of Union troops who arrived in Alexandria the day after Virginia seceded from the Union on May 23, 1861, was to free people living in its notorious slave jails (see fig. 1.1). These prison-like buildings housed enslaved men and women before traders transported them by ship or overland to the Deep South. Northern reporters followed a Michigan regiment that went to two slave jails to free its occupants. At the first facility, they found only one enslaved man from Maryland, whose enslaver had placed him there out of fear that he would flee North at the start of the war. At the second slave jail, soldiers discovered that traders had already removed the men and women kept there. In need of shelter, soldiers converted these buildings into temporary housing, and the unnamed man from the first jail reportedly joined the Michigan regiment as a cook.[6]

In contrast to Northern newspapers' positive reporting on the Union's liberation of the city's slave jails, many soldiers mistreated Alexandria's Black residents, especially during the early years of the war. Former Union soldier Frederick C. Floyd recalled an incident in his memoir in which he and his fellow soldiers asked two men to sing and dance for them. Instead of responding with appreciation, his regiment ridiculed the men, most likely comparing them to caricatures from blackface minstrelsy that circulated widely in the North.[7] Sometimes, Union soldiers even turned to violence. Henry Whittington, a pro-Confederate resident who remained in Alexandria for the entirety of the war, described in his diary several occasions in which soldiers attacked African Americans from May through August 1862. "The ill feeling existing between the US soldiers stationed here and the negroes in our midst," he wrote, "is exhibiting itself daily by attacks upon the latter for the slightest conceivable cause, and I saw one this morning who gave evidence of a terrible castigation at their hands."[8] The *National Republican*, a Washington-based newspaper, confirmed Whittington's observations of white on Black violence.[9]

Despite these abuses, Alexandria's free and enslaved residents recognized that the arrival of Union soldiers provided an opportunity to alter local racial dynamics. A free carpenter prior to the war, John A. Seaton in a deposition for the Southern Claims Commission in 1873 recalled a conversation about the Union army with Robert H. Dogan, another free Alexandrian. Seaton, who was testifying so that Dogan would be reimbursed for buildings commandeered and later torn down by the Union army, noted that Dogan "felt good when he saw the Union troops come into Alexandria. . . . He felt as though a ton [of] weight had been lifted off from him." Seaton went on, claiming that "in fact I don't know a colored man who did not sympathize with the Union side." Politically astute men such as Seaton knew what to say to ensure that federal authorities compensated Dogan for his lost property, but both men also understood what the alternative was to the Union army's presence during the war. Seaton's support of the Union army and later the Republican

Party led to his political appointment at the US Capitol where he worked as a police officer.[10]

One of the first changes triggered by the Union's presence in Alexandria was the reopening of schools. Fears driven by Nat Turner's Rebellion (1831) had led to the passage of legislation in Virginia that made it illegal to educate free children, whose education, whites argued, would enable the circulation of rebellious ideas among all African Americans. Schooling, however, continued in Alexandria, which was part of the District of Columbia at the time. When the federal government retroceded Alexandria to Virginia in 1846, all schools for free Black children closed.[11] Black women stood at the forefront of local conversations about the reopening of Alexandria's schools at the beginning of the war.[12] Four women—Anna Bell Davis, Mary Chase, Sarah A. Gray, and Jane Crouch—established schools in the summer of 1861. Although the historical record is scant, these women most likely came from different backgrounds. Gray and Crouch were from Alexandria's wealthiest free families. Davis, who had fled slavery to Alexandria, lived temporarily in one of the city's slave jails, where she most likely started teaching. Nothing is known about Chase's background.[13]

The embarkation of Union troops and supplies to points farther south and west also created numerous employment opportunities. The Union's railroads, hospitals, commissaries, bakeries, and even burial grounds needed laborers, and Black men and women were willing to do the work. In September 1862, the *Alexandria Gazette* reported that African American men were "work[ing] on the wharves in unloading the government transports and loading the government cars."[14] Albert Webb, who fled to Alexandria in August 1862 after the Battle of Cedar Mountain, recalled that he was employed on the railroad near Washington's Navy Yard but returned home to Alexandria each night.[15] Charles W. Brown, a ship caulker from New York City, was boarding in Alexandria when troops arrived. He took a position with the Union's Commissary Department.[16]

Despite the need for workers, the Union army did not treat African Americans well, especially those who were enslaved. The Confiscation Acts of 1861 and 1862 declared enslaved men and women in Confederate territory to be "contraband," a term coined by General Benjamin Butler that was used to justify not returning enslaved individuals to enslavers.[17] These laws, however, did not grant rights to the enslaved and instead enabled the exploitation of these Black individuals by the military. The writings of Black and white abolitionists and missionaries provide important insight into the work conditions that African Americans experienced during the first two years of the war. These individuals also became advocates for Alexandria's self-emancipated refugees who had recently arrived in the city. As early as fall 1861, an anonymous writer for *The Liberator* quipped that there was "no freedom nor justice for the slave, only a change of masters" in Alexandria.[18] By August 1862, Harriet Jacobs, who had fled to the North in 1842 and documented her story in *Incidents in the Life of a Slave Girl* (1861), moved to Alexandria to support the city's refugees. She wrote to white abolitionist William Lloyd Garrison that she had met a group of men who worked for the federal government but who had received only food rations, not wages. She explained, "All expressed a willingness to work and were anxious to know what was to be done with them after the work was done. All of them said they had not received pay for their work, and some wanted to know if I thought it would be paid to their masters."[19] A month later, in a letter to US senator Charles Sumner, white abolitionist Samuel G. Howe criticized the Union army after visiting Alexandria on behalf of the US Sanitary Commission. Howe recounted, "They are employed but *not paid their* wages: their claim would not be admitted. Those whom I saw at Alexandria, marched under guard to and from their work. And locked up in jail at night, and who get only rations, and sometimes clothes as a gift, are specimens of the whole."[20] Howe hoped Sumner would convince his fellow senators to pass legislation ending this practice and grant African Americans the right to make contracts and earn wages as free workers.

In conjunction with the military's unfair employment practices, the federal government had to grapple with the large number of refugees streaming into the city. Beyond offering jobs and rations, government officials did little to address the refugees' needs, many of whom only brought what they could carry. Dr. John R. Bigelow, a Union army surgeon, described the enormity of the emerging humanitarian crisis to the American Freedmen's Inquiry Commission in spring 1863. In a letter, Bigelow narrated what he observed outside of his window: "And now here comes one hundred and fifty more of these suffering ones this very night and places are all full and our hearts too, but we will do all we can and hope on."[21] Several abolitionists and missionaries also documented the inadequacy of Alexandria's housing, food, and clothing supplies and requested aid from Northern organizations. In the same letter to Garrison in which Jacobs documented the lack of wages, she described how refugees had converted an old foundry into a shelter, but it did "not afford protection from the weather." Many people living in the structure were sick, "lay[ing] on boards on the ground floor." Some had received blankets from individual Union soldiers, but otherwise the federal government had given them only rations.[22]

As a result of the federal government's inaction, newly arrived African Americans lived wherever they could find shelter. White residents who had fled to Confederate controlled Virginia had left homes and businesses empty, but the Union army used these properties for themselves. The city's best homes were converted into military and civilian offices with sleeping quarters upstairs. Some Black and white residents rented out rooms, but most refugees did not have money to pay for housing. Instead, abandoned and decrepit schools, factories, and tenements functioned as makeshift shelters. Julia Wilbur, a white abolitionist from upstate New York and a friend of Jacobs, wrote in her diary in November 1862: "Little can be done for them until they have better places to live in."[23] Two days later, she described one of the shelters that refugees had improvised: "I found them in places unfit for brutes to live in. Many rooms had no windows, some no chimneys, & fire was built on a pile of stones, & [the] room [was] full of smoke."[24] Refugees also lived in Alexandria's most infamous buildings, the slave jails. Jacobs wrote with some irony as to the social inversion enacted in these spaces: "The habitable part of the building is filled with contrabands, the old jail is filled with secesh [Confederate] prisoners—all within speaking distance of each other. Many a compliment is passed between them on the change in their positions."[25] For the first time, African Americans enjoyed the freedom of mobility in these places that had previously been used to hold enslaved men and women before their sale and transportation to the Deep South.

One solution to Alexandria's humanitarian crisis was for federal authorities to provide housing, but government bureaucracy slowed down local efforts. Even among white abolitionists in the US military, change was slow. In September 1862, Alexandria's mayor, Lewis McKenzie, petitioned Secretary of War Edwin M. Stanton, an Ohio-born lawyer who supported abolition, to construct shelters for refugees.[26] McKenzie, a native Alexandrian and president of a railroad company, was one of Alexandria's few enslavers who supported the Union throughout the war. In fall 1861, Alexandria's remaining white residents elected him to be mayor, and the Union military approved his selection.[27] Stanton forwarded McKenzie's letter to Alexandria's military governor John P. Slough, who, like Stanton, was a former abolitionist lawyer from Ohio. Slough then requested that the city's provost marshal, Capt. John C. Wyman, investigate Alexandria's housing situation. Wyman, who came to Alexandria with the 33rd Massachusetts Infantry Regiment, reported that many refugees lived in dangerously overcrowded conditions and submitted a plan to build four barracks. After no response, Wyman wrote again, "ask[ing] for authority to build some cheap Barracks, in which they could be made

Comfortable" along with "approval [to have] a few buildings which were very much dilapidated and had been deserted prepared for the accommodation." Perhaps to win over his superiors, Wyman suggested that federal housing allowed the government to provide both "supervision" and "control" over new arrivals.[28] Slough's response is unknown, but the first refugee barracks opened in February 1863.[29]

A month earlier, President Abraham Lincoln's Emancipation Proclamation officially ended slavery in Alexandria, addressing some of the murkiness surrounding the status of self-emancipated refugees and the city's enslaved population. In April 1862, the federal government passed the Emancipation Act, which ended slavery in the District of Columbia and compensated pro-Union enslavers, but this legislation did not abolish slavery in Union-controlled areas of northern Virginia. Alexandrians had to wait for the Emancipation Proclamation, which Lincoln announced on September 22, 1862, and would be enforced on January 1, 1863. Lincoln, however, listed Union-controlled areas that were exempted from the Proclamation. This list included the newly established state of West Virginia and the counties of Accomack, Northampton, Elizabeth City, York, Princess Ann, and Norfolk, and the cities of Norfolk and Portsmouth in Virginia. Alexandria was not on the list.[30] On December 31, 1862, Wilbur documented in her diary a conversation with Wyman about the city's "contrabands" and the impending change in their status. Wyman reportedly responded, "There are no slaves here."[31] A few days later, the *Alexandria Gazette* complained that the Proclamation affected Alexandria "to a merely nominal extent, as all the slaves have already been driven off, or brought into the contraband camp."[32]

By spring 1863, education, employment, and housing saw palpable changes in response to the abolition of slavery. Increasing numbers of missionary and abolitionist groups from the North sponsored teachers to open schools in addition to the home-grown ones already in operation. African American women continued to dominate education, with at least twenty-one women, including the four who first taught in Alexandria in 1861, working in the city (see table 1.1).[33] In 1864, the city's most renowned teachers, Harriet Jacobs and her daughter, Louisa, established the Jacobs Free School with donations from the New York Freedmen's Aid Society and their newly freed neighbors. On the first day of class, the Jacobs School had one hundred students. Within a few months, she and her daughter had 235 pupils (see fig. 1.2).[34]

Three Black men who taught in Alexandria went on to establish Baptist congregations, another assertion of rights that retrocession had taken away. Each had arrived in Alexandria in 1862, and within a few months had turned

Table 1.1. Gender and racial breakdown of Alexandria's teachers during the Civil War.

Race	Male	Female	Unknown
African American	9	21	2
White	4	9	0
Unknown	2	2	0

Source: Butchart, "Freedmen's Teacher Project."

to preaching. Like other teachers, they all had different statuses prior to the war. Clement Robinson and George W. Parker opened the Select Colored School together in spring 1862. Born near the Virginia–North Carolina border, Robinson had migrated to Philadelphia prior to the Civil War where he first taught. Parker and his family, who had been enslaved, fled from Petersburg, Virginia, to Alexandria during the war.[35] Within a year, both men started congregations—Robinson at Second Baptist (now known as Beulah) and Parker at Third Baptist.[36] In November 1862, Leland Warring began teaching in Alexandria's abandoned Lancastrian school building where many refugee families lived. Warring, who had also been enslaved, reportedly studied with a minister, eventually developing his teaching skills. He moved his school to one of the federal government's barracks where he not only continued teaching, but also founded Fourth Baptist (today known as Shiloh).[37]

The establishment of schools and churches created a sense of community in wartime Alexandria, but problems with the federal government persisted. Employment was a particularly contentious issue. By the final year of the war, Black workers directly engaged federal personnel, turning to petitions and work stoppages to change employment practices instead of relying on white abolitionists and missionaries to be their advocates. In February 1864, J. G. C. Lee in the quartermaster's office wrote to Washington requesting more money to pay his workers. Lee noted that these wages were used "to support their families" and that some workers were so frustrated that they had "grown mutinous." Based on a note on the front of his letter, Lee had already borrowed $20,000 from the Commissary Department to pay back wages.[38] The Colored Laborers of Alexandria, a nascent union organization of men who worked in the Commissary Department, petitioned their commanding officers to end a tax on their wages that only Black workers had to pay. All workers were taxed to cover any medical expenses, but Black employees paid an additional tax to cover social services for refugees. The Secretary of War refused to alter the policy.[39]

Figure 1.2. Harriet and Louisa Jacobs's school in Alexandria, 1864. A handwritten inscription under the original photograph reads, "Coloured school at Alexandria, 1864, taught by Harriet Jacobs and daughter, agents of New York Friends." Robert Langmuir African American Photograph Collection, Stuart A. Rose Manuscript, Archives, and Rare Book Library, Emory University, Atlanta. https://digital.library.emory.edu/purl/023vt4b8mw-cor.

By 1863, African American women also appeared on federal employment rolls. A military hospital at St. Paul's Episcopal Church, which cared for both Union soldiers and Confederate prisoners, hired at least three women to work as seamstresses. Another woman was a nurse at the Clermont Smallpox Hospital, which cared for Black and white civilians and soldiers just outside the city limits.[40] Like their male counterparts, women had to confront federal officials who did not pay them for their work. In 1864, an army doctor refused to pay African American women for nursing wounded soldiers. Wilbur wrote in her diary, "The women have been told that they will get no pay, & this morning they refused to work."[41] Wilbur did not document whether the women's work stoppage was effective. Civilian employers were not more generous, and ironically the US military often interceded in these situations. Amanda Coats, who worked as a domestic servant, reported to Wilbur that her last two employers had not paid her, and one even "threatened to shoot her if she left." Wilbur reached out to the provost marshal's office on Coats's behalf, and Coats received some of her back wages.[42]

As in other Union-controlled areas, men in Alexandria joined the United States Colored Troops too. By 1864, J. G. C. Lee reported that 790 men had mustered into the army, and 500 were ready to be drilled. Some even joined a special company that protected northern Virginia from Confederate incursions.[43] Pro-Confederate Alexandrians viewed Black soldiers negatively, foreshadowing future conflicts in the city. Whittington wrote in his diary about a military recruitment poster: "Another Mass Meeting of the Colored People, who are determined to assert their manhood & prove to the world their title to a name [of] honor." Whittington refused to comment on the sign but wanted to "record this as a history of the times."[44] A few weeks later, he complained of newly mustered troops causing "general indignation" among white residents, calling them "poor[,] ignorant, deluded creatures, where certain death awaits them."[45]

For soldiers who could no longer fight, the military provided jobs in supportive positions. L'Ouverture Hospital—named after Toussaint L'Ouverture, the revolutionary leader who ended slavery and brought about Haiti's independence from France—opened in spring 1864 to care for sick and injured Black soldiers. L'Ouverture was one of the first military hospitals to care solely for African Americans, setting the precedent for segregated federally funded medical facilities. Dr. Edwin Bentley, who ran the hospital, wanted to hire disabled Black soldiers to work there. In a letter, he explained the variety of responsibilities that these men filled:

> A large number of them have been wounded in battle, and have thus proved themselves brave and gallant men. Among those disabled by wounds etc. there could by care be selected a competent company of colored invalids, who would in a short time do the guard duty of this hospital in a very efficient manner, and be able to replace and relieve the company of white soldiers, by making themselves useful as guards, funeral escorts, attendants, etc.; a company of disabled Blacks, who do not wish their discharge, yet are able to do this duty, although disqualified for the field.[46]

L'Ouverture contained over 600 beds and was often filled to capacity. By the end of the war, it had cared for over 1,000 patients.[47]

Like Black laborers in the city, soldiers directly engaged military officers to address injustices by the end of the war. The burial of Black soldiers in a segregated, nonmilitary cemetery was a flashpoint. Reverend Albert Gladwin, a Baptist missionary from Connecticut who was appointed Alexandria's Superintendent of Contrabands in 1863, refused to allow Black soldiers to be buried in the city's Union military cemetery, known as Alexandria's Soldiers Cemetery (present-day Alexandria National Cemetery) and founded in 1862. In late December 1864, Wilbur recorded in her diary that Black soldiers had argued with Gladwin over the issue, wanting deceased members of the United States Colored Troops to be buried in the Soldiers Cemetery. Gladwin not only refused to respect the soldiers' wishes but also arrested one of them for insubordination. In response to Gladwin's callousness, more than 440 patients at L'Ouverture Hospital signed a petition that demanded they be granted the right to be buried in the Soldiers Cemetery. Military Governor Slough admitted to Harriet Jacobs that he had been misinformed as to the wishes of African American soldiers and would ensure that all soldiers were appropriately buried. Slough also reinterred 125 soldiers in the Soldiers Cemetery, but in a segregated section dedicated to the United States Colored Troops. Gladwin was fired a few weeks later.[48]

Gladwin's abuse of African Americans also included the mismanagement of refugee housing. As Superintendent of Contrabands, he oversaw the federal government's barracks and other temporary housing options. Instead of seeing his job as a humanitarian one, he treated refugee housing as a money-making venture that supposedly instilled self-reliance and independence. All refugees were required to pay rent, and if someone could not, Gladwin jailed them. When numbers of renters declined, Gladwin sent out soldiers to round up possible tenants.[49] Gladwin even required that African Americans pay rent to live in abandoned buildings, but white refugees had no such requirements. Again, African Americans directly voiced their concerns to federal officials. In a letter, Edward Smith complained to Secretary of War Edwin M. Stanton that Gladwin forced him to pay thirteen to fifteen dollars a month while a white family, who occupied the other half of the building, paid nothing.[50] This practice can be found elsewhere. John T. O'Brien notes in his research on post–Civil War Richmond that the federal government required African Americans to work to receive support, while white residents, especially middle-class women, had only to claim Union allegiance.[51]

In reaction to Gladwin's administration of refugee housing, African Americans tried to avoid living on federal properties. In a letter to a friend, Wilbur described meeting a refugee who wanted a little wood to "live by himself & be independent." He had no interest in living in the federal government's barracks. Wilbur sent him to a Mr. Pierce who supplied him with building materials.[52] A month later, Wilbur met families living near an abandoned mill. Their housing was substandard, "but few of them are willing to go to the barracks." Although she did not mention Gladwin, Wilbur commented that they had "various objections" to going there.[53]

Instead of relying on federal housing, most able-bodied refugees built their own homes on Alexandria's outskirts. By fall 1863, 100 to 200 new houses containing one to two rooms, each with a little yard, had been constructed. The ground rent was one dollar a month, much cheaper than what Gladwin charged.[54] White writers described the self-sufficiency of residents in Grant-ville, a neighborhood named either for General Ulysses S. Grant or Peter Grant, a formerly enslaved shoemaker who built one of the earliest homes. In October 1864, Samuel May Jr., a Unitarian minister and abolitionist from Massachusetts, described Grantville in a letter to the *National Anti-Slavery Standard*. The neighborhood, he noted, was "composed of small and humble dwellings, yet *their own*, very many (I believe the most) of them *built and paid for* out of the proceeds of their own labor."[55] The Executive Committee of the New England Yearly Meeting of Friends visited Grant and his neighbors and noted "the appearance of neatness and comfort," which they attributed to the work of Jacobs and Wilbur.[56] By the end of the war, the neighborhood, which would be renamed Petersburg, was home to more than 1,500 people.[57]

The flow of wages into African American pockets facilitated home con-struction and land purchases in other parts of the city. The ability to purchase property was one of the hallmarks of freedom for newly emancipated men and women, an idea that would be passed down to future generations. African Americans had owned property in Alexandria as early as the late eighteenth century, and white Quakers had also rented and sold homes to free families throughout the antebellum period.[58] As other scholars have argued, urban dwellers tended to be more willing to sell property to prospective Black buyers because their occupational options were not necessarily tied to the land. Fluctuations in the economy also forced Black and white property owners to sell.[59] Newly emancipated families pooled their incomes together to pur-chase property during or immediately after the Civil War. Luther Porter Jack-son documented that free African Americans in Alexandria prior to the war owned forty-one properties worth over $27,000.[60] Five years later, that number jumped to almost $77,000, with more than 370 families owning homes or land. Tax ledgers show that recently freed African Americans owned most of these properties, and more than 280 of them were small, wooden dwellings worth $25 to $50. A handful of Alexandria's prewar free residents owned property worth more than $300.[61]

The importance placed on homeownership among African Americans received little support from federal officials. During the war, the US govern-ment confiscated more than 140 properties for delinquent taxes and disloyalty among Alexandria's pro-Confederate population, but it refused to use its power to reallocate that same property to African Americans. Instead, the profitability of real estate speculation influenced federal auctions. White inves-tors, including federal employees, bought almost all available property sold in Alexandria. They also resold it for a huge profit. Lucius E. Chittenden, registrar of the US Treasury, purchased several properties during the war. In 1864, he resold one lot, which he had bought earlier that year for $250, to George L. Seaton for $1,000. Seaton, a carpenter and father to John A. Seaton, was one of the wealthiest free men in Alexandria prior to the Civil War.[62] There is no evidence that Seaton complained about the inflated price of the property.

From among the properties sold at federal auction, African Americans only bought three. Nothing is known about William Washington prior to the war, but he purchased a home for $390 and appeared in the tax records in 1865.[63] Paris Simms purchased property a few streets over from his prewar home for $320. He had been enslaved in Alexandria.[64] In only one instance did the federal government attempt to address past wrongs. Harriet Williams, a formerly enslaved woman, had paid taxes on her home since the 1850s. The US Marshals' office confiscated the property, worth $800, after its pro-Confederate owners had not paid taxes for several years. In 1864, Williams bought it back for the nominal fee of $10.[65]

The Union military's presence in Alexandria throughout the war meant that it was the primary adjudicator of African American rights; however, long-time residents and recent arrivals had a stake in the articulation of freedom and equality and made their opinions known to federal officials. Almost as soon as Union soldiers arrived, Black residents reestablished schools and churches, both of which had been banned fifteen years earlier due to retrocession. Later in the war, protests by African American workers led to some improvements in employment practices. Black soldiers even criticized the mistreatment of their fallen brethren, demanding that they be buried as soldiers, not contraband. Finally, although the federal government provided housing, refugees chose to build houses and purchase land, making Alexandria, at least for the moment, their home.

The years immediately after the Civil War saw the continued exercise of agency on the part of African American residents who strove for equality. And again, the federal government played an important role in postwar Alexandria.

RECONSTRUCTION

During Virginia's Reconstruction, Black Alexandrians continued to turn to federal officials to address infringements on their newly acquired rights; such infringements were largely driven by the return of former Confederates. An unknown number of pro-Confederate Alexandrians had lived elsewhere in Virginia for the entirety of the war and were utterly alienated by the new racial order that had emerged during their absence. Their goal was to return to the social and economic structures of the antebellum period by denying that local law and custom had changed during the war as a consequence of the abolition of slavery and the articulation of equal rights. As such, African Americans recognized that they needed to be politically active to stop the many attempts at rolling back their newly acquired rights, and they created a coalition of Black and white Radical Republicans who advocated for equality. They also partnered with the Freedman's Bureau and other humanitarian organizations as a strategy to manage white efforts to reinstate Black Codes. However, changes in the postwar economy combined with former Confederates' political influence among conservative politicians made equal rights difficult to sustain. By the end of Virginia's Reconstruction in 1870, race relations in Alexandria had changed dramatically but unevenly, and it was uncertain what the future might bring without federal oversight.

By April 1865, Black residents worked with white Radical Republicans on both sides of the Potomac River to hash out what postwar freedom and equality would look like. They worried that returning Confederates would attempt to roll back all reforms instituted by the federal government during the war and refuse any further changes that supported full citizenship for African Americans. To protect themselves, Black Alexandrians petitioned Virginia's military governor, John P. Slough, to remain in his post until both municipal and state officials overturned racist antebellum legislation.[66] A few months later, Black and pro-Union white residents formed the Union Association of Virginia with the goal of promoting a loyal government, withholding the franchise from former Confederates, and granting African American men the franchise.[67] That same year, Alexandria hosted a statewide convention at which African Americans argued for the end of Virginia's Black Codes and the passage of legislation guaranteeing full political rights. Participants also agreed to collaborate with the Freedmen's Bureau to establish schools for African American children. Virginia would not offer public education until 1870.[68]

Concerns expressed by Black residents were well founded. Within a few months of the war's end, former Confederates attempted to reinstate the racial practices of the past. In June 1865, several civil court cases came to the attention of the Freedmen's Bureau. In these cases, a local judge refused to grant African Americans the right to testify against white defendants. In one case, the judge told George L. Seaton that "William[']s [the white plaintiff] testimony would be taken while that of the witnesses for the defense would not."[69] Henry E. Alvord from the Freedmen's Bureau, a Union army veteran from Massachusetts, notified Alexandria's civil court that it no longer had jurisdiction over cases involving African Americans. In a letter to his superiors,

Alvord explained, "The Mayor and civil magistrates of this city boldly declare that they will never receive the testimony of a negro and state that if the laws even oblige them to do so they will promptly resign."[70] Headquarters recommended that Alvord find someone to adjudicate cases involving African Americans and arrest any local authorities who "may interfere with the discharge of your duties."[71]

Racial tensions finally exploded on Christmas Day 1865 when former Confederates attacked several African American men, some of whom were Union soldiers, in multiple locations throughout Alexandria. One resident named John Anderson was shot twice and died five days later. The size and tenor of the unrest, which included violence against military personnel, required special treatment by the federal government. The US Military Commission, which had been created to adjudicate Confederate war crimes, established a court and brought charges against eleven white residents. The trial included at least twelve African American witnesses plus Union soldiers on duty that day. White Alexandrians also testified, but only on behalf of the defense. They claimed either to be unable to identify the instigators or blamed the victims for the violence perpetrated against them. The court found the eleven men guilty of "disturbing the peace, committing an assault with intent to kill, and finally of murder." Their prison sentences, however, were shortened on a technicality, and all were free a few months later.[72]

Black Alexandrians remained undeterred in their demands for racial equality, but they quickly learned that they needed a new approach to navigate Alexandria's postwar racial realities. The biggest challenges involved housing and employment. The drawdown of Union troops ended many jobs that had been created during the war, and confiscated properties were returned to their Confederate owners. Structures constructed by the military were also torn down, including refugee housing and military hospitals. In response to these changes, many African Americans felt compelled to leave. The Freedmen's Bureau helped individuals and families by functioning as an employment agency and providing transportation to those who either had lined up a job or wanted to reunite with family members in other parts of the country.

By the end of the war, the Quartermaster General and Freedmen's Bureau managed a sizable number of properties, including 135 tenements and 4 barracks, that housed refugees (see table 1.2).[73] Between 1865 and 1867, these buildings were either returned to their former Confederate owners or torn down. Surplus building materials were sold at auction or repurposed.[74] Those refugees who needed special assistance—the elderly, disabled, and orphaned—and who had no family nearby to provide care moved to the

Table 1.2. Number of residents in Alexandria's barracks, July 1866.

Name of barrack	Number of households	Number of persons
Prince Street Barracks	52	113
Sickle Barracks	45	158
Seward Barracks	13	39
Construction Barracks	25	85
TOTAL	135	395

Source: Monthly Reports of Tenants Occupying Tenements, Records of the Bureau of Refugees, Freedmen, and Abandoned Lands, Virginia, 1865–1872, M1912, roll 50, RG 105, NARA, Washington, DC.

Freedmen's Village in nearby Alexandria County (now Arlington County) or to Barry Farm in Washington, DC. By 1868, the Freedmen's Bureau had relocated at least eighty individuals to federal properties outside Alexandria.[75]

The election of former Confederates to the municipal government in 1866 only compounded problems for indigent refugees who had arrived during the war. Virginia's Poor Laws allowed men and women to request local assistance after a year of residency; however, Alexandria's newly elected mayor, Hugh Latham, complained about the number of African Americans in need and claimed that refugees had "no legal residence among us."[76] Latham, another former enslaver and member of the newly formed conservative party, had fled Alexandria at the beginning of the war when Union troops arrived. In 1863, the federal government found him guilty of treason and confiscated his property, but he returned in May 1865, facing no further prosecution.[77] Oliver Otis Howard, a former Union general and commissioner of the Freedmen's Bureau, responded to Latham that his department would care for refugees who needed long-term assistance but that local leaders needed to come to terms with their responsibilities to Alexandria's newest residents. Howard explained, "Those indigent freedmen who are resident at Alexandria, are regarded as forming a part of the Alexandria poor, whether they came into the city during the War, or not."[78] Latham, however, was not persuaded and refused to provide aid to Lucinda Jackson, the spouse of a Union soldier who had moved to Alexandria. To pressure Latham into helping Jackson, the Freedmen's Bureau offered to provide meat to the city's soup kitchen. Latham finally complied.[79] Problems with Latham persisted until spring 1868 when Virginia's military governor removed him from office. For the next two years, William Berkley, a local white Radical Republican, served as mayor.[80]

The shrinking of the federal government's physical presence after wartime mobilization also meant that residents needed to find employment in the private sector. The return of Confederates created jobs in domestic and agricultural work, but most whites continued to view Black employment through the lens of slavery. Black men and women, many of whom had already fought for worker rights, wanted contracts with clearly stated wages and protections from exploitation. To mediate conflict among workers and employers, the local office of the Freedmen's Bureau tried to ensure that all able-bodied African Americans found jobs and assisted them with contracts. In January 1866, Samuel P. Lee, another Freedmen's Bureau employee, reported that he had a list of over 300 positions available in the area and had already helped ninety-three people find jobs.[81]

Alexandria's postwar job market still could not support the thousands of people who had migrated to the area during the war, most of whom the US government had employed. It is unknown how many African Americans left; however, the Freedmen's Bureau's correspondence files provide a glimpse of postwar out-migration. George Long, a patient at L'Ouverture Hospital, requested transportation funds to return home to Georgia so he could work on a cotton plantation.[82] Emma Brown wanted to go to Philadelphia where she said that she had a job waiting for her.[83] Transportation requests were often for locations where men and women already had family.[84] Benjamin Thomas looked forward to going to Augusta, Georgia, "where his family lives and he can get work to support himself and them."[85] The Libby family planned to travel to Gordonsville, Virginia, where they had relatives. Jackson Libby "ha[d] been sick for some time, and he hoped" his father would care for his family.[86] In a few cases, Black residents requested that the Freedmen's Bureau bring family members to Alexandria. James Pryor asked for assistance to provide transportation for his daughter, Elizabeth Weden, who had been sold away twenty-two years earlier, and her children from Alabama. Oliver Otis Howard, however, requested an investigation to ensure that Pryor, who was seventy-seven years old, could support his family.[87]

In 1866, George W. Van Beek sent agents to Alexandria to recruit workers for his cotton plantation near Helena, Arkansas. Federal oversight was limited where the plantation was located, but Black Alexandrians with few employment options welcomed the opportunity. When they arrived at Van Beek's plantation, workers faced overcrowded housing conditions, no medical care, and a lack of food. A few men attempted to go to a nearby Freedmen's Bureau office to complain about their situation, but a group of white men working for Van Beek chased them down and imprisoned them. Black workers on an adjacent farm freed the men, and they finally reached federal authorities. In response to complaints, Van Beek claimed that the men had been unproductive, unlike the "faithful hands" on nearby plantations, and refused to pay them. Samuel P. Lee, writing from Alexandria, demanded that Van Beek fulfill his contract that the Freedmen's Bureau had helped to write. It is unknown whether Van Beek ever paid his workers.[88]

The Freedmen's Bureau also mediated conflicts between laborers and employers in and around Alexandria. In December 1865, a Mr. Ayres complained about an unnamed married couple breaking a contract to work on his farm. The husband had reportedly found a better paying job in Maryland, and his wife, who stayed behind in Alexandria, refused to work for Ayres. The Freedmen's Bureau wanted the couple to fulfill their contract, but federal officials admitted that they could not force them.[89] While receiving medical treatment at L'Ouverture Hospital, Alice Phinney filed a complaint against her former employer. Phinney stated that when she "was taken sick," her employer's sister had "misused her and threatened her with a knife [and] called her a stinking Yankee Heifer." They then forced Phinney to flee, threatening "to take her to the barn and flog her."[90] In another instance, protests focused on back wages from the federal government itself. In 1865, Alvord petitioned the military to compensate more than seventy workers who had not been paid for wartime work. Federal officials in Washington refused, stating that it was impossible to verify their employment. Furthermore, they argued that the quartermaster's office had created these positions to keep African Americans productively engaged while receiving federal rations and housing. In Washington's opinion, these men and women did not deserve wages for their work.[91]

As a result of the postwar employment landscape, the number of African Americans listed as property owners declined between 1865 and 1870. As noted earlier, the city's 1865 tax record listed more than 370 Black-owned properties, many of which newly emancipated families had built on land that they rented. Five years later, the US Census documented only around 130 property owners, a sharp decline. Peter Grant, one of the namesakes for the Grantville neighborhood, had moved to Fauquier County, Virginia, to live with son and his family by 1870. He was eighty-two years old.[92] Among Alexandria's remaining families, those who had been free prior to the war owned the most expensive properties. Skilled artisans also more easily transitioned to the private sector and were able to maintain or purchase additional properties. Hampshire Fractious, a plasterer, and his family had migrated from Clarke County, Virginia, to Alexandria during the war. By 1865, he owned two homes on rented land. He later bought more than ten acres just outside of the city limits, presumably to farm.[93] Strother Moten made enough money as a blacksmith to purchase properties worth $2,000 by 1870. His family later used one of his homes as a boarding house to generate additional income.[94]

Black property ownership created rifts among neighbors that played to class and gender divisions. In 1868, Catherine Hansberry bought a home from George L. Seaton, but he never filed the deed at the courthouse because he believed that Hansberry could not afford the house and should rent it instead. In court, Hansberry claimed she had not only paid Seaton $200 in cash but also forwarded to him her husband's military pension plus an annuity. The court sided with Seaton, noting that Hansberry could not afford the house based on her income.[95] Without the recognition of their marital rights, formerly enslaved women faced additional burdens upon the death of their spouses, even after the war. Jemima Harris, who had fled to Alexandria during the war from Manassas, Virginia, had married a free man named Henry in the mid-1840s. When Henry died in 1857, the county appointed an administrator to auction off his property and pay his debts. She noted in an affidavit with the Freedmen's Bureau in 1868 that, while the community recognized their marriage and six children, the county administrator refused to give her or their children any of the proceeds from the sale of his property. The Freedmen's Bureau tried to obtain the monies for Harris, but the archival record is unclear whether her claim was successful.[96]

Harriet Williams lost her home when after the war the federal government refused to stand by the sale of Confederate properties. In 1865, Mary Dixon, the widow of the former homeowner, received a certificate of redemption from President Andrew Johnson, and Dixon reclaimed her husband's property taken during the war. Williams turned to the courts to keep her home, which she had bought at auction a year earlier. The Freedmen's Bureau supported her claim, but local and state judges ruled in Dixon's favor. Black and a handful of white residents were outraged. During Williams's eviction, one white onlooker was arrested for inciting a riot and interfering with the duties of a police officer. Deputy Sheriff Rock later testified, "There was a great deal of excitement among the people, there were great many colored people present, they were very much excited, threatening the vengeance of both the civil and spiritual authorities."[97] In a telegram, Williams wrote to Oliver Otis Howard that "the Sheriff [has] thrown my things out & [I] have nowhere to go. Please send me some kind of protection as I am in a dreadful state." Howard wrote to his Alexandria staff requesting that they help Williams find a new place to live.[98]

The federal government's mixed response to the needs of African Americans after the war meant that residents increasingly had to turn to other organizations and institutions for support. Black churches provided one such space.[99] In addition to caring for their members' spiritual needs, congregations hosted political meetings, lectures, and cultural programming. Third Baptist Church, led by George W. Parker, hosted concerts by the Freedmen's Choir as a fundraiser for the congregation. The *Alexandria Gazette* reported that "the house" was "well filled, and the music excellent." An encore performance was planned for the following week.[100] In 1867, Alfred Street Baptist Church, Alexandria's oldest and largest Black congregation, hosted lectures by Oliver Otis Howard, the commissioner of the Freedmen's Bureau; Reverend John W. Hunnicutt, a former proslavery minister who became a Radical Republican; and John M. Langston, an African American lawyer from Ohio who later represented Virginia in the US Senate.[101] Zion Baptist Church, established in 1864 near Alexandria's waterfront, hosted Radical Republicans on a regular basis. They assembled to discuss local, state, and federal politics and to nominate party members for political office.[102]

The National Freedman's Relief Association, led by high-ranking federal appointees and civil servants, was one of the few organizations operating in Alexandria that continued to fund educational opportunities for Black children after the war. Established in 1863, the association initially focused on the needs of African American refugees who had migrated to Washington and Alexandria. Two Union soldiers taught for the association, and Northern supporters donated clothing, which they mailed to Alexandria.[103] After the war, the organization focused on recruiting white teachers from New York and New England to work in Alexandria and other Black schools in the US South. In June 1865, it opened the First National Freedmen's School, which taught over 160 students. The National Freedman's Relief Association also established other education programs housed in federally owned properties until they were torn down in 1867.[104]

In response to the destruction of federal buildings and limited support from outside organizations, Black Alexandrians decided to raise funds to establish new schools on their own terms for local children. Samuel P. Lee explained to another Freedmen's Bureau official that "several public meetings held by the freedmen of this place to raise funds to purchase land for the purpose of building school houses."[105] Residents organized the First Free School Society of Alexandria to purchase land where, with assistance from the Freedmen's Bureau, they built two schoolhouses.[106] The first school, built in one of Alexandria's oldest Black neighborhoods, incorporated recycled materials from the military's refugee housing, which made it more affordable to construct. It was named the Seaton School after George L. Seaton, with whom the Freedmen's Bureau had contracted to build Alexandria's schools.[107]

The second school, named the Lee School after Cassius F. Lee (Robert E. Lee's cousin) who had sold land to the society, was in one of Alexandria's newer African American neighborhoods. Seaton had to use new materials for this structure, and the Lee School cost around $2,000 more to build.[108] After Seaton completed the two schoolhouses, Oliver Otis Howard gifted them to the society to ensure that they were used for educational purposes regardless of "race or previous condition of servitude."[109] For the moment, African American residents did not have to rely on local white authorities, humanitarian organizations, or the federal government to provide an education for their children.

Arguably, the most important right coveted by African American men during the late 1860s was that of the franchise. As noted earlier in this chapter, Black Alexandrians organized meetings and conventions to discuss political issues as soon as the war ended. They also partnered with the city's small but powerful cohort of white Radical Republicans, many of whom worked for the federal government during and after the war. Some of these white men moved to Alexandria as part of the Union's war effort and decided to settle there permanently. Others came from families who had migrated to northern Virginia from New England or the Mid-Atlantic states during the antebellum period. These families mostly consisted of small-time farmers who were known for their antislavery views.[110] The collaborations among Black and white Radical Republicans created opportunities for interracial political activism, although white Republicans dominated leadership positions and set agendas. Richard Lee Morton in his 1919 study of African American politics in Virginia remarked that "Alexandria was the Radical center of the State" after the Civil War.[111]

That radicalness surfaced in March 1867 when Black male residents, with support from white Radical Republicans, decided to participate in a local election. Although no local, state, or federal legislation had passed that enfranchised African American men, they interpreted the Reconstruction Act (1867) as granting universal male suffrage. Passed a few days earlier, the Reconstruction Act laid out the process by which former Confederate states rejoined the Union, including referenda on new state constitutions that outlawed slavery and incorporated the Fourteenth Amendment. These referenda also required that African American men vote on any constitutional changes.

Black and white Radical Republicans did not want to wait until Virginia's referendum for the franchise and decided to mobilize African American men to run for political office and vote in the spring of 1867. White party members initially put forward a roster of white-only candidates, but Black residents successfully demanded that African American men be included too.[112] They also chose six men, two Black and four white, to be poll watchers and to count any votes that the city election commission rejected. If African American men were turned away, they then voted at alternative polling places. On the morning of the election, Mayor Latham and a local judge traveled to Washington, DC, to meet with President Andrew Johnson and US attorney general Henry Stanbery to discuss whether they should accept Black votes. While Johnson and Stanbery's response had not "given them any definite answer," they decided to throw them all out.[113] Francis H. Pierpont, the governor of the restored government of Virginia, requested that the US military be present during the election to protect Black voters from possible violence. He also argued that "all male citizens over the age of twenty-one years are entitled to vote at all elections except those disqualified," the latter phrase pointing to white men, such as Latham, who supported the Confederacy. Despite being turned away at the official polls, the *Alexandria Gazette* reported that 1,000 African American men voted for the first time in Alexandria on March 5, 1867.[114]

While the local election commission did not count any Black votes, African American men remained undeterred. Six months later, they voted for the convention to rewrite Virginia's constitution so that it included language from the Thirteenth and Fourteenth Amendments. This time, Samuel P. Lee of the Freedmen's Bureau oversaw the election with Black and white Radical Republicans assisting at the polls. Over 1,800 Black men voted, and they almost universally supported the new constitution.[115] In the spring of 1868, Republicans again nominated African American men to run for municipal offices, but none garnered enough votes.[116] A few men, however, became jurors in the federal court for the eastern district of Virginia where John C. Underwood presided.[117] A year later, Black and white voters successfully elected George L. Seaton to Virginia's General Assembly, the first Black Alexandrian to be elected to political office.[118] In 1870, George W. Parker, former school teacher turned preacher, was elected to city council, and Traverse B. Pinn was elected magistrate. Pinn, a free farm laborer from rural Virginia, had fled during the war to Alexandria, where he worked for the quartermaster's department as a teamster. He was also active in Radical Republican circles.[119]

After the Civil War, Black Alexandrians continued to fight for their rights, turning to a combination of white Radical Republicans, the federal government, humanitarian organizations, and each other for support. Returning Confederates attempted to reinstate the racial status quo of the antebellum period, but Black residents had already begun to establish a new racial order in their absence. By the end of Virginia's Reconstruction, race relations had changed dramatically, but it was unknown whether the progress made during the 1860s would last once federal authorities ceded control.

CONCLUSION

In June 1866, Julia Wilbur, a white Quaker from New York who had worked in Alexandria during the war, returned to the city to visit her friend Fanny Lee. Lee and her family lived in one of Alexandria's former slave jails, which had gone through numerous transformations since the war started. Created to hold enslaved men, women, and children before they were sold South, Alexandria's slave jails had become temporary housing for Union soldiers and newly emancipated refugees. They also held Confederate soldiers and sympathizers as prisoners. During their conversations, Lee described to Wilbur "the terror" that the place once held over her family, especially when traders sold her brother. Those feelings, however, had changed over the course of the war as Lee had converted part of the jail into her home. Before leaving, Wilbur asked Lee for a door bolt as a keepsake, and Lee reportedly retrieved an axe to cut one off. The moment was not lost on Wilbur: Lee, "whose family had suffered there when it was a trader's jail was tearing the bolts off the prison door." As Lee and Wilbur struggled to remove the bolt, a disabled Union soldier arrived and helped them. Everyone in the group soon realized that they were enacting the "literal downfall of one of the famous Slave Pens of Alexandria." This act, wrote Wilbur, was "poetic justice."[120]

Wilbur's story of the removal of a bolt from a slave jail's door symbolizes the complex relationship that emerged among old and new Black residents, the federal government, and white abolitionists and missionaries in Alexandria. During the war, thousands of African Americans made Union-controlled Alexandria their home. Some were longtime residents with deep roots in the city, while others had fled to Alexandria from war-torn areas of Virginia. Both mistreatment and opportunity coexisted at the hands of white civil servants, military personnel, abolitionists, and missionaries, and African Americans carefully navigated among them. The immediate postwar period was just as tumultuous, with the drawdown of federal troops and return of pro-Confederate families. African Americans, however, continued to demand that their rights and freedoms be assured, turning to the Freedmen's Bureau, local white Radical Republicans, and each other for support.

By 1870, Black Alexandrians had experienced both the possibilities and limitations that resulted from the Civil War. The failure of the federal government to reappropriate property and provide steady employment undermined their economic stability, but a small number of Black residents continued to purchase homes and pooled resources to construct churches. In collaboration with the Freedmen's Bureau, Black Alexandrians owned two educational facilities, which became Alexandria's first two public schools for Black children. Finally, African American men fought for their political rights and elected their own to local and state office by the end of the decade.

Like the rest of Virginia and the nation, Black Alexandrians struggled to obtain freedom and racial equality during the 1860s. However—the city's proximity to the nation's capital altered people's day-to-day experiences by providing unique relationships with the Union military and federal personnel. Those interactions facilitated the development of future strategies with which to navigate the rise of Jim Crow segregation in the late nineteenth and early twentieth centuries.

CHAPTER TWO

Mobility

In 1927, seven African American men established the Departmental Progressive Club (DPC) to "create wholesome recreation, encourage good character and to foster fellowship among themselves; and by so doing to improve the city by making it a better place for all people to live."[1] Like other Black fraternal organizations at the turn of the twentieth century, the DPC was a place where members socialized, organized sporting events, and engaged in community service.[2] There was, however, one key difference. The founding members named the organization after their employer; "departmental" referred to the various federal agencies in which the men worked in Washington, DC. In fact, the federal government employed all the founders of the DPC, all of whom lived across the Potomac River in Alexandria, Virginia.

The DPC represents one of the many ways, in the late nineteenth and early twentieth centuries, in which Black Alexandrians remained connected to the District of Columbia after Reconstruction ended in 1870. During the late nineteenth and early twentieth centuries, both jurisdictions leaned toward white conservatism, aiming to marginalize African Americans through a variety of laws and practices; however, Jim Crow segregation functioned differently in Washington, DC, which Black Alexandrians leveraged to their advantage. At first glance, the segregation in both jurisdictions shared numerous similarities.

The federal government introduced separate schools for Black and white children in 1862, the same year that slavery in the District of Columbia was abolished. In its early years, separate school boards ran Washington's educational offerings, and it had two superintendents, one Black and one white. By 1874, the US Congress took control over the management of the District of Columbia's political affairs, stripping residents of almost all local control and disenfranchising both Black and white voters. Washington's late-nineteenth-century housing boom, tied to the expansion of the federal government during the Progressive Era, saw neighborhood developments increasingly divided by race and class. Under the guise of protecting property values, white developers and homeowners introduced racially restrictive covenants and white-only neighborhood agreements to the nation's capital.[3]

At the same time, Washington offered unique opportunities that made it distinct from Virginia and other parts of the United States. While Virginia had segregated almost every aspect of people's day-to-day lives by the early twentieth century, the District of Columbia remained under the purview of federal legislators who held a mixture of opinions on Jim Crow segregation. Thus, some aspects of Washington society were racially segregated, and others were not. Schools, restaurants, and many private businesses barred Black residents or provided separate accommodations. Public transportation, museums, and libraries, however, were not segregated. Washington also never passed miscegenation laws, which would have banned interracial marriages. Federal employment mostly relegated African Americans to custodial, construction, and domestic work, similar to positions available in the private sector. These jobs for the government, however, were seen as more secure and by the early twentieth century offered pensions and other benefits. Finally, a handful of well-educated African American men and women obtained clerkships through political patronage or a high score on the civil service exam. The loss of home rule, however, meant that Alexandrians had something that Washingtonians coveted: the franchise. Not until Virginia implemented a new state constitution in 1904, which introduced poll taxes and other legislative tools to disenfranchise voters, did Black Alexandrians face similar limitations on the right to vote.

For Black residents on both sides of the Potomac River, the operation of two segregationist systems side-by-side highlighted the socially constructed nature of turn-of-the-century structural racism. As a result, the experiences of navigating Jim Crow segregation in Washington and Alexandria periodically led to acts of civil disobedience that challenged new segregationist policies. For instance, public transportation, which Virginia segregated in the early twentieth century, became a site of anger and frustration among Black travelers that led to both protests and lawsuits. More commonly, Black Alexandrians used their awareness of the advantages and disadvantages of each jurisdiction to improve their lives and the lives of their families and friends. Black Alexandrians often viewed Washington as offering a modicum of economic stability and even upward mobility through its public school system and federal employment options. At the same time, Black voters in Alexandria attempted to use their access to the franchise to their political advantage, which they hoped would help them land federal jobs.

Several problems emerged with the strategies that Black Alexandrians deployed to manage the impact of Jim Crow segregation at the turn of the century. Not everyone had access to the same resources, and an unknown number of Black residents had to make do with what they had available to them locally. Only individuals with political or social connections could participate in Washington's relative advantages. Some of these opportunities were class-based, and families had to have the right relationships with Washington's Black elite to access them.[4] Economic security was also necessary if a family was to afford sending their children to school in Washington, even with help from DC-based relatives. Extensive kinship networks connected both sides of the Potomac River after the Civil War, but poverty often interrupted educational opportunities. To take down Jim Crow segregation in Virginia and Washington, residents would need to tap into their network of friends, family, and colleagues on both sides of the Potomac River and use both direct action and the intervention of the courts to make palpable change. That phenomenon would emerge just before World War II.

Through an elaborate web of social, economic, and political actors, Black Alexandrians carefully navigated the segregationist systems operating in both Washington and their hometown, weighing the pros and cons of each. Virginia's politicians had embraced white supremacy by the beginning of the twentieth century and replicated Jim Crow laws found elsewhere in the US South. Meanwhile, the District of Columbia was fraught with racial contradictions, as it simultaneously segregated certain sectors and not others. In some cases, its version of segregation, most notably in education and employment, differed from other parts of the country, especially Virginia. For many Black Alexandrians, proximity to Washington during the Progressive Era allowed them to defy segregation in Virginia by acquiring more secure and sometimes better paying federal jobs and by ensuring that their children had access to a quality education in DC schools.

The humiliation of crossing the Potomac River on public transportation, however, provoked the earliest instances of local, cross-jurisdictional activism.

Black Alexandrians' movements between Washington and Virginia underscore the importance of mobility in the Progressive Era. Commuting was a vehicle for change, even though it remained racially charged between the two jurisdictions. In the late nineteenth and early twentieth centuries, new transportation technologies made Washington, DC, more accessible to northern Virginia residents. Public transportation increased overall in and around the nation's capital, allowing people to travel greater distances over shorter periods of time for less money. Train and ferry companies, which had developed in the antebellum period, opened new routes and fare prices declined. A few decades later, electric streetcars and gas-powered buses became the main modes of transportation with newly established commuter lines connecting the region.[5] By the 1920s, it took less than 30 minutes and cost 15 cents to travel one-way between Alexandria and downtown Washington, DC.[6]

Equitable access to new transportation technologies, however, remained a constant issue throughout the period. During the Civil War, US senator Charles Sumner had successfully legislated a ban on racial segregation in passenger cars coming into and out of Washington, DC; however, in 1868, the Washington, Alexandria, and Georgetown Railroad Company attempted to separate Black and white riders. In 1873, the US Supreme Court declared this policy to be unconstitutional.[7] Meanwhile, Virginia's transportation policies pivoted toward other Southern states, which had already introduced race-based segregation on railways after Reconstruction. In 1891, Philip W. McKinney, who argued for white supremacy in his 1889 gubernatorial campaign, proposed legislation to segregate railroad cars in Virginia. In response, Black Alexandrians organized meetings, wrote letters to their representatives, generated public resolutions, and sent men to Richmond to argue against the bill.[8] After weeks of activism, Freeman H. M. Murray (who will be discussed in greater depth later in the chapter) wrote in his diary that he "saw Mr. Bend-[h]eim [Alexandria's state delegate] abt Car Law. He will notify me if Com [mitee] take[s] it up. Thinks it won[']t take up."[9] Black efforts in Alexandria and elsewhere were successful for the moment, and white legislators did not pass laws to segregate transportation.

After the US Supreme Court ruled in *Plessy v. Ferguson* (1896) that segregated public accommodations were constitutional, Virginia passed legislation in 1900 segregating passenger trains and steamboats.[10] In both the District of Columbia and Alexandria, African Americans held meetings to discuss the implications of Virginia's new transportation policies, but leaders "urged their race to abide by the laws." Black Washingtonians used their political connections within the federal government to argue for the invalidation of Virginia's new segregation laws because they impacted interstate transportation, but without success.[11]

Newspaper coverage on the experiences of riders traveling between Washington and Alexandria highlighted the humiliation caused by Virginia's new law. In several instances, white conductors angered African American passengers by refusing to honor their seat assignments, which sometimes resulted in arrests. In December 1900, Alexandria police arrested John Ward from New Jersey for refusing to move to the African American–only car once the train crossed the Potomac River. His wife paid his ten-dollar fine, and they continued to travel south.[12] A few months later, the *Alexandria Gazette* told the story of two women who usually commuted to work on a streetcar but who had chosen to ride the train one morning when the streetcars were delayed. After they bought their tickets, the conductor denied them their seats because they were in the whites-only section.[13] In another incident, a rider hoped that her arrest would lead to the federal courts' overturning of Virginia's segregated train law. In August 1906, police officers arrested Barbara E. Pope, a schoolteacher, writer, and civil rights activist from Washington, and fined her ten dollars in Falls Church, Virginia, located a few miles from Alexandria's border. Pope decided to fight the charge, and with support from the Niagara Movement, she won her case in both the Supreme Court of Virginia and the Supreme Court of the District of Columbia. The US Supreme Court, however, never took up her case, and the segregation of passenger trains remained on the books.[14]

By the end of the nineteenth century, the Washington metropolitan area was introduced to a new form of public transportation: the electric streetcar. In 1894, the Virginia General Assembly chartered the Washington, Alexandria, and Mount Vernon Railway Company to build a streetcar line running from downtown Washington, DC, to George Washington's plantation, Mount Vernon, in hopes of promoting heritage tourism.[15] For northern Virginia real estate developers and land speculators, the arrival of streetcars incentivized the region's suburbanization. Over the next several decades, farms and country estates were converted into modern subdivisions for the region's growing numbers of white civil servants, small business owners, and railroad and factory workers. Like developments outside of other major cities in the United States, they were racially restricted.[16]

Streetcar passengers initially sat wherever they wanted, but Alexandria's new state delegate James R. Caton, urged the Virginia General Assembly to extend the segregation of passenger trains to streetcars in 1902. John Mitchell Jr., editor and publisher of the African American newspaper, *Richmond Planet*, noted that protests against the legislation came primarily from streetcar companies "who could ill afford the expense and inconvenience which [segregated cars] would impose."[17] White drivers from Alexandria traveled to Richmond to testify against the law and threatened to quit if Caton's law passed. The possibility that African Americans could obtain jobs as motormen and conductors on Black-only streetcars most likely influenced white protests.[18] The law passed and was implemented in spring 1902.[19]

The segregation of streetcars led to several arrests of both Black and white riders who refused to move to their designated areas once they crossed the Potomac River. In May 1902, officers first arrested L. M. McDonald, a Black school teacher from Washington. McDonald claimed that she had not heard about the law, and when the conductor asked her to move, she refused, arguing there were no other seats available.[20] The arrest of Mary Custis Lee, Robert E. Lee's daughter, received extensive news coverage, not only because she was perceived to be a respectable white woman but also because Lee embodied her father's white supremacist legacy for Confederate veterans and their families. Lee's arrest outraged white Alexandrians who threatened the police with violence if they attempted to bring her into the station. An anonymous donor paid her fine, and Lee never appeared in court.[21] Nelson S. Spencer, a white attorney from New York, sued the streetcar company over the constitutionality of the law after his experience on a streetcar between Washington and Alexandria. Spencer won the case in the Supreme Court of the District of Columbia; however, instead of abolishing the practice, Virginia expanded the law to the entire state. Individual conductors were also given the ability to designate white and Black seats at their discretion, but passengers were denied due process if they felt their rights were violated.[22]

By the mid-1920s, the popularity of streetcars waned, and gas-powered buses began to dominate public transportation in the Washington metropolitan region. Buses first appeared in the District in 1915 for local service, although one company offered rides to northern Virginia.[23] Washington-based companies initially refused to provide service to Black customers; however, once local government regulated the industry, it required that buses be available to all travelers.[24] Within a decade, the Alexandria, Barcroft and Washington Bus Company offered 117 round trips daily from Washington to Alexandria and neighboring counties.[25] Its regularity and price, especially during the Great Depression, made the bus an affordable alternative to segregated streetcars and trains.

Buses traveled to and from Washington and northern Virginia for almost fifteen years before the Virginia General Assembly decided to pass legislation to segregate gas-powered buses in 1930.[26] Once again, the crossing of the Potomac River created problems for Black riders. In 1931, white police officers arrested a family traveling from Newark, New Jersey, to Hillsboro, North Carolina. Oswald D. Durant, a well-known and respected Black doctor in Alexandria, witnessed their arrest and called a local attorney to help the family. The charges were dropped, and Durant drove the family to the bus station so that they could continue their journey.[27] Two years later, a rider from nearby Arlington County reportedly struck a white bus driver when he was ordered to the back of the bus. He was brought up on assault charges in Arlington's police court.[28] The most well-known case involved two women, Mamie Kinchlow and Bessie Nelson. In August 1932, Kinchlow and Nelson boarded a Greyhound bus in Trenton, New Jersey, and sat in the seats listed on their tickets. Once they switched buses in Washington, DC, the driver warned them that they needed to move to the back of the bus and requested that they do so before they crossed the Potomac River. Both women refused, and when they reached Alexandria, police officers arrested them for disorderly conduct and fined them twenty-five dollars each. Neither paid the fine, and both women went to jail. Kinchlow and Nelson sued Greyhound for breach of contract, wrongful ejection, and false imprisonment. They lost their lawsuits on appeal in 1937.[29]

African Americans living in Alexandria in the late nineteenth and early twentieth centuries relied on new transportation technologies that made the District of Columbia more accessible. The segregation of transportation in Virginia but not the District of Columbia, however, heightened racial tensions for travelers moving between the two jurisdictions. Lawsuits against transportation companies occurred in the pre–World War II period, but without much success. Nevertheless, the courts' perception of "separate but equal" eventually changed. In 1946, the US Supreme Court ruled in *Morgan v. Virginia* that Virginia's segregation of interstate transportation was unconstitutional. Irene Morgan, who was visiting her family in Gloucester County, Virginia, refused to move to the Black-only section of a bus on her return trip to Baltimore, Maryland.

EDUCATION

The quality of public education in Alexandria was one of the many reasons why Black families commuted to Washington, DC, during the late nineteenth and early twentieth centuries. Throughout this period, both jurisdictions provided racially segregated education, but even among segregationist practices, there were clear differences. Public schools for African American children opened in Washington, DC, during the Civil War but were somewhat autonomous, giving teachers, administrators, and parents control over educational quality. For wealthier families, Howard University's preparatory and collegiate programs added to the city's prestige. In Virginia, Black and white men voted in support of segregated public schools in 1867 as part of the state's postwar constitution that included language from the Thirteenth and Fourteenth Amendments. The passage of this constitution was part of the process for former Confederate states' readmittance to the Union. Public schools opened in Virginia in 1870, but it quickly became clear that Alexandria's white superintendent and school board were purposefully undereducating Black children.[30] In response to the educational differences between the two jurisdictions, Black Alexandrians put their children on trains, streetcars, and buses so they received a better education in Washington, DC. Others sent their children to live with extended family who already resided in the District. This latter strategy allowed children to attend public schools without calling attention to their Virginia residency. Of course, turning to Washington, DC, to offset the problems with Alexandria's educational offerings only provided a short-term solution and did not address the bigger issues surrounding segregated schools. Many poorer families, who needed their children to work at an early age, did not reap the benefits of living near one of the best school systems in the country for Black children. Thus, while this strategy addressed the educational goals of some families, the opportunities created by living near Washington reinforced class divisions.

With the establishment of public schools in 1870, Alexandria's white school board wanted to control all the city's educational offerings. To strip Black parents of their influence over education, the school board renamed the two schools gifted by the Freedmen's Bureau in 1867 after white educators: the Snowden School for Boys and Hallowell School for Girls.[31] A few years later, frustrated that African Americans owned the school properties and required the city to rent them, the school board threatened to move Snowden and Hallowell if trustees did not cede their control over the land and buildings.[32] In the meantime, it denied a request to convert a short-lived industrial school into a high school. Board members argued that state and federal laws required the establishment of four high schools, segregated by race and sex, but that Alexandria's student population had not demonstrated the need or aptitude.[33]

For the moment, Alexandria's school board expected all families to send children to private schools if they wanted a high school education.[34]

A handful of students who were educated in Alexandria prior to 1870 were already prepared for high school or college. Virginia had few options, so wealthier families sent their children to Howard University for part, if not all, of their secondary or postsecondary careers.[35] William Henry Madella first studied at Lincoln University in Oxford, Pennsylvania, where he received a bachelor's degree in 1876. When he returned home to Alexandria, he attended Howard University to study medicine. The Virginia Board of Medical Examiners refused to license Madella, but he saw patients anyway. In 1897, Madella finally received a medical license, more than a decade after he began practicing.[36] Harrison L. Harris, whose formerly enslaved mother, Jemima Harris, had demanded compensation for the sale of her deceased spouse's property (as detailed in chapter 1), graduated from Howard University's medical school in 1882. That same year, he moved to Petersburg, Virginia, where residents elected him to be the City Physician and a member of the Board of Health.[37] Harrison's brother, Alfred W. Harris, pursued a law degree at Howard University and was the first Black lawyer admitted to the bar by Alexandria's corporation court. He also moved to Petersburg, where residents elected him to the Virginia General Assembly. He later established the Virginia Normal and Collegiate Institute, today known as Virginia State University.[38]

Among middle-class families, gender played an important role in their decision to send children to prestigious educational institutions such as Howard University. Class expectations promoted the idea that men were to be the breadwinners; in reality, both men and women worked to ensure the economic security of their families.[39] This phenomenon played out among Alexandria's educators, one of the few careers open to Black middle-class women. In the late nineteenth and early twentieth centuries, all of Alexandria's male teachers attended Howard University at some point in their careers. Rozier D. Lyles, born during the Civil War to one of Alexandria's free families, attended local schools before taking classes at Howard University. He taught in Alexandria from 1883 until his death in 1933.[40] John F. Parker had been enslaved prior to the Civil War and began teaching in Alexandria's public schools in 1871. He worked while taking courses at Howard University and finally obtained a bachelor's degree in pedagogy in 1909.[41] In contrast, female teachers had more varied educational backgrounds and, because of familial responsibilities, moved in and out of the workforce at higher rates. Sarah A. Gray and Jane Crouch, who had begun teaching in 1861, attended the Oblate School for Colored Girls in Baltimore, a Catholic institution run by the Oblate

Sisters of Providence, prior to the Civil War. Gray also studied with white abolitionist Myrtilla Miner, who had opened the Normal School for Colored Girls in Washington, DC, in the early 1850s.[42] Only two female teachers attended Howard University during this period. Constance G. Seaton, daughter of George L. Seaton, studied music at Howard University for several years before transferring to the Hampton Institute. She returned to Alexandria where she taught elementary school until her untimely death in 1886.[43] Louisa Tancil studied medicine for two years at Howard University before becoming a schoolteacher. In 1895, she moved to Washington, DC, where her spouse, Dr. George W. Cabiness, had opened a medical practice. She left teaching a few years later, most likely to care for her growing family and to dedicate herself to her increasing social responsibilities among Washington's social elites.[44]

In response to the strategies used by parents to give their children a quality education, white Alexandrians complained about the number of students traveling to the District of Columbia. In 1882, Alexandria's superintendent remarked that Washington could afford to educate nonresident students, but Alexandria was "too poor to be so liberal."[45] Black residents, however, knew that it was more than a lack funds that influenced local education. During a community debate in 1892, a Black resident publicly criticized the school system for not providing children with a decent education, especially girls, whom he believed "should be sent to Washington." A day later, the same speaker issued an apology in Alexandria's local newspaper for his criticisms of the public school system. The same paper also reported that a train had struck and killed a Black female student returning from school in the District of Columbia.[46]

Starting in 1899, Washington's public school system began to assess its nonresident student policy in response to the increasing number of children from Virginia and Maryland in attendance. The US Congress had previously legislated that DC's schools had to make exceptions for children whose parents worked in the District but resided elsewhere. This policy primarily catered to elected officials and political appointments who temporarily lived in the District and who wanted their children to go to school there, at least for part of the year.[47] Alexandrians who worked for the federal government also benefited from this legislation and could send their children to DC's public schools. However, Washington's school board tried repeatedly to limit the number of nonresident students over the next two decades.

In the 1910s and 1920s, Black families without the benefit of federal employment relied on kinship networks to send their children to school in Washington. Oral histories with longtime residents speak to how families navigated residency requirements as Washington's school board tried to limit attendance. Born in 1908, Charles "Buster" K. Williams explained that he went to school in Washington starting in sixth grade. He noted that "you had to give a District address. We had relatives in Washington; we stayed with them." Born a decade after Williams, Elsie Thomas and her brothers, civil rights activists and lawyers Samuel W. and Otto L. Tucker, lived with relatives so that they could go to school in the District.[48] Sometimes, even local leaders expected both Black and white families to send their children to DC for school. In 1912, Alexandria County's school board, located outside of the City of Alexandria, was told that it could no longer expect the District of Columbia to provide a high school education for its residents. The County offered to pay the District of Columbia for sixty students, using taxpayer monies, but immediately faced complaints from parents about the selection process.[49]

By the early twentieth century, the appeal of DC's public schools only increased as the gaps between the educational offerings in Alexandria for Black and white children expanded. While white children attended high school classes, there were no such options for Alexandria's African American families.[50] In 1909, Hallowell's principal obtained permission to start a vocational program, funded by donations from the community, but the school board refused to pay for a teacher.[51] The Snowden and Hallowell Schools also used the same structures built by George L. Seaton after the Civil War (see fig. 2.1), while white children went to newly constructed two-story brick buildings that had several amenities, including electricity and indoor plumbing.

After years of complaints about the condition of the city's Black-only schools, Snowden burned to the ground one afternoon in March 1916, while the children played at recess. The fire started when someone threw a match into a trash can located in a closet under the steps between the first and second floors. The entire building was destroyed.[52] A week after the fire, the superintendent rented two buildings for students in first through fourth grades, but it is unknown whether upper grades were offered.[53] With no discussion of new facilities initiated by white city leaders, Black parents requested that the superintendent purchase land for a new "brick school building for colored boys and girls." They argued that Hallowell, where female students still went to school, was also "practically beyond repair" and needed to be replaced.[54] In February 1919, the newly established Colored School Improvement League again petitioned the school board for a new building, stating that "this petition represented an expression from the entire colored citizenship of Alexandria."[55] After another delay, the school board finally purchased land and began building a school, but it required that residents donate money to pay

Figure 2.1. Hallowell School for Girls, ca. 1905.
William Smith Collection, MS399, no. 1492,
Special Collections, Alexandria Public Library, Virginia.

for furniture and supplies. Officers for the Snowden School Alumni Association wrote newspaper articles asking for donations and noted that teachers were raising money too. The Industrial Equipment Committee had obtained more than $700 in donations that it planned to use for sewing, cooking, and woodworking equipment.[56] Alexandria's new all-Black school opened in fall 1920 and was named the Parker-Gray School after longtime teachers John F. Parker and Sarah A. Gray.[57]

By the 1920s, Washington's school board again attempted to ban students from neighboring jurisdictions, this time arguing that DC schools were overcrowded. And again, their efforts failed. Only the US Congress had the power to legislate public school admissions policies in the District of Columbia. To change the law, DC's school board had to lobby the House Subcommittee on District Appropriations or turn to the federal courts.[58] In 1936, Washington's superintendent of schools denied admission to Lois Kemp, a white student from Arlington County, Virginia, whose father worked for the federal government. The Kemps sued, and the court ruled that DC's public schools had to admit their daughter. A few months after the ruling, the District's leading daily newspaper, the *Evening Star*, reported that Washington's public schools were experiencing an increase in the number of nonresident students.[59]

By the 1930s, Alexandria's public schools had also become overcrowded because of an influx of children whose parents were part of President Franklin D. Roosevelt's New Deal bureaucracy. The increase in Black students finally put sufficient pressure on the school board to open another elementary school and to provide classroom space at Parker-Gray for a high school. Using a federal loan, Alexandria bought a vacant silk factory and converted it into the Lyles-Crouch Elementary School, also named after two other longtime African American teachers, Rozier D. Lyles and Jane Crouch. The new building, however, was not big enough to address local needs. The school board rented two houses for its third-grade classrooms and required high school students to attend school in the evening to alleviate overcrowding.[60]

Despite these improvements, Alexandria's schools still lagged, and Black families continued to look to Washington for an alternative education. One of the biggest issues was the lack of support from the Alexandria school board for the high school, which remained unaccredited throughout the 1930s. In 1936, parents at Parker-Gray organized a book drive to support the school library so that it met accreditation requirements. Three years later, a reporter for the *Chicago Defender* noted that Parker-Gray had made major improvements, such as offering a band and orchestra program and a football team, but it remained unaccredited.[61]

Adding to the school system's problems, Alexandria's superintendent of schools, T. C. Williams, fired Parker-Gray's beloved principal, Wesley D. Elam, for his involvement in the equal pay movement. Elam was born on Virginia's south side, which consisted of several counties near the Virginia–North Carolina border with large Black populations. He studied at the Hampton Institute, unlike most of Alexandria's early teachers, before becoming Parker-Gray's principal in the fall of 1927.[62] In the late 1930s, Elam was elected president of the Virginia Teachers Association, which represented Black educators throughout the state. One of the issues that the association wanted to address was Virginia's race-based pay scale for teachers.[63] Alexandria's Black teachers, like their colleagues throughout Virginia, understood only too well how unfairly they were paid. Alexandria's 1926 school board minutes documented the pay gaps between Black and white educators. For the upcoming school year, all African American teachers made less than $1,000 except for Parker-Gray's principal, who received $1,000. Meanwhile, the most junior white teacher's salary was $900. Black Alexandrians also knew that because Washington's teachers were federal employees, they did not face a race-based pay scale. Anna J. Cooper, well-known Washington-based education activist and principal of the prestigious M Street High School, had a salary of $1,800 a year in 1905, the same as other public school principals.[64] In addition to pay equity, Washington's teachers received significantly higher salaries in comparison to Alexandria's.

As Virginia Teachers Association's president, Elam supported a test case to end Virginia's race-based pay scale for teachers, which infuriated Superintendent Williams, who was an ardent segregationist. In June 1940, the Fourth Circuit Court of Appeals ruled that race-based pay scales were unconstitutional in *Alston v. School Board of City of Norfolk*.[65] A few months later, Alexandria's Negro PTA Council petitioned the city's school board to equalize teacher salaries. Williams claimed that he would adjust salaries slowly over the next three years, although he had neglected to inform anyone about his plans. What Black Alexandrians did know was that Williams had not only fired Elam but also blackballed him. Elam struggled to find employment as an educator in Virginia for the rest of his career.[66]

During the late nineteenth and early twentieth centuries, many Black families relied on Washington, DC, to provide a better education for their children than what Alexandria offered. Washington's accessibility, through kinship networks and public transportation, provided an alternative to Alexandria's underfunded, segregated school system. The federal government also segregated Washington's public schools; however, school segregation operated differently in the District of Columbia where administrators, teachers, and parents enjoyed more autonomy over the quality of education provided. As a result, Washington's schools were recognized as the best in the country during the Progressive Era. Alexandria's Black families wanted nothing less for their children.

WORK

The Washington metropolitan region's growing but segregated job market during the Progressive Era appealed to Black Alexandrians as well as to other African Americans from throughout the country. Like most small Southern cities at the turn of the century, Alexandria offered limited options, relegating most men to heavy industry, construction, and railroads and women to domestic work. A small number of business owners and professionals functioned as community leaders who, when problems emerged, advocated for Black residents.[67] The federal government's expansion during the Progressive Era, however, affected both the types and numbers of jobs available. African Americans found mainly low-paying jobs in departments and agencies in downtown Washington, but a handful obtained political appointments and clerkships. At the same time, government contracting opportunities were expanding, particularly in the development of the region's infrastructure. Streetcar suburbs, supplying housing to white, middle- and upper-class families, and monumental edifices along the National Mall employed hundreds of men in the building trades who worked for federal contractors. Factories and heavy industries also proliferated along Alexandria's waterfront, and at least one catered only to government contracts. With so few well-paying and secure options available, many old and new Black Alexandrians coveted federal employment.[68]

Across all socioeconomic classes, federal employment was the biggest reason to live in the Washington metropolitan region in the late nineteenth and early twentieth centuries. Many scholars have demonstrated that the federal government provided a small number of prestigious clerkships, which motivated well-educated African Americans from across the country to move to DC. Republican administrations, which dominated the White House, appointed African Americans to public office, but again offered limited options. Even teachers at DC's public schools and professors at Howard University were federal employees. The overwhelming majority of Black men and women, however, held low-paying positions in construction, janitorial, and domestic work either directly employed by the government or as contractors. Facing a segregated job market across all sectors of the economy, Black workers often chose to stay in federal positions for life because of the relative advantages that came with government employment.[69] Access to Washington's public schools was one such benefit. In 1920, the US Congress passed the Civil Service Retirement Act, which allowed federal workers to participate in a pension program.

A handful of Black Alexandrians who first experienced federal employment during the Civil War tapped into the Republican Party's patronage system to access a limited number of jobs available to those individuals with the right political connections.[70] As noted in chapter 1, John A. Seaton, a free carpenter before the Civil War, along with his father, George L. Seaton, worked for the quartermaster's office. By 1869, he obtained a position as a laborer in the US Treasury Department and then as a police officer at the US Capitol.[71] Politically active Traverse B. Pinn, who had been elected magistrate in 1870, also worked for the quartermaster's office as a teamster. By the early 1870s, he held a position at the US Treasury Department.[72] Not every attempt to obtain a federal appointment or employment was successful. A delegation of Black Republicans failed to convince President Ulysses S. Grant to appoint Robert D. Ruffin as Alexandria's postmaster. Ruffin had been enslaved in Yorktown,

Virginia, and fled to the Union army in June 1862. In 1874, he moved from Washington, DC, to a nearby county where he had been elected sheriff—the first Black sheriff in the state. At the same time, he was studying law at Howard University; he eventually opened a private practice in Alexandria. Ruffin never obtained a federal position but remained active in the local Republican Party.[73]

The end of home rule in the District of Columbia in the early 1870s also gave Black male voters in Alexandria a political advantage. Unlike Washingtonians, Black Alexandrians could mobilize votes for Republican candidates on the local, state, and federal levels, and they expected to be rewarded for their loyalty. A handful of Washingtonians even claimed Alexandria residency in hopes of either obtaining or keeping positions. William Mahone's election to the US Senate in 1881 led to heated exchanges among his inner circle about patronage positions and Virginia residency. Mahone led the Readjuster Party and, while he caucused with Republicans, he wanted all political appointees from Virginia to be loyal to him. In March 1882, Mahone wrote to a white supporter, David A. Windsor, about individuals who claimed Alexandria residency and held federal employment. Mahone wanted to know whether Douglass Syphax, brother to William Syphax (from chapter 1) and a messenger at the US Patent Office, was an Alexandria resident. Windsor responded that Syphax "is a republican and votes with the readjusters" but "has not lived in the city for eight years."[74] A few weeks later, Robert George Cunningham, a white Treasury clerk, responded to a similar query from Mahone about another civil servant. Cunningham responded that he "presume[d] he is one of the many that I am told claim Virginia as their voting place but reside in the District of Columbia."[75]

Even with these privileges, opportunities in the federal government were limited regardless of who was in power. White politicians often overlooked Black loyalists, especially for prestigious appointments. Rozier D. Beckley, a member of one of Alexandria's wealthier free families, held several positions in the offices of the Quartermaster General and the Freedmen's Bureau during the 1860s and was a Republican Party loyalist. As with Ruffin, Black Republicans traveled to Washington to lobby on Beckley's behalf after Alexandria's congressman ignored requests that he be appointed to the US Post Office. Their initial efforts failed, but Beckley obtained another position a year later.[76] In 1881, William Mahone ran on a platform that included bringing more federal appointments to Virginia; however, both Black and white Alexandrians had already established their own political networks and worried that Mahone would take federal patronage away.[77] George Preston, another Black civil servant, explained to Mahone that Alexandria's Black Republicans did not need him to obtain federal jobs because they already had relationships with other politicians and civil servants. Preston, who lived in Alexandria, understood how this system worked and obtained positions in the US Patent Office and later the War Department.[78] He recommended that Mahone focus on Alexandria's working classes who wanted jobs on the grounds of the US Capitol or on the Department of Agriculture's experimental farm. Many of these men, he noted, traveled to Pennsylvania to do harvesting in the summer and fall, not returning home until after the November election. If they worked locally, then they could vote for Mahone.[79]

The creation of the civil service in 1883 somewhat leveled the playing field for federal job candidates who had previously won and lost positions at the whim of politicians. Political affiliation and racial attitudes, however, continued to impact employment, and many of the practices established during Reconstruction affected African Americans.[80] Freeman H. M. Murray was an exception. Born in Ohio in 1859, Murray grew up in a mixed-race family that supported his intellectual interests, which initially led him to a career in teaching. In 1883, Murray passed the civil service exam and received a clerkship in the US Pension Office. Instead of living in the District, he moved to Alexandria to live near his extended family and commuted on the train or ferry. He thoroughly enjoyed his clerkship, noting in his diary that he was "getting along at [the] office finely" after a few weeks on the job.[81] By the summer of 1884, Murray wrote that his supervisor paid him a "great compliment today saying mine was the best record of my class in the office for Aug[ust]."[82] However, he soon became acquainted with Washington's capriciousness. Like his colleagues, he feared the election of President Grover Cleveland, a Democrat, and prepared to find alternative employment. The president-elect, however, sent a letter to the US Pension Office, "assuring us we will not be disturbed." By April 1885, Cleveland's administration had not fired anyone, and had hired ten new clerks, including two African Americans.[83] Firings did occur two years later, after an article in a Republican-leaning paper portrayed Pension Office employees as "loafers."[84] Murray survived the firings and remained in the civil service for over twenty years. He continued to be active in politics, becoming a founding member of the Niagara Movement in the early twentieth century (see fig. 2.2). After starting his own printing company in Washington, Murray collaborated with W. E. B. Du Bois on the organization's first journal, *The Horizon*.[85]

Few African Americans had opportunities like Murray. Most Black men found other types of jobs, if not through the government itself then through the growing number of federal contractors. At the turn of the century,

Figure 2.2. Leaders of the Second Niagara Movement, 1906.
J. R. Clifford, Lafayette M. Hershaw, and Freeman H. M. Murray
(*standing, from left to right*), and W. E. B. Du Bois (*seated*).
W. E. B. Du Bois Papers, MS 312, Robert S. Cox
Special Collections and University Archives Research Center,
UMass Amherst Libraries, Amherst, Massachusetts.

white-only neighborhood associations and federal politicians embraced the City Beautiful Movement, pushing heavy industry out of Washington, which they believed marred its overall appearance.[86] The region's industrial base moved to Alexandria, which saw the expansion of its fertilizer plants, breweries, textile factories, and brickworks. Potomac Yards, which opened in 1906, was the largest railyard on the Eastern Seaboard, serving five railway companies.[87] Meanwhile, Washington's beautification projects created numerous positions in the building trades, most of which were outsourced to local businesses. Sidewalks and streets were big business as white developers constructed new neighborhoods, and the federal government wanted roadways to match the grandeur of the National Mall. By the early 1910s, local paving companies also sent bids to the Bureau of Public Roads to upgrade streets through Alexandria for automobile traffic between Washington, DC, and George Washington's plantation, Mount Vernon. The Bureau of Public Roads believed that these improvements increased school attendance in rural areas and helped farmers transport agricultural goods to local markets. Automobile travel was also important for tourists going to and from Washington and Mount Vernon. One of these early roads became incorporated into Route 1, which today connects Maine to Florida.[88]

The construction and paving industries relied on Black laborers, many of whom commuted from Alexandria to work in Washington or on other federal projects in the region. For more than sixty years, Cranford Paving Company, founded in 1872, received millions of dollars in federal monies to pave the streets and sidewalks in Washington and northern Virginia.[89] Numerous Black men living in Alexandria listed Cranford's Washington office as their employer on their World War I draft cards.[90] Other laborers worked at Camp A. A. Humphreys (today known as Fort Belvoir), the US Army's Engineers Training School established during World War I in a nearby county. P. F. Gormley Company, who won the contract to build Camp A. A. Humphreys, hired local subcontractors in and around Alexandria to complete the military base. By March 1918, Gormley's subcontractors rented homes in Alexandria for their workforce, but it is unknown whether these laborers were Black or white.[91]

As it had during the Civil War, the federal government depended on Alexandria's waterfront for wartime mobilization during World War I. The depth of the Potomac River's channel allowed for the construction of large steamships for military purposes. In 1917, the US Shipping Board contracted Groton Iron Works, under the name Virginia Shipbuilding Corporation, to build twelve steamships in Alexandria, each costing over $1.5 million.[92] The positions that Black men held at the shipyard are mostly unknown. On their World War I draft cards, Black men almost universally wrote "laborer," providing no specifics as to their responsibilities. There were a few exceptions. Lorenzo Chase, who held a handful of different jobs in Alexandria before joining the Virginia Shipbuilding Corporation, wrote down that he was a cement finisher. Lee Hollin worked as a riveter.[93] Jobs at the shipyard appealed to new arrivals who had moved from the Deep South to the Washington metropolitan region in hopes of finding better employment opportunities. Originally from Sumter, South Carolina, Charles Breisford wrote on his draft card that he worked as a laborer for the Virginia Shipbuilding Corporation. Samuel Jones, also from

South Carolina, found employment as a foreman in the shipyard. After the war, he stayed in Alexandria and worked for the railroads.[94]

Wartime mobilization during World War I brought recruiting agents for northern manufacturers to Alexandria looking for Black workers. By 1916, the *Alexandria Gazette* reported that large numbers of Black men had left the city for jobs in the North, but white businessowners believed that they would soon return home, "Where they are understood by the whites and where they have every opportunity for their betterment."[95] At least 700 men left Alexandria's fertilizer plants to work in munitions factories and on road construction in Pennsylvania. Worried about the impact of Black out-migration on the local economy, Alexandria's city council passed an ordinance requiring recruiting agents to obtain a $500 license and pay a $1,000 bond to guarantee employment contracts.[96] The city council's new legislation did not slow the exodus. Black Alexandrians looking for better job opportunities outside the Jim Crow South continued to move to industrialized cities in Pennsylvania, New Jersey, and New York.

The day after the 1918 Armistice, the Bureau of Ordnance broke ground on the Alexandria Naval Torpedo Station (today known as the Alexandria Torpedo Factory) for the War Department. The factory was one of many facilities owned by the federal government located in northern Virginia in the early twentieth century. Once again, African Americans found segregated job opportunities building this multiblock facility that dominated the waterfront. When the station opened in 1919, it manufactured and stored torpedoes for the US Navy, but it ceased production in 1923. The federal government repurposed the complex as a storage facility for munitions and War Department records.[97] During most of the interwar period, few people worked at the station. George E. Parker, a former house painter, held a position as a janitor there for seven years.[98]

By the 1920s, Black women in increasing numbers found jobs with the federal government too. War work had first enabled white women, along with a handful of Black women, to find federal employment during the Civil War, with the expectation that women would return to their previous lives as daughters, wives, and mothers when the war ended. Many women, however, chose to remain in their positions for either financial or personal reasons.[99] During World War I, Washington also saw an influx of female workers. Like their predecessors, these women decided to stay, often preferring employment over marriage.[100] Most Black women held domestic-related positions in the federal government, but a small number found white-collar positions. Julia Washington left domestic work in Alexandria to become an assistant cook at the cafeteria for the US Navy.[101] Alexandria native Carrie Jackson worked at the Bureau of Printing and Engraving as an assistant printer and then as an examiner.[102] Ethel Hackley moved from Pennsylvania to Alexandria in the late 1920s to work as a card operator, an early form of computing. Her family later moved to Washington, DC, where she continued to work as a clerk for the US Navy.[103] All three women were married to men who also worked for the federal government.

Already familiar with the mechanics of federal employment, Alexandrians welcomed New Deal policies that injected desperately needed funds and jobs into the local economy. Throughout the 1930s, both Black and white residents participated in New Deal programs, although options for Black Alexandrians remained circumscribed in comparison to their white counterparts. In 1934, Samuel W. Tucker, Elsie Thomas's older brother and recent law school graduate from Howard University, worked with local teachers at a federally funded night school for adults.[104] A unit of the Civil Conservation Corps, consisting of 70 to 200 African American men, began to clean up the city's waterfront, which had been marred by decades of industrial abuse.[105] In 1939, Hopkins House, a settlement house founded by Black teachers aimed at helping indigent youth, received National Youth Administration funding.[106]

The expanded federal bureaucracy required to support Franklin Delano Roosevelt's New Deal perpetuated many of the segregationist practices seen among Alexandria's employers since the nineteenth century. Even under the Roosevelt administration, which was known for its more liberal views on race relations, African Americans faced a segregated job market. This pattern can be seen among the founding members of the DPC from the beginning of the chapter. Born in Washington, DC, Jessie Carter moved to Alexandria as a child with his widowed mother and siblings after World War I. Census takers in 1930 listed his occupation as a "private helper" for the US government, and he continued to work various nondescript federal positions for the next twenty years.[107] The employment trajectory of another DPC member, however, reflected changes in Black job prospects that began to percolate in the 1930s. Born and raised in Alexandria, Lawrence Dunbar Day had started working at the General Accounting Office as an "office helper" in 1930. A decade later, he became a clerk. By 1952, he was section chief of the voucher office.[108]

CONCLUSION

The differences in segregationist practices between Alexandria and Washington were once again brought into sharp relief in the spring and summer of 1939.

Both jurisdictions offered public libraries, but only white patrons were allowed to use Alexandria's. Samuel W. Tucker, now a full-time lawyer, had to travel to Washington, DC, to do legal research for his clients, using facilities such as the Library of Congress. The only Alexandria option was the Parker-Gray School's library, but it was geared toward children and its collections were primarily donated. When Alexandria completed a new white-only library building using taxpayer dollars, Tucker decided that it was time to create a scenario in which to challenge Jim Crow segregation in Virginia. The Virginia Public Assemblages Act (1926) mandated the segregation of all public spaces but forbade the outright exclusion of African Americans if a segregated option was not provided.[109] Tucker believed Alexandria's white-only library was a perfect test case.

To challenge the law, Tucker set up two situations that he hoped would end up in the courts. First, he obtained a library card application for his friend, George Wilson, a retired US Army sergeant and Alexandria resident, and asked him to submit it. The librarian refused Wilson's application, and Tucker sued the library. A few months later, Tucker recruited five men to visit the library and request library card applications. Once they were denied, they were to select a book from a shelf and sit down at a table to read it. The librarians, shocked by what was happening, called the police who escorted the men out of the library. Thanks to a few calls by Tucker, a crowd, including reporters from both Alexandria and Washington, gathered to observe the event.[110]

Once the two trials began, the judges quickly realized what was at stake. Judge James Reese Duncan refused to decide on the case and released the men involved in the sit-in. A year later, Judge William O. Woolls threw out Wilson's lawsuit on a technicality but noted, "There were no legal grounds for refusing the plaintiff or any other bona fide citizen the use of the library." Woolls understood that if Wilson applied again and was refused a card, then the outcome in the courts might be different.[111] However, by that time, Alexandria's city leaders had announced plans to build a separate library for Black residents.

Although it failed to overturn the segregation of public accommodations in Virginia, Tucker's legal maneuvers reflected the synergisms that existed between Washington's and Alexandria's Black communities during the Progressive Era. Born in Alexandria, he lived with extended family in Washington to obtain an education, and he later studied law at Howard University. There he learned about civil disobedience through the teachings of school chaplain, Howard W. Thurman.[112] In 1933, Black Washingtonians put civil disobedience to use, establishing the New Negro Alliance, which deployed direct action against white-owned businesses who refused to employ African Americans.

One local grocery company sued, but the US Supreme Court ruled that the alliance's peaceful demonstrations were constitutional, thus setting the stage for future civil rights activism.[113] Tucker also knew about the recent cases of the National Association for the Advancement of Colored People (NAACP) to integrate graduate school programs in Maryland and Virginia. One of his professors, Charles Hamilton Houston, and a former classmate, Thurgood Marshall, had successfully sued the University of Maryland's Law School for refusing to admit a prospective Black student in *University v. Murray* (1936).[114] Tucker's strategy at Alexandria's white-only public library was novel, but it aligned with similar ideas circulating among both Black Washingtonians and Alexandrians: using civil disobedience, combined with the courts, to roll back segregation.

In the period after Reconstruction through the 1930s, Alexandria's proximity to the District of Columbia altered but, like Tucker's sit-in, did not end Jim Crow segregation. In the early twentieth century, African Americans chafed at the experiences of crossing the Potomac River on public transportation, moving between two segregationist systems, only one of which segregated trains, ferries, streetcars, and buses. A handful of both Black and white riders turned to the courts in protest, but with little effect on Virginia's policies. These new transportation technologies, however, facilitated the movements of Black Alexandrians who, in response to local educational conditions, decided to send their children to Washington's premiere public and private schools so that they had more promising futures. As the federal government expanded during the Progressive Era, so too did opportunities to find work in the region. Federal employment, like other job sectors, was segregated, but these positions were seen as desirable because of their relative stability and benefits. The federal government's expansion also created new jobs, most notably with government contractors.

The relationship between Washington and Alexandria provided the spark that led residents such as Tucker to question structural racism and turn to direct action and the courts to fight it. Housing was another such arena where systemic racism impacted Black Alexandrians in the early- to mid-twentieth century. And—it also required the careful navigation of local, state, and federal power structures to fight it.

CHAPTER THREE

Accessibility

On October 10, 1967, A. Melvin Miller, a civil rights leader and lawyer for the Federal Housing Administration (FHA) in Washington, DC, spoke before Alexandria's city council about the housing problems that African Americans faced. A few days earlier, two children had died in a fire; they had been living in a building that he described as a "firetrap." This tragedy, Miller noted, was not the first. In 1962, six children had died in a similar fire a few blocks away. What connected them was that the children were Black, and their families had few safe housing options in Alexandria. He argued that these "families . . . are forced to live in this type of housing solely because there is no other housing in the city available in which they can live." Miller then shared another story about an elderly resident who had taught in the school district for forty-two years and who, after retiring, volunteered to help needy residents. She wanted to downsize from her two-story home but remain in Alexandria to be close to family and friends. One night, she called Miller and cried. Miller explained, "They told her they had just what she wanted until she got there, and she was turned down at virtually every one of them because she is a Negro."[1] Like the families whose children had died in housefires, she could not find a place to live in Alexandria.

Miller's anecdotes drove home a message to the city council and other individuals in the room that night that local practices and policies had to change so that African American residents could access decent housing. Above all other issues facing African Americans, Miller believed that "the problem of inadequate housing and discrimination in housing" was "behind virtually every problem that has been brought forth in the cities of America today." He was uncertain how much longer "this system is going to be permitted," but he decided to speak before the city council in the hope of beginning the process of desegregating Alexandria's housing market.[2]

Miller's speech highlighted the impact of housing discrimination on African Americans in Alexandria, which was partially driven by the city's proximity to the nation's capital combined with local and federal policies and practices. The expansion of Washington's bureaucracy during the Progressive Era led to a housing boom in northern Virginia. Real estate developers built modern subdivisions consisting of single-family homes with small yards along streetcar and train lines to cater to the region's growing workforce. These subdivisions, however, were located outside of Alexandria, which offered more dense housing options and had buildings that dated to the eighteenth century. To appeal to homebuyers interested in a modern suburban lifestyle, white leaders annexed new subdivisions, which introduced racially restrictive covenants to Alexandria for the first time.[3] Meanwhile, federal land use zoning allowed Washington bureaucrats to control all construction within view of the George Washington Parkway, a new road project that connected Washington to George Washington's Mount Vernon and that cut through Alexandria. At the same time, federal officials pressured Alexandria's city council to pass a zoning ordinance that aligned with their policies for the parkway. Alexandria's zoning prioritized single-family, suburban homes, moving the city's industrial sector away from new subdivisions and into Black neighborhoods. Finally, as in other parts of the country, New Deal housing policies adversely affected African Americans by denying access to federally backed mortgages and simultaneously targeting Black neighborhoods with eminent domain to make way for public housing and urban renewal projects.[4] As Miller rightly stated, Black families struggled to find decent places to live and were often forced into dilapidated housing in hyper-segregated neighborhoods or out of Alexandria completely. And federal policies, implemented on both the national and local levels, helped to codify housing segregation.

In many ways, Alexandria's housing problems reflected issues that African Americans and other marginalized communities faced throughout the United States. Many historians have shown how local and federal policies redrew racial boundaries in American cities and suburbs and forced African Americans into hyper-segregated neighborhoods. In turn, African Americans mobilized, often breaking with Black elites, who were more conciliatory toward white politicians, and using direct action to highlight injustice.[5] Alexandria's proximity to Washington, however, allowed activists to engage national politicians and civil servants on housing issues in unique ways. And a handful of African Americans, such as Miller, held critical positions within the federal government. In Miller's case, he worked as a lawyer at the FHA in Washington and later at the Department of Housing and Urban Development (HUD). Nevertheless, African Americans remained limited in their ability to influence federal and local policies that reinforced segregationist practices through the 1960s.

Like Samuel Tucker in the previous chapter, Miller was part of a new generation of activists who changed the ways in which African Americans responded to social injustice. J. Douglas Smith argues that the 1939 sit-in over Alexandria's white-only library was a turning point in Virginia's paternalistic system.[6] The use of direct action combined with Tucker's legal and political acumen, forced city officials to face what was the first of many challenges to segregation during and after World War II. For Tucker, the educational opportunities that Washington offered, first through its public schools and then through Howard University, provided the foundation for such activism. Other historians have pointed to the role that Black military personnel and veterans played in protests during and after World War II, especially in response to the Servicemen's Readjustment Act (1944), popularly known as the GI Bill. The GI Bill provided low-interest mortgages and college funding, but government officials denied African Americans and other marginalized communities access to these programs.[7] By the mid-twentieth century, Alexandria, because of its location, was home to numerous members of the armed services and veterans. Many of these men and women worked at the newly constructed Pentagon, on one of the nearby military bases, or in downtown Washington.

This chapter explores the impact of the federal government on housing in early- to mid-twentieth-century Alexandria and the ways in which local actors navigated segregation by leveraging relationships with Black Washingtonians, civil servants, and military personnel. The expansion of the federal government's workforce during the Progressive Era facilitated the use of racially restrictive covenants in newly constructed subdivisions. Introduced by the federal government, land use zoning also reorganized the city's racial makeup. Finally, housing segregation further accelerated as the federal government implemented public housing and urban renewal projects from the 1930s through the 1960s that targeted African American neighborhoods. In response, civil rights activists and their supporters, many of whom worked for the federal government, mobilized resources on the local and federal levels to fight housing discrimination. Through news coverage, speeches, marches, and legislation, African Americans also raised awareness about housing discrimination and promoted alternatives that would create new opportunities for all residents. By the late 1960s, problems surrounding housing persisted, but Alexandrians could see notable changes in the racial makeup of a handful of neighborhoods.

BEGINNINGS

The construction of turn-of-the-century streetcar suburbs to cater to Washington's growing civil service put new pressures on Alexandria's housing market. White developers purchased large tracts of farmland and country estates, which existed outside of Alexandria, on which to build subdivisions that they hoped would appeal to the region's white middle class. Advertisements and newspaper articles described these neighborhoods as modern developments that offered the most current amenities.[8] To participate in the changing housing market, city boosters turned to three ideas: the construction of new subdivisions, territorial annexation, and land use zoning. These strategies allowed developers, property owners, and city officials to curate Alexandria's preexisting housing stock and construct new neighborhoods, almost all of which had racially restrictive covenants. As a result, the city's overall population increased, but the percentage of African American residents declined until the 1970s (see table 3.1).

Like in education and employment, as discussed in the previous chapter, the federal government's expansion during the Progressive Era impacted Alexandria's housing market too. By the 1890s, white civil servants had moved to northern Virginia in increasing numbers where they purchased newly constructed single-family homes and commuted to work on trains or streetcars. Alexandria's older housing stock, which consisted largely of densely packed rowhouses, was unappealing to most homebuyers. To align itself with new ideas about homeownership in the early twentieth century, Alexandria needed to change the types of housing available and redraw the color line.[9] Most of Alexandria's land was developed, and there was little to no room for the construction of new subdivisions. The city's racial demographics also varied block by block, representing a mixture of Black and white residents.[10]

Table 3.1. Alexandria residents based on race from US Census data, 1910–1970.

Years	Total population	Number of Black residents	Number of white residents	Number of other residents	Black residents in total population (%)
1910	15,329	4,188	11,132	9	27.3
1920	18,060	4,112	13,936	12	22.8
1930	24,149	4,912	19,230	7	20.3
1940	33,523	5,281	28,219	23	15.8
1950	61,787	7,622	54,121	n/a	12.3
1960	91,023	10,353	80,388	282	11.4
1970	110,938	15,644	94,534	832	14.1

Source: US Census population numbers and percentages from 1910 through
1960 are from Social Explorer (www.socialexplorer.com/explore-maps).
Note: In 1950, Social Explorer divided "race" between "white" and "non-white."

To resolve this issue, Alexandria turned to the annexation of land from nearby counties, where racially restricted subdivisions were in the process of being built and vacant land was available for future development. In 1909, the Rosemont Development Company built a new subdivision offering "modern living" along a streetcar line just outside of the city limits. When developers sold houses in "Rosemont," they inserted a "Caucasian only" clause in the deeds for most lots. Impressed by the neighborhood's "beauty" and "value," city leaders argued that the neighborhood should be annexed. In 1915, after a series of court battles, Alexandria annexed Rosemont, along with several other white-only subdivisions.[11] The annexation of additional land from neighboring counties in 1930 included at least thirteen more racially restricted subdivisions and hundreds of acres of undeveloped farmland and country estates.[12]

The federal government introduced land use zoning to Alexandria when it began the construction of the George Washington Parkway in the late 1920s. A federally owned highway that connected the District of Columbia to Mount Vernon, the Parkway was intended to embody for automobile drivers "the dignity, purpose and memorial character of said highway." To improve its overall ambience, federal officials limited land use along the roadway to middle-class residential developments and commercial establishments that catered to travelers, such as gas stations and roadside restaurants. Concerned that the condition of buildings near the parkway might mar the driving experience, federal officials also lobbied Alexandria city leaders to pass a land use zoning ordinance that aligned with federal policies.[13] Alexandria had previously passed a zoning ordinance in 1923, which divided the city between residential and nonresidential spaces, but it did little to police property use.[14] In response to federal pressure, the city council hired Irving C. Root, chief engineer from the Maryland-National Capital Park and Planning Commission, the federal agency that oversaw the construction of George Washington Parkway, to consult on the city's new ordinance and draw up its first zoning map.[15]

In 1931, Alexandria's city council passed its new zoning ordinance that aligned with both state guidelines and federal policies.[16] Like other communities, the new zoning ordinance prioritized single-family dwellings, but it took special care to protect the aesthetics in the area around the George Washington Parkway. In at least one instance, the new ordinance put a local company out of business. West Brothers Brick Company owned land that it planned to use for clay mining a couple of blocks away from the parkway. The city's new land use map, however, zoned the West Brothers' property for residential purposes so that Alexandria could promote a white middle-class image for parkway travelers. The company sued, but the Virginia State Supreme Court affirmed the legality of the city's zoning policies.[17] West Brothers Brick Company sold its land for suburban development, and racially restrictive covenants were inserted into the land deed.[18] Meanwhile, African American households a few blocks from West Brothers' land were rezoned for industrial use on Root's new zoning map.[19]

City officials also used zoning to make older neighborhoods more appealing to white middle-class homeowners. Parks and yard space were believed to increase property values and create amenities that white middle-class families wanted. A city planning report from 1935 noted that parks compensated for the lack of yard space in older neighborhoods and "prevent[ed] the development of slums." When possible, it recommended that zoning policies prioritize yard space and playgrounds so that children did not have to play in the street.[20] The location of elementary schools also appealed to white middle-class families. Best practices meant that young children walked only about a half mile to and from school, and most of Alexandria's white-only elementary schools met these guidelines. African American children, however, had a very different experience. Until the opening of the Lyles-Crouch Elementary School, only two elementary schools were available for Black children, and they were located two miles away from each other on opposite sides of the city.[21]

The expansion of the federal workforce in the early twentieth century led to new policies and practices that limited housing options for African Americans in Alexandria. Racially restrictive covenants combined with annexation expanded the number of white-only suburban neighborhoods. Zoning ordinances, informed by federal policies for the George Washington

Parkway, prioritized single-family dwellings for white middle-class residents. City officials also attempted to make older sections of the city more appealing to white families through the construction of parks, playgrounds, and elementary schools.

Starting in the 1930s, New Deal housing policies also contributed to housing segregation in Alexandria.

THE NEW DEAL

Alexandria (as well as the rest of the Washington metropolitan region) functioned as a metaphorical petri dish where the same white civil servants who wrote and implemented New Deal housing policies also lived. As many historians have argued, these policies did not address everyone's housing needs and exacerbated housing shortages for African Americans by further limiting options in an already segregated housing market. Federally backed mortgages and public housing construction added to the marginalization of Black residents who additionally had to navigate racially restrictive covenants and land use zoning. Furthermore, New Deal programs failed to provide enough housing to address local need; they also limited wealth generation and deemed homes and neighborhoods as either high risk or blighted without acknowledging the role that discrimination played in their physical condition. At times, the rhetoric of blight had no connection to reality, with homes targeted for slum clearance often meeting or surpassing housing codes.[22] Finally, another important issue that impacted Black homeowners and renters in the 1930s: a massive influx of new federal workers and military personnel.[23] African Americans were part of this migration and put down roots in notable numbers, either moving out from Washington or from other parts of the country, especially the Deep South. Black housing options, however, differed significantly from white ones, and new arrivals and longtime residents competed in a circumscribed housing market. These demographic pressures, combined with New Deal policies, made it difficult for African Americans to find a place to live in Alexandria.

FHA real estate appraisers deemed neighborhoods with large numbers of low-income or minority residents as high risk and often refused to insure mortgages from private banks for properties in those areas.[24] The Washington metropolitan region's 1937 FHA grading map (also known as a redlining map) designated Alexandria, except for its recently annexed white-only subdivisions, as high risk, placing it in either the "F" or "G" categories. The "F" category meant that an area "show[ed] effects of negro occupancy; many of the structures are in poor condition and are rapidly tending to become slums if not already in that category"; while the "G" category denoted that an area lacked "homogeneity of property design or racial grouping."[25] Thus, white homeowners in newer, restricted subdivisions had a better chance of participating in the FHA's mortgage programs in the 1930s.

For new subdivisions that received FHA support, real estate developers had to meet guidelines that mitigated what federal officials believed to be risk factors, which included the presence of Black homeowners and renters. As a result, developers inserted racially restrictive covenants in their land deeds in order to receive federal funding. In one instance, the FHA set what language should be used: "No race or nationality other than those for whom the premises are intended, shall use or occupy any building on any lot, except that this covenant shall not prevent occupancy by domestic servants of a different race or nationality employed by an owner or tenant. (The wording of this restriction should not be used in actual restrictions which are to be recorded, but a racial restriction should be properly drawn so that the objectives as above set forth will be accomplished)."[26] In this case, developers modified the covenant language from the FHA and inserted "Caucasian only" instead of the phrase "race or nationality."[27] Playing to eugenical ideas from Virginia's Racial Integrity Act (1924), Alexandria's developers often inserted covenants that emphasized a white/non-white divide as opposed to a Black/white one.

In addition to funding new construction, the FHA provided monies for historic preservation projects. Interestingly, the FHA's grading map for the Washington metropolitan area considered Alexandria's older structures to be high risk, but assessors made exceptions if the structure's historic value could be translated into economic value. As early as 1930, Irving C. Root had noted that "Alexandria's historical appeal is as great" as Williamsburg, but that more needed to be done to "protect the submerged values and attractiveness of the city and save it for the community, which will eventually cash in on it."[28] Root's statement about the undervaluation of Alexandria's older housing stock also occurred in other cities where wealthier white residents began to promote what Cameron Logan argues is "a new form of value, one based in its distinctive legacy of colonial- and federal-era houses and the atmosphere of history associated with them."[29] Federal monies to renovate old buildings went to at least one white homeowner and a local history museum. In 1934, Virginia's governor allocated an FHA-backed loan from Virginia's "better-housing campaign" to pay for the installation of a new roof on Gadsby's Tavern, a late eighteenth-century hotel and eating establishment associated with the Founding Fathers. The local chapter of the American Legion opened

Gadsby's as a museum in 1929.[30] A year later, local newspapers reported that FHA and city officials toured a recently restored colonial-era home that had received an FHA-backed loan. FHA administrators wanted to see whether such projects were a good investment.[31]

Alexandria's federally funded public housing program also figured prominently in the reorganization of neighborhoods along racial lines. From the late 1930s through the early 1960s, white city leaders reworked Alexandria's racial landscape by tearing down residences in racially mixed neighborhoods and replacing them with segregated public housing.[32] To understand Alexandria's housing needs, the city council first asked the Works Projects Administration (WPA) to write a report on the problem. In 1939, the WPA found that 23 percent of Alexandria's 8,076 dwelling units were substandard or in need of major repairs to make them structurally sound. Of these substandard dwellings, 15 percent housed whites and 67 percent housed African Americans.[33] The data from this report also correlated residents living in substandard housing with income level, family size, and access to social services. Overcrowded homes, which totaled 280, affected 2.5 percent of the total number of white dwellings and 7 percent of Black ones. Of the families in substandard housing, 49 percent made less than $1,000 a year. Most low-income families were small, consisting of two to three people. Finally, only 11 percent of whites and 15 percent of African Americans in substandard housing were known to welfare organizations. These final two percentages shocked researchers: public and private charities seemed unaware of the depth of Alexandria's poverty.[34]

Black residents protested the city's decision to tear down houses it deemed to be blighted to make room for segregated public housing.[35] Hannah Nelson, a domestic worker and cook who moved to Alexandria after World War I, owned her home and provided room and board for one lodger. She hired white lawyer Henry P. Thomas to fight her property's condemnation by the city.[36] Thomas argued that Nelson's home was "actually in very good condition, in such condition that it can be repaired." The council voted in favor of Nelson.[37] A letter from railroad worker Lynn W. Ellis, who moved to Alexandria sometime in the late 1920s, spoke directly to the relationship between race-based segregation and local housing conditions:

> You are aware of the fact that sixty per cent of the houses that is
> available for colored people has long out lived their usefulness. But
> if you demolish these houses immediately, then where shall all of
> these people find shelter? This is a matter that deserve[s] your closest

thoughts. Certainly these people do not desire to live in fire traps but if that is the best that [they] can do, then why turn them out in the streets in masses? The majority of the people that has rec'd moving notices has tried in vain to find new homes. Or places to store their belongings in such short time that has been given them.[38]

The city council's minutes note that the letter was received, but no action was taken in response.[39]

In June 1939, the city council created the Alexandria Housing Authority (later known as the Alexandria Redevelopment and Housing Authority [ARHA]) to administer a federally funded public housing program.[40] In its first year, ARHA planned to build about 200 units for low-income families and raze the same number of privately owned homes.[41] A year later, ARHA condemned 240 homes and began construction on two segregated housing facilities. The white-only John Robert Homes was built on vacant land along the tracks of the Richmond, Fredericksburg, and Potomac Railroad and the border of one of the city's poorer, racially mixed neighborhoods. African American families were housed in the George Parker Homes, the construction of which required the condemnation of two city blocks of The Berg, another racially mixed neighborhood. The Berg, shortened from Petersburg and named for a town in southern Virginia, was one of the neighborhoods established by African American refugees who had fled to Alexandria during the Civil War. As noted in chapter 1, these men and women had built their own homes instead of relying on the Union's refugee housing options.[42]

The massive mobilization of Americans during World War II put additional pressures on Alexandria's housing market. Newly arrived military personnel and defense workers had limited options in a region that was already overextended through the influx of civil servants during the New Deal era. For African Americans who already faced a racially circumscribed housing market the situation was even more dire. A 1941 *Washington Post* article reported that "as many as 20 Negroes [were] occupying three and four-room houses" because they had no place to go.[43] In response to the problems that Black families faced, Washington's War Housing Center requested "'every Negro family in this entire territory to go over his household and see if he can "double up" a bit and take in a paying war guest or his family.'"[44]

In addition to requesting that Black families open their homes to boarders, federal authorities built temporary housing and trailer parks for military personnel and war workers.[45] Alexandria's wartime housing, however, continued the pattern of underserving African Americans. Chinquapin

Village (300 units) and Cameron Valley (341 units) provided housing for white defense workers. Ramsey Homes (20 units), built in a racially mixed neighborhood not too far from the city's Black-only public housing units, was for African Americans.[46] White residents and city leaders disliked the federal government's construction of war worker housing, and they especially complained about trailer parks. Trailers, they argued, devalued nearby homes and potentially caused outbreaks of disease. During the war, the FHA condemned Black-owned homes and installed fifty trailers for African American war workers; another fifty trailers were placed in a white-only neighborhood for white workers.[47] Alexandria's city council unanimously passed a resolution denouncing the installation of trailers and then turned to the courts to stop the federal government.[48] After an injunction by the courts failed, the city council refused to supply sewer and water hookups to the trailers without a court order.[49] By summer 1943, after several months of legal battles, the federal government had installed its trailers. A year later, the FHA gave the trailers to ARHA to house African American families.[50]

By the end of World War II, Alexandria's racial landscape had changed drastically. The FHA had only backed mortgages for white homeowners and even required developers to insert racially restrictive language in land deeds. ARHA had destroyed parts of Alexandria's racially mixed neighborhoods and replaced them with segregated public housing units. Additionally, many Black homeowners affected by the public housing demolitions lost any wealth that they had generated through homeownership. Wartime mobilization only exacerbated housing issues, bringing thousands of Black and white war workers and military personnel into the region. The federal government attempted to provide segregated housing for new arrivals, but it failed to address the housing needs of African Americans.

All these problems persisted in the post–World War II period.

POSTWAR HOUSING POLITICS

After World War II, white politicians, civic organizations, and business leaders embraced federally funded urban renewal programs in the hope of continuing to redraw the city's racial boundaries and accommodating the demands of postwar growth in Alexandria. Public housing, restrictive covenants, annexation, and zoning were still important; however, city boosters believed that more needed to be done to appeal to white middle-class families who were moving into the region as part of the US government's Cold War expansion. Leroy S. Bendheim, Alexandria's vice mayor and member of a committee that oversaw ARHA, explained the need for renewal: "Those who cling to ancient customs and moorings in the face of insistent progress will awake some day to find themselves living in a dead city, through which time and events have swept by to come to rest in more receptive climes."[51] Many white leaders, afraid that Alexandria's older housing stock might turn away families looking for a modern lifestyle, sought to reimagine the city as relevant in the postwar consumerist era. African Americans, however, were left out of the new image of a modern Alexandria.

White leaders expressed numerous reasons to pursue urban renewal. The creation of a historic district in 1946, known as the Old and Historic District or Old Town, made redevelopment projects nearly impossible in the oldest sections of the city. All construction in the historic district had to go before the Board of Architectural Review (BAR), which required projects to align with a colonial or early republican aesthetic.[52] Competition from newly built shopping centers outside of the city meant that consumers did not need to venture into Alexandria's congested downtown to go shopping.[53] By the 1950s, the majority of the city's residents did not work within the city limits but were commuting to federal and other office jobs along the region's new highway system.[54] With their jobs elsewhere, these workers needed a greater incentive to live and shop in Alexandria. Finally, the US Supreme Court's decision in *Brown v. Board of Education* (1954) terrified many white parents who feared their children would attend integrated schools. The pairing of federal funds with local authority gave white leaders the ability to manage, if not eliminate, racial integration in Alexandria's public schools through housing policy.

Concerned with increasing Alexandria's modern features and attractions, the city's first attempt at urban renewal began in 1951. ARHA studied an eleven-block area to the west of the city's historic district and found sixty-four homes without private baths and only cold-water plumbing. Thirty of these were reportedly in such a dangerous structural state that ARHA recommended demolition.[55] ARHA, along with the city council's planning committee, endorsed seizing these properties through eminent domain and selling them to a private developer, who would build a shopping center. The shopping center was to become Alexandria's new commercial district so consumers would not leave the city or drive into the historic district to go shopping.[56]

The city's shopping center project upset numerous residents, both Black and white, for a variety of reasons. Business owners expressed outrage that the city council would use eminent domain and then sell the land to a private developer. They also felt that the city government needed to put its resources into supporting preexisting businesses. The president of a white-only citizens association from a nearby neighborhood spoke against the theoretical concept of eminent domain and questioned whether the project addressed any of the city's housing problems or simply made them worse. A representative of a nearby Black congregation argued that the plan would "leave in one corner thereof a Church serving a particular community but move the community away and leave the church there isolated."[57] Finally, attorney Edwin C. Brown, another Howard University–trained lawyer, represented Black homeowners in the area. Originally from Oklahoma, Brown had opened two law firms, one in Washington and another in Alexandria, in the 1940s and represented Black Alexandrians on two key civil rights issues: housing and schools.[58] In response to the proposed urban renewal project, Brown stated that his clients did not believe that city leaders would help them find new homes once they were displaced. Brown, however, went further, connecting the condition of housing in the area with racism: "You know, as I know, that the housing situation as regards negroes is acute. They have low incomes and as a result will have low standards of living and they are not responsible for it! In any job, private or with the municipalities, they are the last ones to be hired and the first ones to be fired. What else can you expect but substandard living?"[59] After much political and legal maneuvering, the city council placed the project on permanent hold.[60]

Within a year, the city council began discussing urban renewal again, this time with the intention to apply for federal funds under the newly revised Housing Act of 1954.[61] To comply with the new law, the city council passed the Minimum Housing-Hygiene Ordinance, which gave the Health and Fire Departments the power to condemn properties not in compliance.[62] At the same time, the city council set up the Community Development Committee, popularly known as the Committee of 77, to analyze the unique needs of Alexandria's neighborhoods. The committee issued a report based on each neighborhood and found that blight was scattered throughout the city. These areas, however, housed a majority of the city's African American residents. To remedy the situation, it recommended the implementation of policies to prevent blight, the hiring of more staff to enforce laws, and measures to make the historic area more accessible to cars. No suggestions were made to address the segregationist policies and practices that had created dangerous conditions in the first place.[63]

Uptown, where the largest concentration of African Americans lived after World War II, remained the biggest concern. Known as Newtown during the Civil War, it was another neighborhood that African American refugees had established. By the mid-1870s, the neighborhood had been incorporated into the city's northwest quadrant and was often called "uptown" in the *Alexandria Gazette*.[64] The Committee of 77 noted that Uptown contained "the most serious blight problems in Alexandria" and had "the highest crime, delinquency and communicable disease rates in the city." Two years earlier, Alexandria's Planning Department also reported that 51 percent of Uptown's housing needed major repairs and that it saw the largest number of social problems. While described as a Black neighborhood, Uptown's demographics were a mixture of Black (60 percent) and white (40 percent) households, but these residents were among the poorest in the city, earning 50 percent below the city average. The Planning Department recommended housing redevelopment in Uptown with federal assistance because "private enterprise has not assumed the responsibility of providing decent living quarters for the people, and more than likely, will not be anxious to do so."[65]

Despite the focus in planning reports on Uptown's housing conditions, Alexandria's first federally funded urban renewal project redeveloped the city's historic commercial corridor (see map 3.1). Named after the eighteenth-century tavern turned museum, the Gadsby Commercial Urban Renewal Project began in 1959. Initial plans included leveling a twenty-block area of Alexandria's downtown and constructing a new commercial corridor in the middle of the city's oldest housing stock. Various versions of the plan included a municipal center, parking lots, green space, high-rise apartments, an auditorium, department stores, a civic center, and a 200-room hotel.[66]

The newly formed Historic Alexandria Foundation, which consisted of white middle- and upper-class residents, were among the most vocal critics of the Gadsby Project. The Foundation, along with preservationist-minded homeowners and other organizations, argued that the project would damage the city's architectural uniqueness and hamper its heritage tourism industry. It conceded that "slums" should be leveled but that other older buildings that its members deemed to be historic should be rehabilitated.[67] In response to these criticisms, city leaders agreed to restore some buildings and to require new construction to match Old Town's colonial and early republican architecture; it subsequently shrunk the project's overall size.[68]

Although not discussed in the press, the displacement of lower-income residents living in and around the Gadsby Project area was a major concern for city officials. A full 75 percent of the individuals and families who were to be displaced applied for public housing, but few African Americans had a chance of finding a slot. In the late 1950s, only 41 units turned over annually in the city's Black-only public housing, which included 459 units. White-only public housing, which had 462 units, turned over at a rate of 210 units

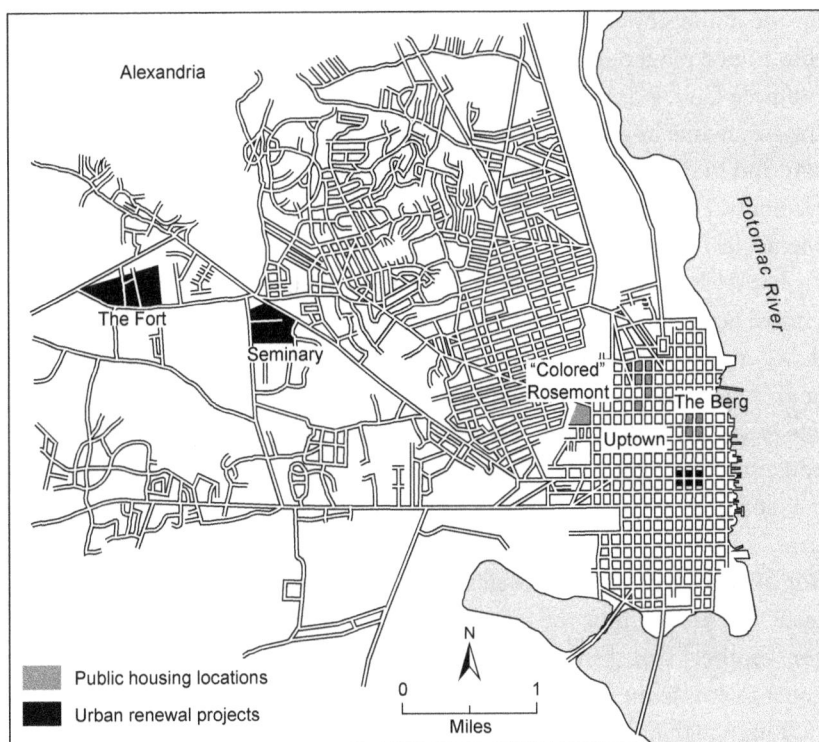

Map 3.1. Alexandria's public housing and urban renewal projects
in relation to Black neighborhoods, 1930s–1960s.
Map by Elisa Luckabaugh, 2023.

per year.[69] Federal funds had been acquired to build additional Black-only public housing; however, these homes would not be available until 1964. For displaced residents unable to obtain public housing, ARHA gave them "assistance" in the form of private market listings of possible rental units and homes for sale.[70]

Around the same time, Alexandria's city council approved two additional urban renewal projects to improve its suburban appeal to white civil servants and other workers: Fort Ward Historic Park and T. C. Williams High School (today known as Alexandria City High School). Unlike Gadsby, which affected Alexandria's urban core, these projects targeted Black neighborhoods recently annexed by the city. After World War II, the Civil War Round Table of the District of Columbia had initiated conversations with white residents about building a park on the remains of Fort Ward, one of the sixty-eight Union forts that remained from the Defenses of Washington. The park would be one of the stops along the Round Table's proposed Fort Drive, a freeway they hoped the federal government would build to alleviate congestion and promote Civil War tourism.[71] With suburban development encroaching on the area, white homeowners petitioned the city council to acquire the property and build a multipurpose park that included recreational and historic elements. Federal funds purchased part of the land, and the park opened on Memorial Day in 1964.[72]

For African Americans, Fort Ward Park further constrained an already limited housing market. A neighborhood known as The Fort had been established on the site after the Civil War, and a handful of families had bought land, which they passed down to their children and grandchildren. By the late 1940s, white developers owned most of the land, but African Americans constituted the majority of the neighborhood's residents. To facilitate the creation of the park, city sanitarians declared all homes at The Fort "substandard," setting the stage for their demolition through the threat of eminent domain proceedings.[73] Maydell Casey Belk, a resident of The Fort, recalled in an oral history how the city pressured her mother to sell: "The city told her [mother] that if she didn't sell it she would lose out because they were going to condemn the houses because they didn't have any bathrooms, no running water and stuff, so that is when she gave in." With their home facing condemnation, the Casey family sold their property in 1965, a year after city leaders had opened the park.[74]

The city slated the Seminary neighborhood, another Black community in western Alexandria, for urban renewal in order to construct a new high school. Residents of the Seminary, like those of The Fort, had settled in the area after the Civil War and worked either in agriculture or at two nearby private schools. Unlike The Fort, African Americans owned almost all the land in the Seminary neighborhood. Its population had also grown significantly because it was one of the few places where Black families could live in what was otherwise a huge swath of racially restricted subdivisions. The Committee of 77 maintained that "Mudtown [the derogatory name whites gave to the Seminary neighborhood] is a problem to the city," and although a few "houses may be rehabilitated, there [were] large numbers that should be removed."[75] By 1960, city leaders decided to level most of the neighborhood and replace it with a "new high school to avoid serious overcrowding in the city's two predominantly white high schools."[76]

T. C. Williams High School opened on the remains of the Seminary neighborhood in the fall of 1965, serving primarily the white-only subdivisions nearby.[77] Desegregation had begun in Alexandria's public schools in

February 1959 after the local chapter of the NAACP successfully sued the city to allow nine children to go to the schools nearest their homes.[78] School officials, however, slowed the implementation of *Brown v. Board* (1954) through the state's pupil placement program, which used academic testing to refuse admittance of Black children to white-only schools. Within a year, the Fourth Circuit Court of Appeals ruled that the pupil placement process was illegal, but Alexandria's school leaders continued to use pupil placement through the spring of 1965. Only the passage of the Civil Rights Act (1964), with the threat that Alexandria would lose $1 million in federal funding, ended the practice.[79] The impact of decades of racist housing policies also meant that only a handful of schools integrated after pupil placement ended. Two of Alexandria's three high schools, including T. C. Williams, catered to white supermajorities through the late 1960s.[80]

Federally funded urban renewal rewrote Alexandria's racial landscape by pushing out Black residents and providing new places for the white middle class, many of whom had moved to the area in response to the federal government's expansion during the Cold War. A new commercial corridor, high school, and historic park all played to postwar standards of suburban living that city boosters hoped would draw white individuals and families to Alexandria. The areas targeted for urban renewal, however, accommodated most of the city's Black residents. Forced out of their homes and neighborhoods, African Americans faced not only displacement but also limited housing options in a competitive, segregated market.

In response to mounting housing pressures, a new generation of Black activists, many of whom also had ties to the federal government, used a variety of strategies to make Alexandria's housing market more accessible.

A NEW GENERATION

The sizable presence of Black civil servants and military personnel living in Alexandria after World War II meant that civil rights activism played out differently than in other regions of the United States. Without question, white city leaders implemented the same segregationist policies and practices that were found in other parts of the country. At the same time, African American residents turned to similar forms of direct action to raise awareness about segregation that they hoped would change the status quo. There were, however, key differences. The federal government was the region's largest employer, and its slow and disjointed desegregation of its workforce, starting with Executive Order 8802 in 1941, gave Black federal workers leverage to criticize

Washington's racist practices. By the mid-1960s, federal agencies, the military, and government contractors actively recruited a diverse workforce, and they needed the housing market to support the region's changing racial and ethnic demographics. African Americans also used their knowledge of the inner workings of the federal bureaucracy and civil rights legislation to put pressure on local government leaders, which had wide ranging implications. A handful of individuals, most notably A. Melvin Miller, held important federal positions and directly challenged discrimination on the local level.

Civil rights activism around housing first appeared in Alexandria in response to nondiscrimination clauses that the federal government inserted into its construction contracts during the New Deal. As early as 1933, the Public Works Administration required that a percentage of African American skilled and unskilled construction workers be on a project's payroll. Government contractors, however, complained that too few African Americans were available and that unions, most of which were white-only organizations, barred them from hiring Black workers. Others tried to avoid hiring Black laborers completely, worrying about the impact of breaking with local segregationist practices. Despite these problems, the federal government's nondiscrimination policy provided opportunities for African Americans to obtain jobs on construction projects.[81]

By 1940, Alexandria's Black leaders reached out to the US Housing Authority (USHA) about possible jobs in the building trades on federally funded housing projects. In response to the federal government's funding of Alexandria's public housing, Samuel W. Madden Jr., president of the Hopkins House Men's Club, wrote that his organization was "hopeful of seeing to it that our group gets their fair and just share of the work." A Howard University alum and a retired schoolteacher, Madden was among a group of educators concerned about the lack of recreational activities for young people in the city. Together they founded Hopkins House, named after a local doctor, as a community center in 1939.[82] To ensure that Black workers understood their rights, Madden invited staff from USHA's Racial Relations Office to speak at one of the Men's Club's meetings. Clarence R. Johnson, the assistant for Negro Labor Relations at USHA, traveled from Washington to meet with club members and learned not only about the Black community's distrust of ARHA but also that white contractors persistently turned away Black skilled laborers.[83] ARHA's contractor argued that there were too few skilled workers in the city and that they had to bring bricklayers from outside of the area. Frank Horne, acting special assistant in the Racial Relations Office, noted that if a contractor had to hire outside labor, then he had to recruit both Black and white outside labor. The Men's Club generated a list of skilled workers living in Alexandria, which the Racial Relations Office forwarded to ARHA's contractor.[84] The same contractor, however, continued to avoid hiring Black skilled laborers. In a note to Horne, a staffer wrote, "Pressure needs to be placed upon contractors."[85]

Most activism, however, focused on the city's use of eminent domain for urban renewal and public housing. Almost all of Alexandria's federally funded projects were built in Black neighborhoods, requiring city leaders to acquire land from African American homeowners and renters. Several individuals and families turned to the courts either to stop the city's acquisition of their property or to demand more financial compensation. In 1952, *The Pittsburgh Courier* reported on the displacement of sixty-five families to build public housing and the impact that the project had on businesses and homeowners. Della Thomas, who lived with her elderly parents in a home that they had owned for forty years, stated that "it seems that the city is taking all the land owned by Negroes in Alexandria." Although her family knew that they could not stop the mass eviction, they hired lawyer Edwin C. Brown to negotiate a better price for their property.[86] Another family displaced by the construction of Fort Ward Park hired white lawyer and state senator Armistead Boothe to represent them against the city. Boothe, a Democrat, was known for his moderate politics and ultimately broke with the Byrd Machine, Virginia's one-party system run by former governor and US senator Harry F. Byrd. He brought in outside appraisers and forced Alexandria to pay more than it initially offered for the property.[87] In at least one instance, African Americans undercut the city's attempt to buy their land by selling it to someone else. The Peters family, who also lived in The Fort neighborhood, sold their land to a Catholic school, despite protests from city planners who wanted to incorporate the property into Fort Ward Park. The city council, however, supported the Ascension Academy and gave them a permit to build a school.[88] The school still stands today and is now St. Stephen's and St. Agnes Middle School.

Residents affected by the construction of T. C. Williams High School turned to more direct tactics in the hope of fighting their displacement. Lt Col. Marion I. Johnson, president of the Seminary Civic Association and vice president of the Alexandria Council on Human Relations, openly criticized white leaders in an interview with the *Washington Post*, which increasingly reported on civil rights issues in the region after World War II. Originally from Texas, Johnson had joined the US Army during World War II and worked at a local military base. He married an Alexandria resident and lived on her family's land in the Seminary neighborhood.[89] Like other residents, he emphasized

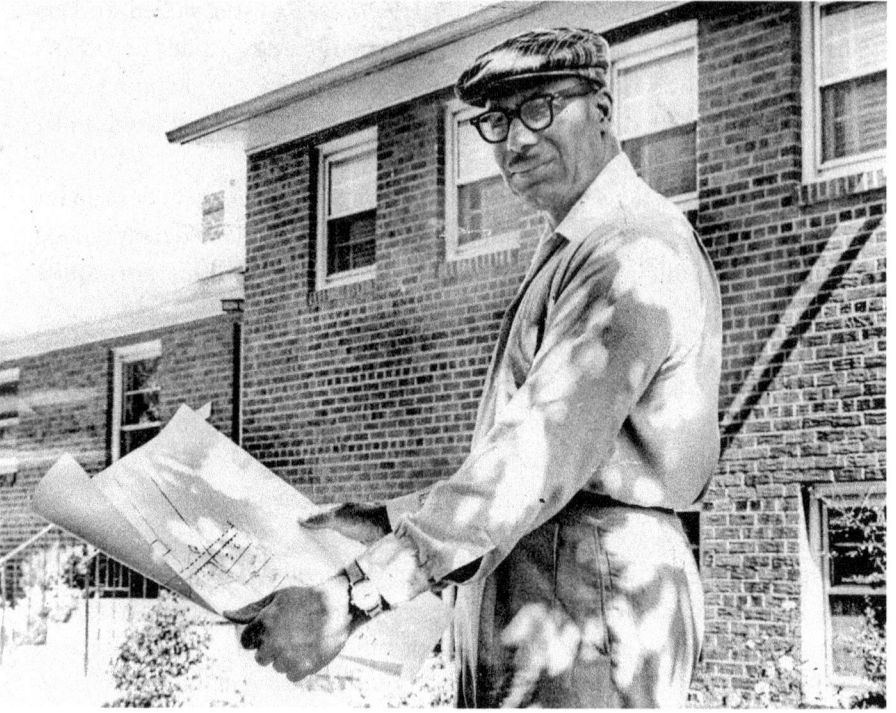

Figure 3.1. Lt. Col. Marion I. Johnson looking over construction plans, 1960.
Photograph by Tom Key, box 1288, Virginia-Alexandria—Houses and
Housing, Star 3 of 3 folder, Washington Star Collection. Reprinted with
permission of the DC Public Library, Star Collection © *Washington Post*.

the fact that white leaders targeted Black neighborhoods for urban renewal
and public housing projects; however, he also argued that Alexandria had
not fulfilled the federal requirements to provide housing for displaced individuals and families.[90] Johnson, with legal support from Boothe, worked out
an agreement with white leaders to set aside land for the construction of a
new Black subdivision (see fig. 3.1). Only sixteen of the fifty-two displaced
families, however, could afford the new homes, even with mortgages backed
by the Urban Renewal Administration. Other families found places to live
in public housing or in the private sale and rental markets. Two families left
Alexandria.[91]

After finding some success in response to the construction of T. C. Williams High School, activists continued to raise awareness about Alexandria's
discriminatory housing practices with the federal government. At a hearing
held by the US Civil Rights Commission on April 12, 1962, Johnson spoke

about the problems in Alexandria: "The most serious problem facing the Negro citizens in the city of Alexandria today is [the] unavailability of decent, sanitary housing on any level because of the unwillingness of the financial institutions, private builders, and other segments of the homebuilding industry to provide housing that is available to the Negroes[,] and the various actions of the city government in its urban renewal[,] highway widening[,] and other Government-sponsored projects."[92]

In front of congressional leaders, Johnson cited racist practices, the lack of new housing options, and the city council's refusal to pass an open housing ordinance as the causes of Alexandria's housing problems. Ultimately, without major governmental changes, he argued, "The Negro will be almost completely driven from the city of Alexandria. Only the public housing residents will remain to serve as a reservoir of domestic servants for the white community."[93] Johnson foresaw the same apartheid state, invoked in the 1968 Kerner Report, already playing out in Washington's suburbs.

By the early 1960s, ARHA continued to operate as it had for over twenty years, segregating public housing, ignoring Black housing needs, and targeting Black neighborhoods as possible construction sites. In 1962, the agency revived a proposal to build 225 new units, and once again all three construction sites were in Black neighborhoods. In front of the city council, A. Melvin Miller argued vehemently against the proposed public housing locations, citing the impact that the destruction of owner-occupied homes would have on the neighborhood. He noted, "The continuous decrease of land space available for Negro occupancy within the City is a most serious problem and the market for safe, sanitary housing above the low-income level is almost non-existent."[94] A few months later, the Federal Housing and Home Finance Agency placed a hold on federal funding for all of Alexandria's development projects until plans to help displaced residents affected by ARHA's proposed public housing were clarified. The new plans included a much leaner public housing program with only ninety units, not even half the needed number, but fewer owner-occupied homes in the neighborhood would be destroyed. Alexandria's revised plans appeased federal officials, and they were recertified in September 1962.[95]

Under mounting pressure from local activists, Alexandria's city council held a closed-door meeting on May 21, 1963, to address raced-based segregation. During this meeting, white city leaders drafted a Human Rights Ordinance that recognized the problems of racial discrimination, including discrimination in housing, for the first time in local law.[96] No notes were taken during the meeting, and it took the *Washington Post* two days to report on the event. Washington's *Afro-American* did not publish an article about the city council's new ordinance for weeks.[97] Once they learned about it, local activists praised the new law. Robert I. Terrell, president of the NAACP's local chapter who worked in real estate, congratulated the mayor and the city council "for rendering a judgment beneficial to the people of our City and the metropolitan area," which he hoped would "influence all private business establishments supported by the public."[98] The Human Rights Ordinance, however, had its limits. The new law put the burden of proof on victims of discrimination and failed to address racism as a systemic problem.

As the city council attempted to address racial discrimination, Metropolitan Life Insurance (MetLife) desegregated its properties, including Parkfairfax, an enormous apartment complex that had been built to address the region's population growth tied to the federal government's expansion during World War II. The property, one of the largest in Alexandria, housed only white renters, most of whom were civil servants and military personnel. In summer 1963, Parkfairfax announced that for the first time African Americans could rent units.[99] Parkfairfax's policy shift, however, was tied not to changes in local housing practices but to negotiations between the national NAACP and MetLife. MetLife owned thousands of apartments throughout the country and had fought against desegregation since the 1940s, especially in northern urban areas, such as Chicago and New York City.[100]

The Civil Rights Act required all federally funded programs to desegregate, including public housing, and Black Alexandrians expected city leaders to implement the new law. ARHA, however, resisted changing its housing practices and blamed white residents for choosing to live apart from African Americans. John Y. Kerr, ARHA's director, went further, projecting that the city's new units in the Uptown neighborhood would "be occupied by Negroes only" because whites would refuse to live in a Black neighborhood.[101] In Kerr's view, segregation was the result of individual choice and not of institutional policies. At the same time, ARHA continued to displace Black homeowners to build new public housing units. Otto L. Tucker, a local civil rights lawyer who participated in the 1939 sit-in (and also the brother to Samuel Tucker), spoke to the *Washington Post* about ARHA's new housing plans. As the *Post* later printed, "The sole reason for the selection of the site was that its inhabitants are Negroes and that '50 per cent of the dwellings are owned by members of the Negro race.' He [Tucker] also contends that in order to condemn properties there, the city must prove the area is a slum, blighted or deteriorated. He said buildings in the area 'provide safe and sanitary dwellings.'"[102] Despite Tucker's criticisms, ARHA tore down several Black-owned homes in "Colored" Rosemont, another African American neighborhood to the north of Alexandria's commercial corridor that dated to the turn of the century. Andrew W. Adkins Homes, named after a late pastor of the Alfred Street Baptist Church, the city's oldest Black congregation, opened in 1967.[103]

By the mid-1960s, activists shifted their focus toward the desegregation of the private housing market in Alexandria and throughout Washington's suburbs. Through the Civil Rights Act, public housing had technically been desegregated; however, the private housing market continued to bar Black families from most suburban neighborhoods. In 1966, an interracial group known as the Action Coordinating Committee to End Segregation in the Suburbs (ACCESS) organized protests throughout the region that focused on the structural hurdles that made it impossible for prospective African American homeowners and renters to find a place to live. To raise awareness and to pressure the real estate industry, ACCESS picketed private apartment complexes in hopes that property owners would sign open occupancy agreements and include the phrase "Equal Opportunity Rentals" in advertisements. Additionally, it coordinated marches along major thoroughfares used by commuters to "dramatize the inferior housing of those poor Negroes and ones who can afford something better but can't find it."[104] ACCESS members walked over sixty miles along the newly constructed Beltway (today known as I-495) that encircled Washington, DC, and made stops in both Black and white neighborhoods. Later that year, ACCESS organized another march along Route 1, beginning in Gum Springs—a neighborhood founded by free African Americans in the early nineteenth century whom the Washingtons had enslaved at Mount Vernon—and running all the way through Alexandria (see fig. 3.2). Finally, because of the military's sizable presence in northern Virginia, ACCESS lobbied the Department of Defense (DOD) to bar all military personnel from renting off-base apartments in segregated buildings. In January 1968, a ban was put in place on segregated apartments around the Pentagon, which included northern Alexandria. A few months later, the coordinator of DOD's off-base housing stated that the military no longer tolerated segregated housing for its service members and expanded the ban to the entire region.[105]

Throughout the 1960s, A. Melvin Miller was the primary leader in the fight against housing discrimination, using his knowledge of FHA and later HUD policies to directly engage white city leaders. His work focused on Alexandria's low-income housing policies, urban renewal, zoning ordinances, and overall race-based housing discrimination. As early as 1962, Miller spoke out against ARHA's practice of displacing homeowners to build public housing units in

Figure 3.2. ACCESS march for open housing in Alexandria, 1966.
Photograph by Owen Duvall, box 830, Negroes—Virginia-Alexandria
folder, Washington Star Collection. Reprinted with permission of
the DC Public Library, Star Collection © *Washington Post*.

Black neighborhoods and recommended the establishment of a commission to suggest alternatives. He advocated for changes in the city's land use zoning policies in Black neighborhoods to allow for the construction of multiunit housing. Around the same time, he proposed the construction of subsidized middle-income housing to help families displaced by urban renewal and public housing construction.[106]

Local activism around segregated housing, along with the tragedy described at the beginning of the chapter, finally compelled Alexandria's city council to pass a voluntary open occupancy ordinance in 1967. "Open occupancy" first appeared in discussions around DC's public housing, which began to desegregate in 1953. Around the same time, the FHA promoted funding for "open occupancy projects," with the understanding that without enforcement powers the federal agency could do little to change local segregationist practices.[107] By the early 1960s, civil rights activists in Alexandria rallied around the concept of open occupancy too, lobbying for local legislation to end discrimination in all forms of housing.[108] Alexandria's legislation was its first attempt to end race-based discrimination in private rentals and sales, but it had limited legal weight because it was voluntary and included no enforcement powers. Nevertheless, Alexandria's city manager planned to hire staff to negotiate with landlords to open apartment complexes to Black renters.[109] Several individuals and local organizations expressed support for the initiative. Eileen Eddy, chair of Alexandria's Economic Opportunities Commission, congratulated the city council on its "assumption of leadership in obtaining voluntary open housing and pledge[d the Commission's] full support."[110]

Chapter Three

The Alexandria chapter of the League of Women Voters, which had made open occupancy a platform issue in 1961, "commend[ed] City Council for unanimously adopting a resolution calling for voluntary Open Housing and hopes this will be enacted as soon as possible." The League, however, wanted more information about the ordinance's implementation and what types of housing would be prioritized.[111]

Federal legislation provided additional pressure to desegregate all aspects of home purchasing and renting with the Fair Housing Act (1968), which was passed six months after Alexandria's voluntary ordinance.[112] A report written by the Kerner Commission on the factors causing civil unrest in major urban centers influenced the act. The US Senate approved the legislation with the hope that allowing African American middle-class families access to suburban homes would offset racial tensions. Within weeks of its passage in the Senate, Reverend Dr. Martin Luther King Jr. was assassinated, and the country witnessed the nation's capital burn. The US House of Representatives signed the Fair Housing Act a few days later as the National Guard protected the Capitol Building.[113]

In the next few months, Alexandria's city council again debated housing, this time under the purview of newly established federal guidelines. Racial discrimination in all aspects of housing was no longer legal, and officials needed to establish stronger local ordinances to support Black residents. By February 1969, in alignment with the Fair Housing Act, Alexandria's white city leaders passed a new open housing ordinance that included enforcement powers.[114]

CONCLUSION

Throughout the early- to mid-twentieth century, Black Alexandrians used a combination of local and federal resources to fight attempts by the city's white leadership to limit their housing options. The earliest forms of structural racism appeared in the racially restrictive covenants of newly built subdivisions, many of which were constructed for Washington's expanding federal workforce. Alexandria's land use zoning policies, generated by a federal employee contracted by city leaders, exacerbated Black housing options by prioritizing single-family homes and delineating parts of Black neighborhoods for industrial use. By the New Deal, the accelerated expansion of the federal government combined with new housing policies under the FHA put additional pressures on the region's preexisting housing stock. City boosters attempted to rewrite the racial landscape through public housing construction and, later, urban renewal projects, all of which, they hoped, would appeal to white suburbanites, many of whom worked for the federal government. As a result of these housing pressures, the options available to Black Alexandrians shrank further, forcing many of them into hyper-segregated neighborhoods or out of the city.

At the same time, a new generation of activists began the slow, stilted process of changing segregationist housing policies in Alexandria. This phenomenon can be seen just prior to World War II when city residents reached out to the Racial Relations Office in USHA to enforce nondiscrimination clauses in government contracts. After the war, Black civil servants and military personnel continued to use their intimate knowledge of the federal government to put pressure on local and federal officials. They spoke to the press about the city's discriminatory housing practices and testified in front of the US Civil Rights Commission. Finally, activists organized marches and pickets to highlight racial segregation in housing and lobbied the DOD to ban all military personnel from renting apartments in segregated buildings. Alexandria's white city leadership finally passed an open occupancy ordinance by the end of the decade, and African Americans began to move into a small number of white-only neighborhoods.[115]

Housing discrimination persisted in Alexandria through the 1970s and 1980s, but Black residents did see major changes in specific neighborhoods. One such neighborhood was Arlandria.

CHAPTER FOUR

Affordability

On October 20, 1969, Alexandria's city council held a special meeting about an assault on a Black teenager by a white police officer in the Arlandria neighborhood and subsequent acts of violence. Located in the northernmost section of Alexandria, Arlandria had originally been a white-only neighborhood constructed to house civil servants and military personnel. By the late 1960s, a growing number of African Americans had moved into the neighborhood, either renting apartments or buying townhomes. During the special meeting, Black speakers noted the repeated abuses of white officers who regularly targeted Black youths, but recent events had gone beyond past aggressions. Leo Burroughs Jr., who had recently moved to Alexandria from Baltimore to work for the Urban League, stated, "The events in the past week and a half in this most historic City, have given rise to some of the most shameful conduct ever demonstrated by any police department anywhere in our State or nation." White residents saw things differently, blaming Black militants for the current violence. Patrick Holland, reportedly a student at a local community college, argued, "It is time that the residents of the City of Alexandria unite in a stand against active terrorism, lawlessness, and intimidation by those elements bent on causing an environment of the destruction and moral decay throughout our community." Another cohort of speakers, however, wanted Alexandria to become a racially integrated city. The Arlandria Neighborhood Committee, a coalition of Black and white residents, emphasized that they lived in an integrated neighborhood and hoped to keep it that way. In a written statement to the city council, the Committee provided a list of criticisms that they wanted city leaders to address, ranging from problems with the police to the lack of safe recreational facilities for teenagers. They ended their statement noting, "There are a number of groups which are constantly trying, for their own purpose, to use race to divide the Arlandria-Lynhaven community. We are still an integrated community. Most of us would like to see it stay that way."[1]

Among all the public comments that evening, one speaker tried to articulate a way forward. Ira Robinson, a newly minted lawyer who had turned down jobs in his hometown of Richmond, Virginia, to work in the legal offices of a northern Virginia defense contractor, had become politically active in the city.[2] In his comments, Robinson noted that Black Alexandrians had already given the city council a list of recommendations to improve race relations, including police reform, after Martin Luther King Jr.'s assassination a year earlier. Furthermore, the issues that Alexandria faced went far beyond one white police officer. "What I would recommend to the City Council is that it get underway not only with the Callahan [the officer] case, not only with police communications with the community, but it get underway with everything that deprives black citizens of the incident of life that belongs to a black citizen in 1969 America."[3] These changes, Robinson knew, would not occur unless the city's leadership became more representative of the community that they served. A few months later, an energized electorate elected Robinson to the city council; he was the first African American to hold public office in Alexandria in almost 100 years (see fig. 4.1).

By the late 1960s, Arlandria had become a flashpoint that reflected broader demographic shifts related to federal policies and racial tensions in the city. Rapid suburbanization and industrialization led to serious flooding problems in the area, causing millions of dollars in property damage. White residents moved out, and large numbers of low- to moderate-income African American families, many of whom were also civil servants or military personnel, moved into the neighborhood. The devaluation of Arlandria's flood-prone real estate, combined with the region's overall population growth and persistent housing discrimination, meant that landlords did not need to maintain rental units to fill them. Meanwhile, Arlandria's affordability, especially the Lynhaven subdivision, appealed to prospective Black homebuyers. Many individuals and families obtained federally insured loans through the Federal Housing

Figure 4.1. Ira Robinson with other newly elected
Alexandria City Council members, 1970.
Photograph by Walter Oates, box 1288, Virginia-
Alexandria—Wire folder, Washington Star Collection.
Reprinted with permission of the DC Public Library,
Star Collection © *Washington Post.*

Administration (FHA) and the Department of Veterans Affairs (VA), particularly after the passage of the HUD Act (1968). These loans sometimes reflected what Keeanga-Yamahtta Taylor calls "predatory inclusion," in which corrupt appraisers and lenders misrepresented housing conditions with no financial risk to themselves. Arlandria's major flooding problems meant that both Black homeowners and renters might lose everything they owned in the next storm.[4]

By the 1970s, Arlandria's affordability and proximity to Washington, DC, made the neighborhood appealing to another wave of new arrivals: immigrants and refugees from Africa, Asia, and Central and South America. Andrew Friedman notes that Washington's interventionist Cold War policies brought many refugees to northern Virginia who had worked closely with the US military, Central Intelligence Agency, or US State Department. These men and women relied on their relationships with federal officials in Washington to lobby on behalf of family members and governments in exile. For individuals living under regimes propped up by the US government, northern Virginia was a popular destination too. For instance, American civil servants and government contractors hired female domestic servants when they were stationed in Central America. They then brought these women home to Washington where they eventually obtained US citizenship. Thus, women, who ordinarily were not the first to settle overseas, became the lodestars for future waves of Central American immigration. Finally, the Hart–Celler Act (1965) dismantled the last vestiges of the National Origins Quota Act (1924) and gave preference to immigrant professionals and other skilled workers. Many highly educated immigrants found employment with the federal government and the region's booming technology and defense industries.[5]

The election of Ronald Reagan in 1980 led to major changes in federal housing policies that impacted *all* low- to moderate-income residents, including Arlandria's racially and ethnically diverse population. Reagan's agenda to cut social services pressed those near the bottom of the socioeconomic ladder to compete for dwindling resources. The US Department of Housing and Urban Development (HUD) lost much of its funding, and local programs vied for financial support through block grants given to state governments.[6] Not all politicians, however, accepted the federal government's dwindling support of social programs. Pierre Clavel, in his study of Boston and Chicago during the 1980s, argues that activist mayors with alternative visions of the role of government found new ways to serve residents. Alexandria, however, initially did little to address the needs of low- to moderate-income neighborhoods, especially those as racially and ethnically diverse as Arlandria.[7]

Simultaneously, college-educated Americans from a variety of racial and ethnic backgrounds moved to the region and were also looking for apartments and homes within commuting distance of employers in Washington or northern Virginia's growing defense and technology industries. While the US economy stagnated in other parts of the country in the early 1980s, job opportunities in northern Virginia soared as the Reagan administration expanded the military-industrial complex in order to defeat the Soviets.[8] To address the federal government's defense needs, retired military and members of the intelligence community found work as contractors, making billions of dollars selling products and services to the Defense Department and other federal agencies.[9] Service industries, responding to the region's affluence, flourished along with construction jobs, domestic work, and clerical positions.

As a result of changes under the Reagan administration, Arlandria was again central to debates about the region's demographic changes, job opportunities, and housing affordability. As employment opportunities expanded, so too did living expenses, with rich and poor competing for places to live in the region. Developers bought undervalued apartments like those in Arlandria in hopes to convert them into high-end rentals or condominiums, which appealed to a new class of white professionals known as "yuppies." Virginia had few regulations protecting renters from predatory practices of landlords and developers, leaving lower-income residents with little legal recourse. Alexandria's city government, without a steady stream of funding from HUD, argued that it was beholden to developers who promised to expand Alexandria's tax base and provide public amenities.[10]

The history of Arlandria in the late twentieth century provides a case study into the ways in which race relations, class politics, and immigration collided, propelled by both the implementation of new federal policies and the continued expansion of Washington's bureaucracy.[11] For low- to moderate-income residents, Arlandria was their home, and with few inexpensive alternatives, these residents wanted to stay. Tapping into past and present activism, Black Arlandrians refused to accept the rolling back of social services or the lack of support from the local government; but to make change happen, they needed to build coalitions not only with white residents but also with the city's immigrant and refugee populations. All Arlandrians expected city officials to respond to their needs, despite declining financial support from the federal government and a lack of legal precedent. In addition, immigrants and refugees from around the world wanted to be included in conversations about Alexandria's present and future, bringing new ideas about the role of government and notions of diversity.[12] The results of local activism were mixed. Many residents staved off displacement, while others, frustrated by the local political climate and the possibility that they might be evicted at any moment, left Arlandria to live elsewhere.

THE ORIGINS OF ARLANDRIA

The expansion of the federal government in the Washington metropolitan area during the 1930s and 1940s laid the foundation for the creation of Arlandria. White federal workers enjoyed Arlandria's new garden apartments, townhomes, shopping centers, and other suburban amenities established along the northernmost edge of Alexandria. Like many neighborhoods, the apartments and townhomes provided modern services to those who could not afford a single-family home in one of Alexandria's swankier subdivisions or who were uninterested in living in Alexandria's older housing stock. Unbeknownst to local boosters, environmental and socioeconomic forces would bring radical changes to the neighborhood over the next fifty years. By the late 1960s, a series of massive floods drove white homeowners, renters, and businesses out of the neighborhood, and African Americans, with few housing options elsewhere, moved in.

Unlike other neighborhoods in Alexandria, Arlandria was relatively new. Located in Alexandria (later Arlington) County, for most of its early history, the area functioned as a marginal space between Alexandria and Washington, DC. Four Mile Run, a stream that included a large swamp and estuary near its terminus on the Potomac River, defined the space. In the early nineteenth century, a handful of white families built farms and mills along the stream.[13] By the 1890s, discussions about streetcar lines between Washington and Alexandria led to the region's first wave of suburbanization.[14] Real estate developers established new communities on the flats between Four Mile Run and Alexandria. Del Ray and St. Elmo, which merged in 1908, became the Town of Potomac. Potomac prided itself as a white-only town and celebrated its racial exclusivity. In 1924, local boosters wrote, "It is perhaps the only municipality in the United States in which ownership of real estate is limited to persons of the Caucasian race, and it is also the only municipality so far as we know, that does not number among its residents persons of African descent."[15]

By the 1870s, a small number of Black Alexandrians rented and owned property along the south side of Four Mile Run, just west of where Arlandria would be established. Ham(p)shire and Maria Fractious, who had fled from western Virginia to Union lines during the Civil War, lived in Alexandria before they bought thirteen acres near Four Mile Run at auction in 1876.[16] Although it is unknown whether Thornton Hyatt (also spelled Hyett) fled to northern Virginia during the war or had been previously enslaved in Alexandria, he rented farmland in the area through the local office of the Freedmen's Bureau as early as 1866. By the 1880s, the county government hired him to run the almshouse, which was located near a farm that he rented.[17] Finally, the Watson family, who were free prior to the war and also lived in Alexandria, bought ten acres of land in 1870. In 1905, they platted "Sunnyside," an unrestricted subdivision for Black families. In the early twentieth century, the number of Sunnyside residents remained relatively small, with only twelve homes appearing in the *1930 US Census*; however, over forty families owned land in Sunnyside by 1934.[18]

Suburban development along Four Mile Run began in earnest during the New Deal and World War II to house Washington's white civilian and military personnel. Alexandria had annexed the land from nearby Arlington County in 1930, with plans to use it to expand the city's housing options. By 1938, Hechinger Enterprises built Presidential Gardens, which included 540 garden apartments. Another developer constructed Beverly Plaza, the area's first park-and-shop, with additional apartments and townhomes nearby.[19] African Americans did not live in these new developments, which the real estate market had designated as white-only. Commercial and residential construction geared toward white federal workers and military personnel continued immediately after World War II. The Arlandria Shopping Center, a mash-up of the words "Alexandria" and "Arlington," opened in 1947 with the capacity to serve 100,000 customers. It is from this park-and-shop that the neighborhood received its name.[20]

After World War II, Arlandria mirrored the region's suburbanization that developers had curated for white families who had moved to the area in response to the federal government's expansion. A former white resident nostalgically recalled that "they shopped at the Arlandria Shopping Center, sent their children to the Mount Vernon movie theater for the Saturday matinee and kept busy on weekends planting rose bushes and azaleas and putting up picket fences."[21] Arlandria's suburban paradise, however, soon disappeared as the neighborhood became embroiled in the region's socioeconomic and environmental transformations of the 1960s.

A PERIOD OF CHANGE

The breakdown of structural forms of segregation, combined with the neighborhood's environmental degradation, led to major demographic shifts in Arlandria by the 1960s. As noted in chapter 3, Alexandria had passed its own open housing policies, which, along with the Fair Housing Act (1968), began the slow process of desegregating the city's neighborhoods. In Arlandria, African Americans began to live outside of Sunnyside by the 1960s, moving into apartments and homes that had previously housed white civil servants and military personnel. At the same time, the region's rapid suburbanization and industrialization led to major floods in the neighborhood. White residents moved out at an accelerated rate by the end of the decade.

Throughout the 1960s and early 1970s, the lack of housing options continued to plague Alexandria's Black community, which consisted of a mixture of longtime residents and new arrivals. The majority of African Americans lived in the Uptown neighborhood, with smaller enclaves around the central business district.[22] Seminary to the west and Sunnyside to the north were the only other neighborhoods with sizable numbers of African American households.[23] Legislation, both federal and local, accelerated changes in housing options, but it would take time to dismantle decades of structural racism. Progressive organizations, such as the National Association for the Advancement of Colored People (NAACP) and the League of Women Voters, worked with local officials to address housing barriers. The 1969 *Bulletin* for the Alexandria chapter of the League of Women Voters listed housing discrimination as the biggest issue facing the city.[24]

As elsewhere in the United States, the frustrations tied to the city's segregated landscape erupted into violence by the late 1960s. As its overall racial makeup shifted, Arlandria became the site of two incidents, both of which highlighted the Black community's frustration with the lack of changes in the way that Alexandria operated. Unlike the uprisings in Washington, DC, after the assassination of Martin Luther King Jr., Alexandria saw minor property damage in spring 1968; however, the assault of a teenager a year later in Arlandria ignited the community.[25] While walking his beat, a white police officer, Claiborne Callahan, chased and pistol-whipped a teenager, whom Callahan claimed had yelled obscenities at him. A group of young men arrived at the scene of the initial attack and went to the police station to explain what they had seen. Callahan accused the eyewitnesses of assault and arrested them too.[26]

As in other cities where uprisings had occurred, many white politicians and residents refused to recognize that Callahan had overstepped his authority. White Alexandrians wrote letters of support to the city council and even organized a dinner in Callahan's honor. At the same time, African American residents protested outside of city hall and the police department. Tension filled the city. The *Alexandria Gazette* reported on rocks thrown at police cars and on the supposed disorderly conduct among teenagers. Two weeks later, police harassment of Black teenagers at a high school football game set off violence throughout the city. Firebombings occurred for the next two nights, and teenagers who tried to congregate in the streets were told to go home. If they refused, they were arrested. By the end of the weekend, the governor had sent state troopers to assist local law enforcement.[27]

In response to statements made at a city council special meeting (discussed at length at the opening of this chapter), white leaders hired consultants from the National Center of Police and Community Relations at Michigan State University to investigate complaints against the police department. Their findings confirmed what Black Alexandrians had known all along: police abuse was a major issue, particularly toward Black teenagers. The consultants, however, went further in their analysis of local race relations and invoked the findings of President Lyndon B. Johnson's Kerner Commission, the 1968 study that pointed to racism as the main cause of recent uprisings in several major cities. The consultants noted that Black residents "want[ed] a voice, a share in shaping their community lives," but if local trends did not change, Alexandria would become what federal commissioners feared: an "apartheid" state.

To rectify these systemic problems, Alexandria's police needed to become more professional, with a fully trained force that did not simply focus only on "crime suppression." More importantly, Alexandria had to develop a more inclusive kind of governance that allowed all residents to be heard and their needs addressed.[28]

Before the city council decided which recommendations to implement, another violent incident in Arlandria highlighted once again Black frustrations with systematic racism. Several weeks after the release of the Michigan State report, a white store clerk at an Arlandria 7-Eleven killed Robin Gibson, an African American teenager, who had supposedly shoplifted razor blades with his friends. The clerk said that it was self-defense. The victim's friends, however, recounted how the clerk had asked them to turn their pockets inside out, and when they had put their hands into their pockets, he pulled out a gun and shot at them. Later that night, violence broke out in Arlandria. Black residents threw rocks and bricks at cars and windows. Someone set small fires, and a handful of people blocked the police from entering the neighborhood. To compound matters, a group of white residents established the Alexandria Citizens Defense League and began to patrol the streets while armed with guns.[29] Violence swept through Alexandria again, and the city council declared a state of emergency.[30]

The city council finally agreed that it needed to implement the suggestions from the Michigan State report and began to articulate the changes necessary for a more inclusive city government. Reforms included the hiring of a new police chief and the development of a community relations program. A Chief's Advisory Committee would suggest reforms to the police department and facilitate communication between the police and neighborhoods. The city council also admitted that the impact of racism went beyond the police; local government had to reorient its relationship with Black residents, fixing what it called "the credibility gap." Based on statements at neighborhood meetings held by the city council, residents recommended more citizen participation in the Parks and Recreation Commission, which they hoped would better serve youth across racial and economic lines. A June 1970 city council meeting ended with an agreement to hold more discussions about reforms.[31]

Arlandria, which had primarily catered to white residents who had moved to northern Virginia to work for the federal government, became the site of major demographic shifts in the 1960s. The partial breakdown of structural racism facilitated the in-migration of African Americans, giving rise to tensions with white residents that erupted into violence. In response, African American residents and activists argued that the city needed to commit itself to systemic reforms and share power with those who had been disenfranchised. As the city struggled to imagine what a more inclusive government would look like, it also had to address another major problem in Arlandria: flooding.

FLOODS ON FOUR MILE RUN

Despite the social, political, and economic problems affecting Arlandria, there was one issue that everyone agreed had to be addressed: flood control. As Adam Rome asserts, rapid suburbanization prompted "an environmental catastrophe" throughout the United States after World War II.[32] In northern Virginia, storm water had few places to go because newly constructed shopping centers, apartment complexes, and tract housing covered soils that had previously absorbed the rainfall. Using new technologies, developers also built houses on steep hillsides and in wetlands, leading to additional erosion. Bridges blocked the flow of water on Four Mile Run and prevented it from reaching the Potomac River. Major storms also caused tidal surges that pushed water upstream, further exacerbating flooding. It took time for Alexandrians to realize the environmental impact of northern Virginia's suburbanization; however, like many Americans in other parts of the country, they demanded action to address what had become a human-made environmental disaster.

Although periodic flooding had occurred along Four Mile Run in the nineteenth century, floods had increased in both intensity and frequency by the 1960s.[33] The 1963 Arlandria flood caused over $32,000 in damages to city property, $1.5 million in damages to commercial property, and $1.8 million in damages to residential property (see fig. 4.2).[34] The storm drove 100 people from their homes and closed 31 stores. The US Army Corps of Engineers studied the incident and decided against any federally funded preventive measures because it believed the cost of the project would outweigh the cost of the damages caused by future floods.[35] Three years later, another major flood "caused a review of the costs and benefits [by the Corps] and it now appears that such a project is economically feasible." Local governments, however, had to assent to the Corps' plans, which included new bridges, levees, culverts, channel widening, and a pumping station, before it went forward to the US Congress for funding.[36]

Alexandria agreed to the Corps' plans, but local, state, and federal authorities did little to address Arlandria's immediate flood control needs. In the summer of 1969, another series of floods hit the area. With assistance from their congressman, Arlandria residents and business owners testified in front of the House's Subcommittee on Public Works to demand that the federal government move quickly to implement the Corps' plan. A. E. Brill, who had operated a grocery store in Arlandria since 1944, tried to express to the committee the level of devastation to his business. He stated, "The whole store was wiped out completely. It [flood waters] got into the registers, the scales, all the refrigeration, $46,000 worth of merchandise, which had to be shoveled out and carried out, which was no good at all." In total, he faced $172,000 in damages, plus he still owed $80,000 on a loan that he needed to reopen his store after the 1963 flood. A loan from the Small Business Administration had helped, but it covered only $100,000 in damages and still had to be paid back. He concluded by noting, "So my building is laying idle there with a lot of mud and nothing to do with it, and you can't do anything with it because the threat of water might come at any time, you see, so you cannot put money on it."[37] Other Arlandria residents and businessowners similarly described to the subcommittee members the damage caused by Four Mile Run's flooding.

With persistent flooding problems, property values in Arlandria declined. In a study conducted by the Virginia Water Resources Center at Virginia Tech, researchers collected data from real estate sales in flood-prone areas along Four Mile Run and compared them to nearby properties in flood-free zones between 1960 through 1974. They found that Arlandria's homes sold for an average of 22 percent less in comparison to similar properties outside of the flood plain. Researchers also surveyed residents to see what they knew about falling home prices and flooding. They reported that 60 percent did not know that their home was built on a flood plain when they purchased it. Furthermore, while 25 percent were unconvinced that their home would ever flood, 83 percent decided to buy flood insurance and hoped that it would protect home prices. A new zoning ordinance passed in 1970, which banned any further development near Four Mile Run, had done little to improve prices. Only 50 percent of Arlandria residents were aware of the new ordinance.[38]

In response to Arlandria's flood-prone real estate, banking institutions relied on federally insured mortgages for home purchases near Four Mile Run. These monies came primarily from two sources: the Cold War GI Bill (1966) and the HUD Act (1968). The Cold War GI Bill expanded the Department of Veteran Affairs' mortgage program to Korean and Vietnam veterans and active service members, insuring mortgages up to $7,500 and offering direct loans up to "$17,500 if private financing is not available."[39] Section 235 of the HUD Act created a new mortgage market through the FHA that allowed low- to moderate-income families to purchase homes with a small down payment and interest rates as low as 1 percent. The FHA provided a 100 percent guarantee for each loan so that private lenders had no risk. The possibility

Table 4.1. Study of mortgage recordings in Alexandria, September 1971–August 1972.

	Number of loans	Amount of loans (US$)	Average loan (US$)
S&L associations—conventional	355	14,135,900	39,819
S&L associations—FHA	21	473,100	22,529
S&L associations—VA	12	385,700	32,142
Mortgage bankers—conventional	125	8,563,900	68,511
Mortgage bankers—FHA	93	1,947,000	20,935
Mortgage bankers—VA	214	6,010,400	28,086
Bank & Trust companies—Conventional	177	10,637,400	60,098
Bank & Trust companies—FHA	4	100,900	25,225
Bank & Trust companies—VA	6	196,700	32,783
Insurance companies—conventional	2	2,014,900	1,007,450
Insurance companies—FHA	0	0	0
Insurance companies—VA	2	54,500	27,250
Individuals	7	155,000	22,143
Others	3	73,500	24,500
VA direct loans	1	23,000	23,000
TOTAL	1,022	44,771,900	43,808

Source: Rufus S. Lusk and Son Papers, George Washington University, Washington, DC.
Note: Dominion Bankshares Corporation from Roanoke, Virginia, hired Rufus S. Lusk
and Son, a real estate statistical firm in Washington, DC, to collect this data. It is
unknown to what purpose this banking institution used this information.

of free money for lenders made these programs ripe for corruption, which Keeanga-Yamahtta Taylor and Christopher Bonastia have documented in several major cities.[40] By fall 1972, over 30 percent of mortgages issued in Alexandria included guarantees from either the FHA or the Department of Veterans Affairs (VA) (see table 4.1). A majority of these federally insured mortgages came from the VA, a phenomenon tied to the large number of military personnel and veterans living in Alexandria who worked either for the federal government or for defense and intelligence contractors.[41]

The federal government's loan policies made homeownership available to low- to moderate-income Black families in and around Arlandria, but a close review of federally insured property transfers from 1969 to 1972 (see map 4.1) shows several problems. White flight combined with Four Mile Run's flooding facilitated Black in-migration to Arlandria using federally insured mortgages to purchase these properties. In contrast, property transfers using FHA- and VA-insured loans in western sections of Alexandria remained primarily white-only. The two Black homebuyers in Sunnyside during the same period had no mortgage financing at all.[42] Arlandria's low- to moderate-income

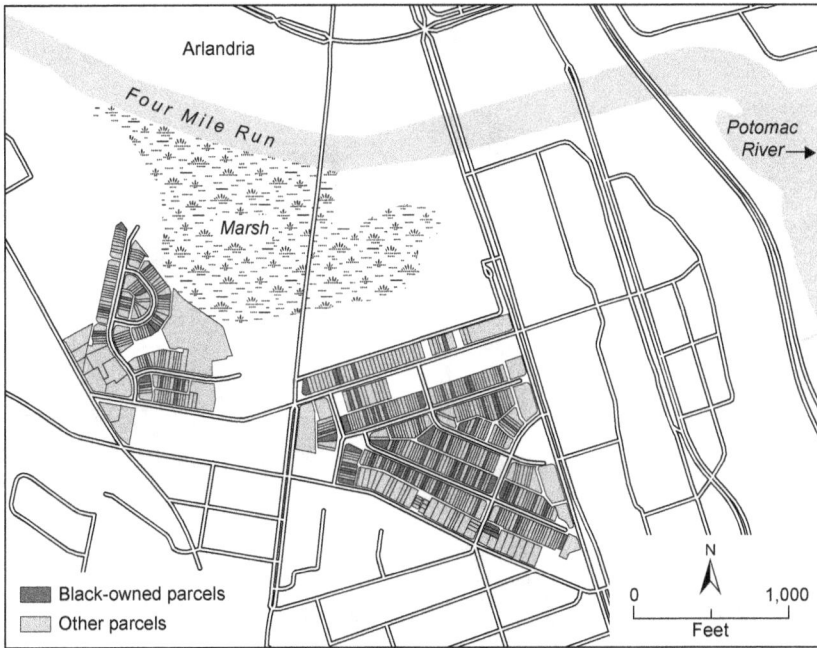

Map 4.1. Black property transfers in Arlandria and neighboring subdivisions with FHA- or VA-backed loans, 1969–1972.
Map by Elisa Luckabaugh, 2023.

homebuyers were also targets for potential criminal activity. Potomac Valley Homes Inc., a real estate company that specialized in assuming FHA- and VA-insured loans for properties in distressed neighborhoods or homeowners facing foreclosure, bought several properties in Arlandria in the late 1960s and early 1970s. In 1979, the company's leadership, including a deputy assistant secretary for the Department of Labor, was found guilty in federal court for misleading investors about the company's real estate ventures. Potomac Valley Homes had also exploited low-income homebuyers by selling them second mortgages, fully aware that they would not be able to pay them back. They then not only foreclosed on properties but also pocketed the money. Federal charges against Potomac Valley Homes, however, focused on their misleading of investors, not on their predatory lending practices.[43]

In June 1972, Arlandria's new Black homeowners and renters faced one of the worst flooding events in local history when Hurricane Agnes hit the Eastern Seaboard of the United States. The lack of permeable surfaces compounded the impact of the storm's heavy rainfall and the Potomac River's

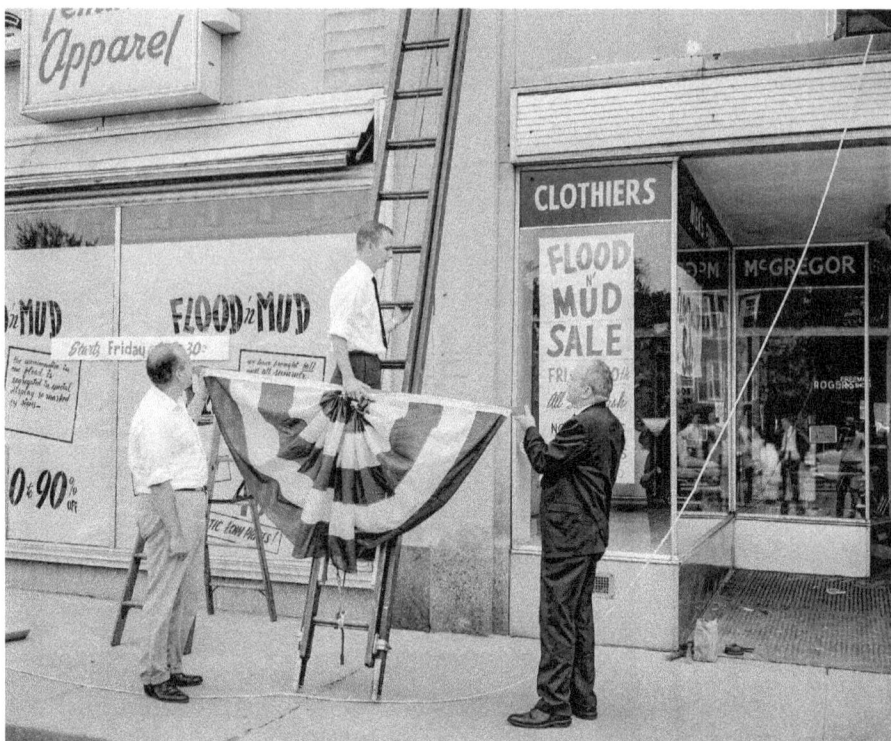

Figure 4.2. Arlandrians help to decorate for the Flood 'n' Mud Sale, August 1963.
Photograph by Don MacAfee, *Alexandria Gazette* Negative Collection,
MS332, no. 29, Special Collections, Alexandria Public Library, Virginia.

tidal surge. Arlandria was almost completely under water, and one resident drowned.[44] Meanwhile, the US Army Corps of Engineers frustrated local leaders, business owners, and residents by continuing to debate flood mitigation responsibilities. The Richmond, Fredericksburg, and Potomac Railroad, which had installed the original culverts that controlled Four Mile Run's drainage into the Potomac River, was now required to rebuild the conduits through their property. The State of Virginia, which maintained one of the roads across Four Mile Run, needed to rebuild a bridge that also blocked the flow of water. Only once everyone agreed to the Corps' plans would it go forward with its implementation of the plan. It finally broke ground in 1973.[45]

Environmental degradation caused by rapid suburbanization in northern Virginia led to massive flooding in Arlandria in the 1960s. Floods occurred along Four Mile Run with increasing frequency and intensity, damaging and even destroying homes and businesses. As Arlandria's racial demographics

Chapter Four

transitioned from white to Black, residents recognized something needed to be done to stop the floods if their neighborhood was going to have a future. The Corps completed the Four Mile Run Flood Control Project in 1980, which cost over $10 million.[46] With flood control addressed, it was only a matter of time before Arlandria would experience additional socioeconomic changes tied to late twentieth-century Cold War politics and Alexandria's proximity to the nation's capital.

NEW ARRIVALS

By the 1970s and 1980s, Arlandria's affordable housing, along with its proximity to federal employment and public transportation, made it a popular destination for the region's Cold War immigrants and refugees. Changes in American immigration policies after World War II transformed the racial and ethnic demographics of the Washington metropolitan area. By 1970, over 130,000 immigrants lived in the region, about 50,000 of whom were Cold War refugees. More than two-thirds of the refugees were Cuban with close ties to the US government. The rest came from Eastern Europe, Asia, and Africa. These new arrivals lived in the suburbs, avoiding the enclaving found in older immigrant-receiving cities. A *Washington Post* reporter noted, "Most area exiles . . . tend to live near each other, but seldom next door; to socialize together, but not exclusively; to intermarry, but less with each generation."[47] Within the next decade, this pattern expanded and diversified, with no one nationality dominating the region's foreign-born population.

Immigrant populations found in Alexandria generally reflected the region. The 1960 US Census listed only 10,291 foreign-born people in Alexandria (a little more than 3 percent of the overall population), the majority of whom emigrated from the United Kingdom, Germany, and Canada. Because of Alexandria's proximity to several military bases and the nation's capital, these numbers included the spouses of US military personnel and government contractors who had been stationed overseas, or members of the American diplomatic corps. The large number of Europeans and Canadians also reflected the quota system that had been in place since 1924, which privileged immigrants from western and northern Europe. No quota existed for white Canadians.[48]

By the mid-1960s, Cuban refugees began to settle in Alexandria and advocated for more inclusive local governance. Local residents, who primarily operated in a Black-white racial system, had never seen immigrants, even those who were perceived to be "white," complicate constructions of difference and inclusion. Luis Vidaña, a Cuban refugee who found employment with the federal government, and others established the Spanish-Speaking Committee of Virginia in 1966 to provide social services for new arrivals in partnership with local governments.[49] In a 1979 survey, the Committee found that individuals from more than twenty-one countries were represented in the state, and most of them lived in northern Virginia. No one group dominated, although the largest populations came from Cuba followed by Bolivia, Peru, and Colombia. All immigrants noted difficulties finding employment and complained about the lack of English language classes for adults. Over 15 percent of Spanish speakers were unemployed, more than triple the state average unemployment rate (5 percent) and almost double the national average (8 percent).[50]

By the late 1970s, the Committee established a community center at a Catholic church in the western section of Alexandria to cater to the city's growing Latino community. Vidaña, however, had to fight for resources from the city government. In a letter to a local official, he argued that the Spanish-Speaking Committee should receive a portion of a federal grant to fund its job training program. He explained, "The insensitiveness toward the needs of the Spanish-Speaking community which are as great as those of any other minority group and toward our achievements which are as great as those of the greater groups."[51] Officials claimed that they supported the Committee, although they felt that its work did not fit the model of a traditional job training center. By 1980, the center's services expanded beyond job placement and included translation services, transportation, application assistance for federal programs, and information on low-income housing.[52]

Alexandria did not offer refugee services until large numbers of Southeast Asians arrived in the late 1970s. Its federally funded Indochina Refugee Assistance Programs focused on employment "to ensure self-sufficiency" but ignored the social and cultural dissonances tied to living in the United States and the psychological trauma of war.[53] In response to the lack of support, northern Virginia's first wave of Vietnamese refugees, led by Jackie Bong Wright, established the Indochinese Refugee Social Services to offer a broad range of social services. After meeting two homeless farmers, Bong Wright opened Welcome House in a townhouse just south of Arlandria to provide temporary housing for refugees. The Indochinese Refugee Social Services operated out of the townhouse for the first few years. Bong Wright, who came to the United States in 1975 and had trained in social work, found that refugees not only needed help applying for social services and finding jobs but also struggled to locate housing when their sponsorships ended. Welcome House provided temporary shelter for two to three families and a handful of single

Figure 4.3. Arlandria's Metrofood, 1984.
Jim Wilson Photograph Collection, MS400, no. 316,
Special Collections, Alexandria Public Library, Virginia.

people for about a month while they looked for more permanent places to live. With funding from the Department of Health and Human Services, Bong Wright hired Laotian-, Cambodian-, and Vietnamese-speaking staff to work with local agencies and manage her expanding caseload.[54] The overworked Bong Wright, reportedly in response to conflicts with city agencies, shut down Welcome House in 1980 and moved out of Alexandria.[55]

Despite its closure, Welcome House reflected Arlandria's changing racial and ethnic demographics. The neighborhood's affordable housing stock was popular among refugees and other immigrants (see fig. 4.3).[56] For instance, Vidaña of the Spanish-Speaking Committee of Virginia rented an apartment in Arlandria in 1968. A year later, military personnel bought homes with their Korean immigrant spouses.[57] By 1975, immigrants from the Dominican Republic, El Salvador, Iran, Peru, Philippines, and Turkey also lived in Arlandria.[58] That same year, the Stolberg family from Kenya rented an apartment; they were one of the neighborhood's first African immigrants.[59] Ethiopian and Eritrean refugees also settled in Arlandria after fleeing the Derg, a socialist military junta that overthrew Emperor Haile Selassie (1974), and Mengistu Haile Mariam's Red Terror (1977–78). Most of these refugees had been business owners or professionals but now worked as taxicab drivers, primarily shuttling passengers to and from Washington's National Airport.[60]

By the 1980s, city officials and newspaper reporters struggled to capture Arlandria's fluctuating racial and ethnic demographics. Arlandria had historically been a white-only neighborhood but had been described as a racially integrated one by the late 1960s. Over a decade later, it was one of the most diverse neighborhoods in Alexandria and, arguably, northern Virginia. Alexandria's 1986 annual report stated that Arlandria's population had shifted to mostly foreign-born. "The predominant groups are Hispanics, Laotians, Cambodians, Vietnamese, Ethiopians, and Nigerians."[61] Reporters for the *Washington Post* portrayed the neighborhood differently, describing Arlandria as home to "thousands of Hispanics and Southeast Asians, as well as some black and some white low-income people, who work at the lowest-paying jobs in the area."[62]

Mary Jordan, a *Washington Post* reporter who worked the northern Virginia beat, gave Arlandria a new nickname in 1986, "Little Salvador," because of the number of Salvadoran refugees in the area.[63] Central Americans had lived in the Washington metropolitan area since the 1960s, at first finding employment with foreign service personnel, active service members, and defense contractors stationed in their homelands who sponsored their immigration to the United States. El Salvador's civil wars starting in the late 1970s forced many young men northward who feared conscription by either the military or guerrillas. Those who came to Washington turned to family and friends who were already established in the area for support.[64] Oscar Zambrano, originally from Chirilagua, El Salvador, left his family's farm in the late 1970s. He ended up living with his brothers, who were already renting an apartment in Arlandria.[65]

By the 1970s, Arlandria's affordability made it a popular home not only for low- to moderate-income Black residents but also for immigrants and refugees, most of whom came from Africa, Asia, and Central and South America. Alexandria's newest residents wanted to be close to the nation's capital so that they could advocate for fellow exiles, participate in the region's robust job market, and access public transportation. They also wanted an affordable place to live, and the flooding of Four Mile Run combined with white flight drove Arlandria's housing prices down. Like local Black families who moved into the neighborhood in the 1960s, the city's newest residents saw Arlandria as their adopted home.

By the late 1970s, a surge in the number of residents made affordable housing increasingly difficult to find. In addition to Alexandria's immigrant and refugee populations, Americans from throughout the country moved to the Washington metropolitan region because of federal, military, and defense contracting opportunities. Employment rates in Alexandria increased by 30 percent between 1975 and 1980, exceeding percentages in Washington, DC, and the rest of northern Virginia. During the same period, the cost of housing exceeded inflation, jumping 19.4 percent.[66] The completion of flood control along Four Mile Run in 1980 meant that Arlandria's undervalued real estate was ideal for mid- to high-end redevelopment catering to this subset of wealthier white-collar workers. For city government, redevelopment also meant increased tax revenues and fewer social services, for which the federal government would cut funding during the Reagan administration. To survive gentrification, Arlandria residents needed to become creative to protect one of the city's last low-income housing neighborhoods.

Starting in the late 1980s, American scholars began to use the term "gentrification," coined by Ruth Glass in 1964, to describe how middle-class home buyers pushed out low-income residents in American cities. In these studies, real estate developers and wealthier white residents turned to urban centers, where property had become undervalued, either to renovate historic structures or to build new commercial or residential properties. This process was believed to unleash the economic value of these locations, but it simultaneously dislocated low-income residents.[67] Although receiving less attention, suburban neighborhoods experienced gentrification too. In the case of Arlandria, federal policies that expanded the numbers of civil servants, military personnel, and contractors living in the Washington metropolitan area, combined with cuts to social services, put new pressures on housing. Class, racial, ethnic, and citizenship dynamics also foregrounded real estate speculation, which continued to cater to white middle- to upper-class families.[68]

The 1970s saw significant changes in local housing policies and the city government's relationship with low-income residents. By the late 1970s, city leaders began to rehabilitate and sell older houses in Arlandria, where some owners had either abandoned their property or neglected it after the floods. By 1975, Alexandria received its first Community Development Block Grant from the federal government, which funded renovations of current residential buildings and an expansion of public facilities, such as streetlights, trash cans, and park benches. At the same time, housing inspectors aggressively cited landlords for unsafe housing conditions. The Residential Rental Permit Program and later Operation CAN (Compliance in Alexandria North) required that certain properties be inspected annually for structural deterioration. Finally, the Alexandria Cooperative Extension Service offered classes and activities for Arlandria residents in order to rebuild a sense of community after the floods.[69]

Despite community investments made in the 1970s, changing federal housing policies during the Reagan administration accelerated the breakdown of affordable housing. Reagan's cuts to HUD's housing subsidies for low-income families directly impacted Alexandria residents at a time when population growth was putting additional pressure on the housing market. Alexandria's 1983 annual report noted, "Federal housing subsidies, which the City has used to stimulate a remarkable growth in housing opportunities over the past decade, have declined considerably in the past few years." Section 8 Certificates, which the Alexandria Redevelopment and Housing Authority (ARHA) had offered soon after the creation of the program under the Housing and Community Development Act (1974), announced that it expected a decrease in the number of rent subsidies. HUD had also reduced the income eligibility limit for public housing and Section 8 units completed after October 1981. In response to federal cuts, city leaders began discussing selling city-owned properties to maintain current levels of low-income housing construction and rehabilitation.[70]

To compound matters, the region's booming economy and expanding workforce put further pressure on Alexandria's limited housing stock. Many aging buildings in the oldest sections of the city needed renovations, and Alexandria's Board of Architectural Review (BAR) required that renovations in the historic district comply with certain aesthetics. These policies added to the overall expense of the area, making Alexandria's oldest properties primarily affordable only to wealthier families. Developers, interested in making profits in a shifting real estate market, also purchased apartment complexes for condominium conversions or to be replaced with new construction. Renovations, new construction, and conversions, however, did not keep up with demand. Even in Arlandria, housing prices soared. Townhomes, which had previously sold for $12,000 in 1975, went for $52,200 a decade later.[71]

In June 1986, Artery Organization Inc. purchased over 1,000 apartment units in Arlandria, creating a firestorm among city officials and residents. Two additional development companies, Potomac Development Inc. and Freeman/Cafritz, bought other complexes in the neighborhood with the intent to renovate.[72] These sales constituted 74 percent of the neighborhood's apartment offerings. All three developers were interested in condominium conversions, displacing current residents in hopes of renting or selling units to middle- and upper-income individuals and families. A month earlier, a new neighborhood organization, the Alexandria United Tenant Organization, had received monies from the city council to study the possibility of residents purchasing their apartment complexes and creating cooperatives. Unfortunately, their efforts did not stop the sales. An Arlandria resident and Guatemalan immigrant Magda Lopez Mijango Gotts told reporters, "It's going to be an exodus of people. There is no place for these people to go. I'm speechless." Alexandria's mayor Jim Moran, who had moved to Alexandria in the early 1970s to work for the Department of Health, Education, and Welfare, noted this would be "the largest displacement in the city's history." Local officials believed little could be done to stop developers.[73]

Tensions over housing displacement in Arlandria pitted racial and ethnic groups against each other, which sometimes resulted in violence. In June 1986, police found the remains of a Nigerian refugee in Sunnyside whom a coworker from Sierra Leone had strangled. Both worked together in Arlandria.[74] The incident sparked an outcry from African Americans living in Sunnyside, whose criticisms were directed at immigrant and refugee households. Complaints focused on the transient nature of apartment dwellers and housing density, with Black residents requesting that the planning commission rezone a nearby vacant lot to stop apartment construction. A longtime Black resident explained to a reporter, "We want neighbors, not transients. . . . We want to know the people who live near us."[75] A few weeks later, upward of forty African American and Latino men brawled in the street. Federal authorities decided to investigate both the murder and fighting, believing that pending displacement triggered both acts of violence. Meanwhile, the National Conference of Christians and Jews organized community meetings to develop a list of issues that affected residents and mitigate neighborhood tensions.[76]

One African American renter recognized that interracial and interethnic cooperation was needed if residents were going to successfully stop displacement. In an oral history conducted through the Office of Historic Alexandria, local housing and labor activist Jon Liss recalled that Jacob T. Hughes offered his home for meetings of low-income residents across racial and ethnic lines. Born in Clinton, Kentucky, Hughes had migrated to Alexandria sometime in the early 1930s. He found employment with the WPA and later the army and navy. With the monies saved through federal employment, Hughes bought a home, but ARHA condemned it in 1952 in order to construct public housing.

His family found another place to live in Uptown before moving to Arlandria.[77] Liss noted that, at first, Black renters, "who sort of were schooled in struggle and come out of both union and civil rights struggles," attended meetings at Hughes's apartment. But Hughes felt that Latino residents needed to be involved too, and he invited them into his home. Over 100 people attended one of his gatherings.[78] Hughes, who was eighty years old, could not sustain these collaborations and passed away later that year.[79]

At the same time, there were few local and state laws that protected low-income residents from displacement. Only one city ordinance forced developers to provide low-income housing in the private rental market: a tax-exempt bond program, which required that participants put aside 20 percent of their units for low-income residents.[80] To halt displacement, local leaders had to develop new laws and policies. First, the city council pressured developers to increase the monies given for the relocation of current tenants based on age, income, and disability.[81] Second, ARHA purchased a building from developers using city bonds. Its goal was to provide public housing units in Arlandria. Third, code enforcement cracked down, noting that conditions in some buildings "constitutes an immediate serious danger and hazard to the life, health, and safety of the occupants." They accused developers of acting as slumlords, all the while increasing rents.[82] Fourth, the city council put aside $500,000 in federal funding to find housing for those displaced and to put together a subsidy program to offset rent increases.[83] Fifth, the city manager established the Northern Virginia Housing Coalition to lobby Richmond for housing subsidies.[84] Finally, believing that condominium owners relied on cars for transportation, the city council passed an ordinance that barred the construction of additional parking for apartment conversions unless developers put aside units for low-income residents.[85]

A handful of Arlandria residents argued that city officials should use eminent domain to acquire apartment complexes, noting that providing low-income housing was for the public good.[86] As noted in chapter 3, eminent domain had displaced large numbers of Black and low-income white residents in Alexandria from the 1930s through the 1960s. Advocates believed that the practice could also be used to their advantage, but only if city government prioritized housing for all residents regardless of income level. They also argued that city leaders still needed to embrace more participatory forms of governance, giving residents more control over policy decisions. In the 1980s, other municipalities engaged in similar discussions. Pierre Clavel's *Activists in City Hall* describes how Boston went so far as to give eminent domain powers to the Dudley Street Neighborhood Initiative.[87]

Some renters and homeowners refused to accept the city leaders' responses and turned to housing advocates in Washington, DC. This group of residents argued that decent housing was a right, and they maintained that the fact that most of the displaced residents were people of color made the displacement a civil rights issue. The Arlandria Community Campaign to Save Our Homes, a newly established, interracial/interethnic housing organization, asked Lawrence Kamakawiwoʻole and others from the Institute for Public Representation at Georgetown Law Center to assess the sale and conversion plan. Fighting against displacement was not new to Kamakawiwoʻole. Born in Honolulu in 1943, Kamakawiwoʻole studied at the Pacific School of Religion in Berkeley, California, where he joined the Third World Liberation Front with Black, Latino, and Asian American seminarians. When he returned to Hawaiʻi in the late 1960s, he unsuccessfully fought Hawaiʻi's largest landowner from forcibly removing farmers in Oahu's Kalama Valley to build a luxury resort. This event, among others, led to the Hawaiian Renaissance in the 1970s.[88] In front of Alexandria's city council, Kamakawiwoʻole argued that Arlandria developers had not complied with Alexandria's Housing Conversion Assistance Policy, which was supposed to stop large-scale displacements and subsequent homelessness. He also made a series of recommendations to assist residents, such as having tenants move out during the summer months when people who worked in the hotel and restaurant industries usually had more money. Finally, Kamakawiwoʻole asked developers to provide more specifics on the cost to re-rent apartments and to generate a list of alternative places with similar rents.[89]

In the meantime, residents and housing advocates organized protests to raise awareness and demand that city officials and developers be held accountable. Arlandria Community Campaign to Save Our Homes and another new group, United Tenants Organization, rallied African American, Latino, and white tenants to speak out.[90] Within weeks of the first sale, 200 residents walked through the streets singing "We Shall Not Be Moved," using the tune of the Civil Rights anthem, "We Shall Overcome."[91] Renters also held a candlelight vigil outside of city hall and another demonstration at one of the developer's headquarters in Maryland.[92]

In February 1987, residents and activists organized a large-scale and interracial/interethnic march from Arlandria to city hall. While giving speeches on the city hall's steps, Mitch Snyder, a Washington-based homeless activist from the Community for Creative Non-Violence, suggested that protesters take over city council chambers, symbolically displacing local government. It was the first and only time in Alexandria's history in which protesters shut down the city council. Frustrated by the presence of protesters, Mayor Moran threatened to send agents from the Immigration and Naturalization Service to arrest immigrant and refugee protesters, and the mayor almost came to blows with Snyder. Patricia S. Ticer, another city council member, sympathized with residents but ultimately saw their tactics as misguided. She recommended that they protest instead outside the White House for cutting HUD's budget.[93]

Arlandria residents, however, had already turned to the federal government, arguing that their displacement conflicted with the Fair Housing Act. In February 1987, District of Columbia congressman Walter E. Fauntroy presided over a congressional hearing on possible civil rights violations and stated that the federal government should support the idea that a "decent home and suitable living environment [be available] for every American family."[94] Residents, city officials, and activists testified about housing issues in northern Virginia, noting that the majority of those affected were low-income African American and Latino residents. Rena Brown, an Arlandria resident who helped to organize fellow renters, complained about the declining number of African Americans in the neighborhood and argued that local white leaders were driving them out of the city.[95] A handful Latino residents wrote letters, stating that they faced discrimination like their Black neighbors.[96] Mercedes Márquez, a colleague of Kamakawiwoʻoleʻs at the Institute for Public Representation who later became the assistant secretary for Community Planning and Development at HUD, ended the hearing by detailing an alternative plan that appealed to both renters and housing advocates. They wanted landlords to sell their properties to a public-private partnership—which included an incorporated tenant organization, a nonprofit developer, and a civil rights organization—that would provide low-income housing. The National Council of La Raza supported the project and agreed to work with tenants and landlords.[97]

Rena Brown and eleven other residents filed a civil rights lawsuit in Washington's District Court, a court that housing advocates knew to be more friendly to renters.[98] Based on legal precedent that had emerged after the passage of the Fair Housing Act, Judge Harold H. Greene agreed to hear the case later that summer. The legal question that the court hoped to address was whether developers racially discriminated against tenants, even if it was recognized as not deliberate. The court also wanted to explore what remedies the law offered. One developer's past project, which included another condominium conversion in Alexandria that displaced 90 percent of its tenants, demonstrated to the court that it targeted low-income neighborhoods that housed African Americans, immigrants, and refugees.[99] Greene declared the case was class-actionable and affected all renters from marginalized communities. The court asked the plaintiffs to generate a list of names of those residents who wanted to sue. By April 1987, 136 renters added their names to the lawsuit.[100]

Meanwhile, the city government tried to put together a plan to help as many renters as possible. By the end of the summer, it had worked out a compromise with developers: for the next five years, they were to put aside one-quarter of their apartments for renters with Section 8 vouchers. ARHA also renovated a 152-unit apartment for public housing.[101] Religious and housing advocates tried to find solutions to Arlandria's housing problems too. Local Episcopal congregations established Carpenter's Lodgings (now Community Lodgings), a nonprofit to address homelessness in the neighborhood. In addition to housing, it offered job training, childcare, and other social services.[102] Another group of residents wanted cooperative housing, in which they owned the building together with support from public and private funds. The Tenants Support Committee, established in 1989, used the bankruptcy of one of the developers to acquire 300 units. Ten years later, it created the Arlandria-Chirilagua Housing Cooperative, named after a town in El Salvador from which many residents had emigrated.[103]

Media portrayals of residents along with alliances and conflicts among African Americans, Latinos, and whites had other long-term consequences that impacted the neighborhood. Kim Cook, a Vietnamese American activist, noted that Vietnamese, Cambodian, and Laotian refugees felt excluded from tenant organizing and left Arlandria for other parts of northern Virginia.[104] African immigrants and refugees also moved to other neighborhoods. Elizabeth Chacko, in her study of Ethiopian immigration patterns, found that her subjects tended to live in western portions of Alexandria by the beginning of the twenty-first century.[105] By the end of the 1980s, journalists for the *Washington Post* reported on the predominance of Latinos in Arlandria, specifically Salvadorans, whose presence had begun to define the neighborhood for both insiders and outsiders.[106]

In the end, Arlandria's housing problems in the mid-1980s demonstrated the multifaceted ways in which African Americans along with Latino and white residents deployed their connections to Washington, DC. Cuts in HUD funding during the Reagan administration combined with population pressures tied to the federal government's expansion created a situation in which Arlandria, a low-income, racially and ethnically diverse neighborhood, was targeted for redevelopment. Frustrated by the lack of local and state support, residents turned to Washington-based resources to fight possible displacement. Well versed in civil rights activism, African Americans also worked with newer residents from across the globe to protect the neighborhood. Some residents, however, did leave, including many of the neighborhood's Asian immigrant and refugee neighbors. Those who remained believed that they had fostered a new sense of belonging and community. Mohamed Conteh, a refugee from Sierra Leone who had lived in Arlandria since 1981, told a reporter that his "family [was] more comfortable now" and that he felt a "greater sense of community" around him.[107]

CONCLUSION

The attempted gentrification of Arlandria highlights the larger social and economic forces at work in the suburbs outside of Washington, DC, in the late twentieth century. An expanding regional economy driven by an increase in defense-related jobs, combined with cuts in federally funded housing programs, led to a hyper-inflated housing market. Virginia's lack of tenant protections also fostered a climate in which unscrupulous developers could purchase undervalued apartments, evict their current tenants, and raise rents as high as the market could bear. Municipalities such as Alexandria, which would have benefitted from increases in tax revenues, struggled to stop mass removals of residents.

Many of Arlandria's residents believed that affordable housing was a right, and that all people should have a place to live regardless of their income. To fight evictions, they used local resources, creating interracial and interethnic housing organizations, speaking at city council meetings, and protesting to raise awareness. At the same time, they turned to the nation's capital to hire representation from Georgetown's Institute for Public Representation, organize congressional hearings, and sue in federal court for civil rights violations. What emerged from the frenzied energy surrounding the potential displacement of Arlandria's residents was a call not only for more inclusion but also for more creativity from government officials and community leaders. The establishment of the Arlandria-Chirilagua Housing Cooperative and Community Lodgings reflected these goals.

Arlandria's racial and ethnic demographics, however, continued to shift over the course of the 1980s. Neighborhood organizations attempted to bring people from different backgrounds together, but not everyone felt included. Interracial and interethnic tensions eventually flared again.[108] By the end of the decade, Arlandria retained some of its diversity from the 1970s, but it also began to be called by a new name, Chirilagua. The presence of Salvadorans in Arlandria redefined the neighborhood, despite its broader racial and ethnic diversity.

CHAPTER FIVE

Memory

The blockbuster film *Remember the Titans* (2000) retells the story of Alexandria's public school system's integration through the success of its high school football team. Set in 1971, the movie opens with the selection of Herman Boone as the head coach for T. C. Williams High School's newly integrated football team, and the relegation of Bill Yoast, the head coach of one of Alexandria's nearly all-white high schools, as his assistant. Boone and Yoast must not only work through their personal and professional differences but also bring their players together to create a team. Despite racial tensions at the high school, the Titans become an unstoppable football team, so much so that Alexandrians, both Black and white, rally around them. In the end, the success of the Titans, who win the state championship, unites Alexandria across racial lines, transcending the political rancor of the time.

A football film with a message, *Remember the Titans* received much commentary in the local press from residents who lived in Alexandria in the late 1960s and early 1970s. Robert Luckett, who had played on the 1971 team, emphasized the film's message about overcoming racial conflict for a common cause. "'We had differences in how we dressed, in what music we listened to, in what schools we were from. We were dealing with a whole lot of things that you are dealing with today. And we came together as a family.'"[1] Hazel

Rigby, who taught at T. C. Williams, focused on the film's social commentary seeded in the relationship between Boone and Yoast. "What matters is that if these two coaches had not been able to resolve their differences as they did. . . . I'm not sure that the rest of us would have accomplished the task [of desegregating Alexandria] either."[2] While well-aware of the many historical discrepancies in the film, Boone himself explained to a reporter that "this wasn't a movie about a state championship. It was about how human beings can come together, and a state championship was just the icing on the cake."[3] Alexandria's integration story in Remember the Titans was acclaimed locally and nationally as a triumphant depiction of racial understanding and belonging, celebrating those who lived through the event and providing an alternative universe where racism could be overcome.

Remember the Titans' box office success, however, created other problems beyond its fictive tropes that played to its feel-good messaging. The film obscured the complex and contested nature of remembering Alexandria's Black past, for which African Americans had fought since the nineteenth century. Black residents demanded that they be included in a more accurate portrayal of the city's history so that current and future Alexandrians could better understand the community in which they lived. At least one audience member spoke openly about this issue after watching Remember the Titans. Patrick Welsh, another former teacher from T. C. Williams, complained about the film's Disneyfication, noting that it was an "oversimplification of the tremendously complex issues of race."[4]

While Remember the Titans inserted Alexandria's high school's integration story into the national psyche at the beginning of the twenty-first century, the recognition of an African American past in Alexandria required both grit and gumption: the way in which history was taught, preserved, curated, and commemorated had to change. And once again, Black Alexandrians turned to Black Washingtonians and to the federal government to challenge the ways in which local history was told. Throughout most of the late nineteenth and twentieth centuries, white residents celebrated Alexandria as "The Hometown of George Washington and Robert E. Lee," playing to a unique form of civil religion that combined the Founding Fathers with the Cult of the Confederacy. These individuals tended to focus on the city's history prior to the Civil War, a period when Alexandria's economy had supposedly flourished; however, these narratives remained mostly silent about one of the major forces behind white residents' prosperity: slavery and slave trading. By the early twentieth century, white city boosters recognized the potential economic value to be gained through the restoration of Alexandria's older housing stock.

Class and racial politics, however, dictated who decided which structures were designated "historic" and thus saved for posterity. The saving of homes and businesses owned by Alexandria's pre–Civil War white elite became a subject of pride for white historic preservationists.[5]

Although circumscribed by segregation, Alexandria's Black residents found ways to document and celebrate their histories in private and public spaces too. As in other parts of the country, families wrote genealogies in their Bibles, listened to history lectures, marched in the streets, and wrote about the past.[6] However, the damage caused by narratives that emphasized white superiority made it difficult for some to believe that African Americans had a history worth remembering.[7] A small group of scholars provided a corrective lens by inserting African Americans into interpretations of the past and recognizing the power relations inherent in slavery that were later used to justify segregation. Historian Carter G. Woodson, who had moved to Washington, DC, after establishing the Association for the Study of African American Life and History (ASALH) in 1915, made it his life's mission to write African American history and help other historians publish their scholarship. In 1926, he created "Negro History Week" for Washington's public schools, which quickly became a national event, including in Alexandria.[8]

By the late 1960s, the Black Power Movement began the process of reimagining African American history through its emphasis on pride, beauty, and culture. Curricular offerings at colleges and universities, community museums, and preservation efforts facilitated new conversations about the past. White-dominated colleges and universities throughout the United States witnessed student protests about course content, majors and programs, and overall campus climate. In 1968, strikes at San Francisco State College led to the creation of the first College of Ethnic Studies, which included programs in African American, Indigenous, Chicano/Latino, and Asian American Studies. Meanwhile, major metropolitan areas, such as Chicago, Detroit, and Washington, DC, saw the establishment of community museums that focused on African American culture and history. With limited support from municipal governments, community museums relied on collections donated by residents and worked creatively to find exhibition space. In Washington, DC, Robert and Vincent DeForrest also established the Afro-American Bicentennial Corporation (later known as the Afro-American Institute for Historic Preservation and Community Development) in response to preparations for the nation's bicentennial to ensure that African American history was included. They identified sites tied to important individuals and events in Black history for the National Park Service's National Register of Historic Places. Finally, the 1976 publication of Alex Haley's *Roots* and the subsequent television series led to a flourishing of genealogical activity among African Americans that complemented Black historical writing on the popular and academic levels.[9]

In Alexandria, Black history reflected broader trends within the Black Power Movement that played to the city's history and especially its unique relationship with the District of Columbia. As colleges and universities grappled with student demands for a more inclusive curriculum, high school students rallied around the inclusion of Black Studies in Alexandria's public schools. Alexandria's teachers, however, had limited curricular support in Virginia but found resources through ASALH. Over the next decade, what would become "Black historic preservation" emerged in response to the region's gentrification, which—as noted in the previous chapters—was tied to the federal government's expansion in the late twentieth century. Longtime residents also called for a community museum like the Anacostia Neighborhood Museum, which was founded in 1967 in the easternmost section of the District of Columbia. Continuing work begun by the Smithsonian Institution in 1965, the city's newly established community archaeology program exposed the public to objects associated with the everyday lives of enslaved and free African Americans, creating opportunities for Black residents and white archaeologists to partner together and rewrite the history of Alexandria, DC, as well as Alexandria, Virginia.[10] The rediscovery of a late nineteenth-century cemetery led to discussions about commemoration and the need for city government to protect burial grounds from desecration.[11] The culmination of these debates led to the establishment of the Contrabands and Freedmen Cemetery Memorial, which recognized the self-emancipated men, women, and children who fled to Union-controlled Alexandria and died there during and immediately after the Civil War.[12]

This final chapter documents how several grassroot movements initiated by Black residents used a combination of local and federal resources to reimagine Alexandria's past. Since the nineteenth century, Black Alexandrians had engaged African American history on both the local and national levels, but it was not until the late 1960s that broader changes occurred in the ways that the past was researched, curated, and circulated. Starting with demands by high school students for Black Studies classes, residents used Washington- and Alexandria-based resources to address the gaps in history education, historic preservation, museum programs, and commemorative practices. These changes injected Alexandria's history with new interpretations of the past, but the process remained piecemeal. Even today, instead of creating a more inclusive, overarching narrative, the city's interpretation of the past remains driven by reactions to specific incidents within the community. Furthermore, certain white residents and organizations have clung to older narratives, refusing to recognize the erasures that they have caused and denying their role in the perpetuation of white supremacy. Despite these shortcomings, the city's narrative of itself had finally begun to address its African American history by the late twentieth century.

The inclusion of African American history in the city's broader understanding of its past started with education. Throughout the late nineteenth and early- to mid-twentieth centuries, most public and academic histories marginalized or erased the contributions of African Americans, playing to notions of white supremacy that were used to justify segregationist practices. African American history also existed, but it primarily fell to individual writers, historically minded community organizations, or Black-serving institutions of higher education. For Alexandrians, Washington-based organizations such as the Bethel Literary and Historical Society and ASALH provided early information about Black history. By the late 1960s, students called for a more inclusive discussion of the past in Alexandria's public school curriculum, and teachers, once again, turned to Washington, DC, for resources. Student demands for Black history in the classroom laid the foundation for future activism in the late twentieth century centered around historic preservation, museums, and memorials.

After the Civil War, Alexandria's African American middle classes were already engaging in discussions about history, which played to their relationship with Black Washingtonians. In 1884, Freeman H. M. Murray, a clerk in the federal pension office (see chapter 2), traveled with friends to Washington, DC, to attend lectures at the Bethel Literary and Historical Society, one of a handful of African American historical societies in the District of Columbia at the turn of the century. Murray and his fellow Alexandrians also presented research or debated contemporary issues in meetings at each other's homes.[13] At the same time, Magnus L. Robinson organized the Frederick Douglass Library Association to promote literacy and intellectual development among Black residents. Robinson came from one of Alexandria's free families and had been active in Alexandria's Radical Republican Party. By 1888, he began to edit the *National Leader* in Washington, DC, which he later moved to Alexandria and renamed the *Weekly Leader*.[14] Frederick Douglass, who lived in Washington, DC, lectured on behalf of the organization as a fundraiser for a public reading room, which opened a year later. In addition to its library, the Frederick Douglass Library Association organized celebrations of the twenty-seventh anniversary of the Emancipation Proclamation on January 1, 1890.[15]

By the 1930s, African American educators created an alternative history curriculum, parts of which they shared with the public. The Departmental Progressive Club put together Alexandria's first African American history program as part of Carter G. Woodson's newly established "Negro History Week" in 1930. A year later, students "presented interesting facts of Negro history" for their school's History Week celebrations.[16] In 1937, African American educators from northern Virginia met in Alexandria and listened to a presentation by Woodson entitled, "The Place of Negro History in the School Curriculum." Wesley Elam, Parker-Gray's principal, later reported to ASALH that his teachers had "fine results using *The Negro History Bulletin* in teaching of American history."[17]

Throughout this period, scholars published books, articles, and other materials on African American history. Not only did these publications provide important information that countered white-centric interpretations, but they also contained local history, which connected Alexandria to the nation's capital. Luther P. Jackson's *Free Negro Labor and Property Holdings in Virginia, 1830–1860* (1942) and *Negro Office Holders in Virginia, 1865–1895* (1945) included entries on prominent Alexandrians. In 1946, Jackson presented his research in Alexandria, sharing information on a local office holder.[18] The transcription of an 1890 letter from Frederick Douglass to Magnus L. Robinson regarding the Douglass Library Association appeared in *Journal of Negro History* in 1953.[19] In 1962, the *Negro History Bulletin* published a biographical essay on DC judge Joseph C. Waddy, whose family had lived in Alexandria in the 1920s.[20]

The most significant research on Black Alexandrians prior to the late 1960s appeared in Constance McLaughlin Green's *Washington: Village and Capital, 1800–1878* (1962), for which she received a Pulitzer Prize. Green, a white Michigan transplant who lived in the District of Columbia, based her book on the work of the Washington History Project, which she directed starting in 1954.[21] Green's research on the capital's enslaved and free populations in the early nineteenth century provided substantial information on Alexandria, including the city's prominent role in the domestic slave trade and the negative impact of the 1846 retrocession on free residents.[22] In his review of Green's book, Howard University professor Williston H. Lofton noted, "It is almost lost to history that Alexandria, Virginia, was originally part of the District of Columbia."[23] Green's book became the foundation of numerous future studies that looked at early republican and antebellum race relations in the District of Columbia, all of which included Alexandria.[24]

In contrast to Green's and others' research, Virginia's official history textbooks ignored developments in African American history. Francis Butler Simkins's *Virginia: History, Government, Geography* (1957) replicated pro-segregationist narratives, which Harry Byrd's Democratic political machine had argued was an imperative after the US Supreme Court's decision in *Brown v. Board of Education* (1954). For civil rights organizations, the political and legal battles surrounding school desegregation made it difficult to leverage resources and personnel to fight how white politicians wanted history to be taught. Virginia's NAACP lawyers focused primarily on dismantling Massive Resistance, a policy to shut down schools that attempted to desegregate in the late 1950s and early 1960s. In 1963, the Virginia Teachers Association, which represented African American educators, spoke publicly against "the use of textbooks which do not present the Negro properly," but it had little clout with white politicians in Richmond.[25] The association's merger with the Virginia Education Association, the state's white-only education organization, in 1966 also muted activism. Simkins's *Virginia* textbook remained in circulation in public schools through the early 1970s.[26]

Frustrated by Virginia's new textbook, at least one Alexandria teacher decided to incorporate African American history into his classroom on his own terms.[27] Carlton A. Funn, a seventh-grade teacher, used educational materials that he had collected from specialty bookstores in Washington and from ASALH to teach his students and make posters for his classroom. Born in Alexandria in 1932, Funn had attended the city's public schools before graduating in 1953 from Storer College in Harpers Ferry, West Virginia, with a degree in elementary education.[28] After serving in the US Army, he returned home and obtained a teaching job in Alexandria in 1957. Looking back at the early years of his teaching career, Funn recalled that he "wanted the black children in my class to leave my room at the end of the year with positive self-esteem, able to raise their heads high and be proud of themselves as black Americans." He continued, noting that promoting pride in children "was very hard to do using that Virginia history book," a reference to Simkins's *Virginia*.[29]

By spring 1969, high school students insisted that Alexandria's public schools, like white-dominated colleges and universities, offer Black Studies courses. In response to student demands, the school board admitted that teachers and staff were already developing a course, and that librarians had begun to acquire relevant books and other resources.[30] The superintendent agreed to invite interested students to curriculum development meetings and contacted ASALH's executive director to act as a consultant. Students, however, wanted the course to be a requirement that all high school students had to take. When this demand was not met, students staged a sit-in during a school board meeting in April 1969. Ferdinand Day, the board's first African American member, took it upon himself to deescalate the situation. He intimately understood the frustrations that drove the students to protest. Also a native Alexandrian, he commuted to Washington, DC, to receive a high school education and later studied to be a teacher. Unfortunately, there were too few opportunities in Alexandria's segregated job market to become an educator, so Day, like his older brother, Lawrence Dunbar Day (see chapter 2), became a career civil servant. While he worked at the State Department, Day remained focused on improving educational opportunities for Black children, and he became an integral member of Alexandria's Secret Seven by the 1950s and 1960s.[31] Day attempted to comfort the students, letting them know that a course would be made available soon; he, along with other school board members and the police, sent the children home.[32] A month later, school administrators submitted a draft curriculum (see appendix) for a new high school course, titled "Afro-American Studies," to Virginia's Department of Education. The Director of Secondary Education approved it and recommended that its content be incorporated into other disciplines.[33]

To prepare for the 1969–70 academic year, the school board decided that teachers should pilot the course over the summer. Three teachers, two Black and one white, agreed to team-teach "Afro-American Studies." No high school textbook existed, so teachers had to develop their own course materials. To do that, they used Funn's personal collection and conducted research at the Library of Congress, ASALH, and other federal agencies. Funn's collection also became an exhibit in one of the schools, and he opened the exhibit to the public. The summer course was a huge hit. One student told a reporter, "It's the best course I've ever taken!"[34]

News about Funn's collection quickly spread among teachers, politicians, activists, and religious leaders who wanted to educate the public about African American history. By the winter of 1970, Funn received several requests from outside of Alexandria to install his collection as a temporary exhibit and give lectures. Panels in the exhibit included information on African American military service, biographies of prominent historical and contemporary individuals, and everyday life in West Africa. Over the next two years, Funn visited the University of Virginia, the University of Maryland, Virginia State College, and a handful of high schools. Funn also exhibited his collection at the Virginia General Assembly, the Washington Metropolitan Council of

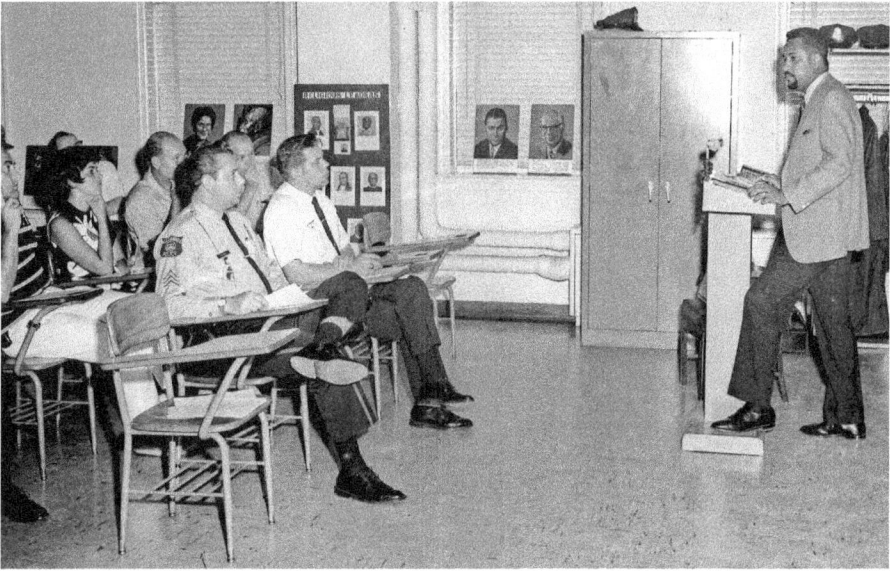

Figure 5.1. Carlton Funn lecturing to Alexandria police officers, 1970.
Carlton A. Funn Sr. Collection, Alexandria Black History Museum, Virginia.

Governments, the Virginia chapter of the NAACP, and the US Army at Fort Lee, Virginia.[35] Teaching Alexandria's police department after the murder of Robin Gibson by a white clerk (see chapter 4) received significant local press (see fig. 5.1). The four-part program was intended to "increase the predominantly white force's awareness of the black people of America." The chief of police later wrote Funn that he hoped to partner with him again.[36]

By the early 1970s, Funn revamped his collection to include other underrepresented communities, about whom he also hoped to educate the public. This decision reflected the rise of multiculturalism and a shift away from focusing solely on African Americans to include other groups who had faced similar forms of marginalization and exclusion.[37] "The History and Culture of Minorities" exhibit consisted of materials on Latinos, Native Americans, Asian Americans, Pacific Islanders, women, the disabled, the elderly, immigrants, and African Americans. In 1974, Funn traveled to the University of Pittsburgh to showcase his expanded exhibit. He explained to a reporter, "My collection is for people. Not just Blacks. We all need to know more about each other. We all need to meet and relate to each other. . . . Then maybe we can begin loving each other."[38] Two years later, the Office of Equal Employment and Opportunity at the US Department of Labor hired Funn to install his exhibit in their main building and to give lectures. A photograph published in the *New Pittsburgh Courier* shows Funn explaining the content of his collection to Secretary of Labor W. J. Usery Jr.[39]

By late 1960s and early 1970s, Alexandria's public schools had begun the process of rewriting its curriculum to be more inclusive, a reflection of the Black Power Movement's emphasis on pride, beauty, and culture. A small cohort of Black Alexandrians, however, had already been learning about African American history since the nineteenth century, to which they had been exposed through the work of historically minded individuals and organizations, especially ASALH in Washington, DC. Meanwhile, Funn functioned as a bridge, using his personal collections from DC and elsewhere not only to provide teaching materials for Alexandria's first Black Studies course but also to develop traveling exhibits to re-educate the public, including the federal government itself.

HISTORIC PRESERVATION

By the early 1970s, new scholarly and popular research about the past informed what would become Black historic preservation. Led by the Afro-American Institute for Historic Preservation and Community Development (previously known as the Afro-American Bicentennial Corporation) in DC, Black historic preservation initially focused on the lack of representation among the historic properties owned by the National Park Service as it related to the nation's bicentennial celebrations.[40] However, low- to middle-income Black Alexandrians argued for a different conceptualization of historic preservation, one that would stop the displacement of families who had lived in the city for generations. Historic preservation, in their minds, meant protecting contemporary neighborhoods from redevelopment, including the city's public housing and urban renewal projects (see chapter 3) and white historic preservation efforts. In the 1970s and early 1980s, Black Alexandrians argued for this new form of historic preservation, one that was focused on people, not structures. And, once again, residents turned to the federal government for support. Federal and city policymakers, however, had no means to make such ideas a reality, and they continued to promote preservationist ideals that aligned primarily with the goals of wealthier white residents.[41]

Throughout most of the twentieth century, white historic preservationists promoted protections for neighborhoods and structures that they deemed "historic" without acknowledging the class and racial implications of their actions. By the 1960s, historic homes in Alexandria had become a valuable commodity, leading to a highly speculative real estate market and increased tax revenues for city coffers. At the same time, Black families, many of whom had lived in Alexandria's older housing stock for several generations, could no longer afford to live in the neighborhoods where they had grown up. Although not necessarily an explicit goal, white historic preservation functioned as another form of gentrification that adversely impacted Black families.[42]

In the late twentieth century, the goals of Black historic preservation overlapped and, at times, conflicted with its white counterpart. For white residents, organizations such as the Mount Vernon Ladies' Association (1853) and the Association for the Preservation of Virginia Antiquities (1889) inspired their preservation efforts in Alexandria. In 1903, the Society for the Restoration of Historic Alexandria opened Carlyle House, owned by Scottish colonial merchant John Carlyle, to display objects tied to George Washington. Over two decades later, the American Legion and the Landmarks Society of Alexandria launched Gadsby's Tavern and the Stabler-Leadbeater Apothecary, respectively, as business history museums. By the late 1920s, the federal government's zoning policies along George Washington Parkway required that Alexandria's colonial and early republican aesthetics be maintained. At the same time, preservation-minded white residents and city boosters were looking for ways to protect Alexandria's oldest housing stock and increase property values. To achieve this end, the city council established the Old and Historic District (O&HD) in 1946. The new ordinance created the Board of Architectural Review (BAR) to certify the appropriateness of all new construction and oversee any renovations in Alexandria's newly designated historic neighborhoods.[43]

To keep pace with growing interest among white would-be homebuyers and with redevelopment pressures, city officials hired a consultant to inventory all historic properties and prioritize preservation efforts; the study was published in 1970. For the first time in the city's history, buildings in Alexandria's African American neighborhoods were documented as historically significant based on the ages of the structures.[44] As noted in previous chapters, earlier property assessments ignored the historical value of African American neighborhoods and targeted them in favor of public housing and urban renewal projects. As late as 1967, Alexandria's HUD Model Neighborhood Grant application to redevelop Uptown described the neighborhood as "residences that once housed slaves, dock and railroad roundhouse laborers, and tanyard and brewery workers," but these properties reportedly "offer[ed] scant economic incentive for historical restoration."[45] Uptown, established during the Civil War and named Newtown, housed the highest concentration of African American families by the 1960s.

While Alexandria's 1967 Model Neighborhood Grant failed, white city leaders and historic preservationists argued for the expansion of the O&HD into Uptown, using the new 1970 historic properties inventory to justify their proposal. The expansion, they believed, would preserve the neighborhood's historic character from redevelopment, as in other white-majority neighborhoods in the O&HD. African American residents, however, quickly mobilized against the proposal. In a planning commission meeting, John Valentine, a newer Uptown resident, criticized both historic preservation and the city's notion of history, which excluded Black voices. Residents were "not interested in the historic value of Old Town," Valentine maintained and, he continued, "If the City wants to include history in this proposal, then include some black history." Reverend John O. Peterson from Alfred Street Baptist Church, who later ferried his congregation through debates around the destruction of its original chapel, argued against the BAR's class- and race-based power. "It was [not] fair to tell a man his house must be altered, just because it does not meet the 'pseudo-architectural styles of years ago,' after he has spent time and money fixing it up for his own comfort." He also noted that "very few [Black residents] were consulted," and that any policy changes "should be done together." Eudora Lyles, a life-long resident, explained her perception of historic preservation: "For the last 30 years everything had been done to harass the blacks; and . . . this proposed extension was just another tool to push the blacks out of the area." Lyles's family had already lost their home to public housing construction, and she worried that the O&HD would displace her family once again. This time, she decided to organize neighborhood residents and fight white city leaders and historic preservationists (see fig. 5.2).[46]

In response to concerns voiced by Black Alexandrians, the city council agreed to study the impact of historic preservation on African American and low-income white residents and to consider alternatives.[47] White city staff met with stakeholders about the project but repeatedly misunderstood how residents viewed their neighborhood. Lawrence Jointer, president of the Inner-City Civic Association, a neighborhood organization that represented Black residents in older sections of Alexandria, explained that city leaders needed to focus on people, not buildings. In a letter to the city manager, he argued that the project should "include studying and developing strategies designed to preserve a community confronted with speculative development spurred by many forces, historic preservation being only one of them." Jointer

Figure 5.2. Eudora Lyles, 1985.
Photograph by Carol G. Siegel, Carol G. Siegel Photograph
Collection, Alexandria Black History Museum, Virginia.

also believed that any study of the impact of historic preservation should not be limited to buildings but focus on "*neighborhood preservation*."[48]

Jointer's argument that historic preservation functioned as a form of gentrification was not unfounded. Funded by the NEA, Alexandria hired a consulting firm to study the relationship between gentrification and historic preservation in 1974. The report, issued a year later, documented how the popularity of the O&HD with wealthier white homeowners had already led to a decline in the number of lower-income white and African American residents (see table 5.1). Starting in the 1960s, lower-income white residents left the O&HD, selling their homes to wealthier white residents who wanted to restore them. While a few African American families benefited from this out-migration, by the early 1970s they began to compete with wealthier white homebuyers. Researchers found that class and racial politics, along with the increasing value of Alexandria's older housing stock, had the potential to convert the O&HD into an exclusive, primarily white, neighborhood unless Alexandria instituted policy changes.

Table 5.1. Changes in occupant households in historic downtown Alexandria, 1960–1975.

Year	Number of Black households	Black households (%)	Number of lower-income white households	Lower-income white households (%)	Number of higher-income white households	Higher-income white households (%)	Total number of households
1960	2,100	42	2,000	40	900	18	5,000
1970	2,250	46	1,050	21	1,600	33	4,900
1975	1,800	40	400	9	2,300	51	4,500

Source: Hammer, Siler, George Associates, "NEA Study Report to the City of Alexandria, Virginia," December 31, 1975, box 199200101, Department of Planning and Zoning, Alexandria Archives and Records Center.

The saturation of O&HD's housing market meant that real estate speculators and homebuyers would soon target Uptown unless the city government intervened. Other pressures, such as the energy crisis, subway construction, and the rerouting of Route 1, added to residential concerns. Instead of expanding the O&HD, consultants recommended a "voluntary community cooperative" created by Black homeowners to manage future occupancy so that "historic black households [could] financially compete for available housing."[49] With this type of cooperative, residents would be able to ensure that their families and neighbors had the right to purchase homes before they went on the market. The prioritization of African American residents in home sales would also guarantee the continuation of Uptown as a "historic black neighborhood."[50]

The same forces that led to Uptown's hyper-segregation doomed the proposed cooperative. Early 1970s federal housing policies prioritized integration, and city attorneys worried that a cooperative that supported Black residents would be viewed as a violation of the equal protection clause of the Fourteenth Amendment.[51] In a memo, attorneys argued that Alexandria would "be vulnerable to attack in a lawsuit alleging a violation of civil rights."[52] Most Black residents also did not support a cooperative. In a mail-in ballot initiative, Uptown residents rejected the cooperative 201 to 49. City officials believed that residents did not want to miss out on potential profits that they might make in the highly speculative housing market. The proceeds from selling a home in Uptown could help families buy bigger, newer homes in other parts of Alexandria or nearby jurisdictions.[53]

Although Uptown's present and future remained unresolved, debates about preserving African American neighborhoods did not disappear. While city leaders had failed to receive a Model Neighborhood Grant for

Uptown, in 1968 they successfully applied to the US Department of Housing and Urban Development (HUD) for the DIP Urban Renewal Project. Known historically as the Bottoms, the DIP was one of Alexandria's oldest African American neighborhoods, dating to when the city first became part of the District of Columbia. Unlike other urban renewal projects, the DIP focused on housing, with ARHA working with residents to ensure that they were provided with temporary homes and could return to the neighborhood after the project's completion. By the early 1970s, the project faced numerous hurdles. In 1972, the Nixon administration implemented deep cuts in HUD's urban renewal budget as part of its austerity measures to slow inflation and stabilize the economy. The US Congress had already appropriated most of Alexandria's funding, but any future monies were in jeopardy. Additionally, Nixon used a corruption scandal to shut down the Federal Housing Administration's mortgage program for low- to moderate-income households, which city officials had planned to use to help DIP residents buy new homes. Without federally insured loans, ARHA had to reevaluate the project's apartment-to-townhome ratios. The increase in the number of rental units led to complaints from white O&HD residents who argued that increased density hurt their home values. To appease them, apartments were given "special design features . . . not normally feasible within the cost constraints of federally subsidized housing" that echoed the O&HD's aesthetics.[54] The first group of residents moved into the DIP's new apartments in 1976. As with past urban renewal projects, African American homeowners became renters, often relying on Section 236 vouchers to pay for housing.[55]

In addition to providing new housing, the DIP Urban Renewal Project contained funding for the restoration of a handful of older properties, but Alfred Street Baptist Church, arguably the neighborhood's most significant structure, did not receive preservation monies.[56] Free African Americans had founded the congregation around 1803, when Alexandria was part of the District of Columbia. At first, founding members met in each other's homes before leasing the church site in 1818.[57] By the 1960s, the congregation had outgrown its facilities and wanted to build a new chapel that included a daycare center, offices, and multipurpose rooms. To make this goal a reality, church leaders negotiated with federal officials to demolish the old chapel along with two nearby homes in exchange for a new building. A new city ordinance, however, protected buildings over 100 years old from destruction. The congregation hired an architect who claimed that the old chapel had been built in the 1880s to prove that it was not historic.[58]

In 1980, an interracial group led by Roger C. Anderson, an Alfred Street Baptist Church trustee, organized the Alexandria Society for the Preservation of Black Heritage (ASPBH) to stop the destruction of the old chapel.[59] Another longtime resident, Anderson had attended Parker-Gray High School before working at the newly constructed Pentagon and then joining the US Army. By the 1950s, he was a clerk with the US Post Office.[60] Anderson and a vocal minority of church members worried about the historical implication of destroying the old chapel, which was slated to be replaced with a parking lot. The Afro-American Institute in Washington, DC, had recently published new information about the old chapel, dating it to the 1850s and highlighting its overall historical significance.[61] Alexandria's newly hired city archaeologist, Pamela J. Cressey, provided additional context on the material culture of free African Americans who lived in the neighborhood around the church. Hired in 1977, Cressey had recently moved to Alexandria to run the newly established Urban Archaeological Program, funded in part by the US Department of the Interior. She also argued that urban renewal destroyed Black historical and archaeological resources: "The DIP demonstrates that there is much that can be lost of Afro-American heritage from recent urban development."[62]

This new information divided residents across racial lines, with both sides claiming to have history on their side. During a public hearing, one church member explained why the old chapel's destruction did not mean that the congregation did not support Alexandria's Black past: "The differences of views before you tonight [are] not reflective of whether some believe in preserving black culture, pride and achievement and some do not. I contend that all those who speak in favor of demolition of the Old Alfred Street Baptist Church believe just as strongly in the cultural preservation of Black achievement as anyone else. The differences may very well rest in the philosophy of how that preservation should take place and under what conditions."[63] At the same time, a memo to the city manager argued why it was critical to protect the old chapel: "For contemporary and future generations of black Alexandrians, the Church is an important cultural and historic symbol; should it be preserved, it will contribute to the entire community's understanding and appreciation of black history in Alexandria—a history that records the largest and one of the strongest free Afro-American populations in the state. The Church can represent Alexandria's black heritage more than other extant structures, since it occupied a central place in black society through to the present day."[64]

Nelson Greene Sr., one of two African American city council members, orchestrated a compromise to avoid the alienation of both parties. Owner of a local undertaking business, Greene had moved to Alexandria from Danville,

Virginia, in 1953 and became active in local politics, including the Secret Seven.[65] He suggested that the city council offer the Alfred Street Baptist Church a temporary occupancy permit for its new chapel and authorization to use a nearby vacant lot for off-street parking. Instead of tearing down the old chapel, ASPBH would be given three months to find preservation monies. The city council approved Greene's proposal unanimously.[66] While boarded up for almost a decade, the old chapel was incorporated into the new Alfred Street Baptist Church complex by 1989.[67]

After the tentative future of the old chapel was resolved, residents and city officials revisited the question of Uptown's preservation. In 1983, the Washington Metropolitan Area Transit Authority opened a handful of subway stations in Alexandria, bringing renewed concerns about gentrification.[68] Additional housing pressures caused by new arrivals, combined with cuts in HUD's budget, contributed to local anxieties. In response, Alexandria's city manager reproposed the expansion of the O&HD, which Uptown's new white homeowners supported.[69] The area in question, however, was not the entire neighborhood but only those city blocks owned primarily by white residents. These residents had already created a separate civic association, the Northwest Old Town Citizens Association, to lobby for the expansion of the O&HD. They also argued that inclusion in the O&HD would provide social and cultural cachet to their properties and increase their property values.[70]

African American residents and activists, however, argued instead for a new idea: a separate district, named Parker-Gray, "to promote the general welfare of its residents." The Sixteenth Census Tract Crisis Committee, named after the US Census Bureau's tract designation for Uptown and which included Roger Anderson and Eudora Lyles, explained to city officials that preservation protections were already in place through ordinances passed in the 1970s. The protections supposedly supplied by the O&HD were no longer relevant. What Black residents wanted were policies that created employment opportunities and helped the elderly to remain in their homes. In addition, the Committee argued that the term "Parker-Gray" was particularly meaningful to Black Alexandrians because it helped to "preserve the memorial character of the Parker-Gray High School and the heritage that it represented to the community."[71] A week later, the city council approved the Parker-Gray Special Historic Preservation District, but without a clear articulation of what protections the new district offered.[72]

After the naming of the district, residents and city staff strongly disagreed about the nature of the Parker-Gray Historic District. A vocal cohort of white homeowners still demanded that they belonged in the O&HD, while African

American residents were split between those who wanted Parker-Gray to function as a neighborhood conservation district and those who were open to having some historic protections. Robert L. Crabill, director of the Department of Planning and Community Development, admitted that local laws allowed for the preservation of historic buildings only. To focus on residents, city government had to either amend its current historic preservation ordinance or write a completely new one.[73]

A year later, the Sixteenth Census Tract Crisis Committee filed a complaint with HUD that the new district, along with several other local policy decisions, discriminated against Black homeowners and renters. At first, HUD officials decided that the suit had no merit; however, they reopened the case once HUD received data that demonstrated a significant decline in the number of Black residents in the neighborhood. The suit argued that a variety of structural forces had led to the concentration of Black residents in the neighborhood, which was 90 percent Black in 1980. At the same time, Parker-Gray lacked a sizable number of historic buildings, warranting neither inclusion in the O&HD nor creation of its own historic district.[74] HUD officials concluded that the Parker-Gray Historic District "was specifically intended to displace low- and moderate-income blacks" and attempted to mediate a solution between residents and local government.[75] Unable to find a compromise, HUD closed the case in 1988.[76]

Starting in the 1970s, African American residents began to articulate a new understanding of historic preservation, one that addressed the needs of residents, especially low-income individuals and families, as opposed to focusing on the protection of buildings. White versions of historic preservation, they argued, had facilitated gentrification by conflating historic and economic value and making older neighborhoods unaffordable. Both the NEA-funded study and HUD's mediation attempted to address residents' concerns, but city leaders were unwilling to make the policy changes necessary. Gentrification continued to affect Alexandria's older neighborhoods.

MUSEUMS AND MEMORIALS

By the 1980s and 1990s, debates about Alexandria's need for a more inclusive interpretation of the past culminated with the establishment of a Black history museum and cemetery memorials. Many scholars have demonstrated the importance of both museums and cemeteries in the legitimization of Black history that provided critical counternarratives to a white-dominated landscape. In the late twentieth century, Black community museums faced major limitations, serving only specific neighborhoods with inadequate access to resources and audiences. These same institutions, however, not only instilled self-esteem and pride but also educated Black and non-Black museumgoers about African American history. Memorialization in the form of cemeteries, however, addressed a deeper issue: that white government leaders and residents had systematically erased Black sacred spaces that represented their deep roots in the city. Because of the destruction of Black communities combined with northern Virginia's rapid suburbanization in the early- to mid-twentieth century, burial grounds were often all that was left of slave quarters, farms, and neighborhoods where African Americans had lived and died. Descendants and activists, empowered by changing attitudes about the significance of Black history and preservation efforts, demanded the restoration of these cemeteries and an acknowledgment of their neglect and abuse.[77] And, once again, Washington, DC, played a unique role in Alexandria's attempt to address past wrongs.

In late twentieth century Alexandria, Black and white activists exercised their social and political connections to make the case for the use of public funds to support a new museum and two cemetery memorials. Alexandria's Black History Museum, established in 1981, was a community driven enterprise that operated on a shoestring budget and was run by a cadre of volunteers. Despite local enthusiasm, it took almost a decade for the museum to be fully operational, and it ultimately required city management. In contrast, the African American Heritage Park (1995) and Contrabands and Freedmen Cemetery Memorial (2014) needed substantial local and federal monies from their inception. These memorials functioned both as markers of forgotten African Americans who were buried in the city and as educational tools highlighting past and present actions toward Black cemeteries and, by extension, Black Alexandrians.

The mobilization for an African American history museum began in the 1970s in response to the closure of the Parker-Gray School, which had served the community from 1920 to 1965. In 1976, the Parker-Gray Alumni Association organized a reunion, which included a display on the history of the school. A welcome letter from the alumni association's president explained, "We believe that a history of the Parker-Gray experience is necessary for present and future generations. We want to honor the proud legacy of an institution that was vital to our black community."[78] A year later, Alexandria's Planning Commission received a request from a resident to obtain federal monies to convert one of the city's recreation centers into a "Black Cultural Recreation Center," which the Parker-Gray Alumni Association would operate. The proposal was denied.[79] Over the next three years, other buildings associated with African American history were suggested as possible centers or museums.[80]

In December 1981, the city council agreed to convert what was once the city's Black-only library—established after a 1939 sit-in attempt to desegregate Alexandria's only library (see chapter 2)—into a museum and community center. The library had closed almost a decade earlier, and city leaders had planned to sell the property to developers. Its location near the former Parker-Gray School appealed to alums who partnered with ASPBH to operate the facility. The city charged the two organizations one dollar per year to rent the building.[81]

Like other early community museums, Alexandria's Black History Resource Center operated on a minuscule budget.[82] The Parker-Gray Alumni Association and ASPBH received donations from residents for their exhibits, and volunteers to manage the center. Two ASPBH members conducted archival research at the National Archives in Washington, DC, to write new narratives about local history. Annie B. Rose, a founding member of ASPBH who was nicknamed the "grande dame of black history in Alexandria," did outreach with public schools and offered lectures and walking tours. Like other activists, Rose had deep roots in the city, although she did not move to Alexandria until after World War II. Finally, the Kennedy Center donated display cases. The museum, which opened in 1983, was to be for everyone. Roger Anderson explained, "We want everyone to know our experience."[83]

One city department provided additional support for the center: the Alexandria Urban Archaeological Program. Inspired by the ideals of the Civil Rights Movement and late twentieth-century multiculturalism, white archaeologists led by Cressey used new evidence to describe a much more diverse and complicated pre–Civil War Alexandria.[84] By the late 1970s, artifacts uncovered during excavations captured the day-to-day lives of Alexandria's enslaved and free populations. One of the earliest excavations was the home of Harriet Williams, an enslaved woman who rented and temporarily owned her home (see chapter 1). A well at the back of her property was filled with artifacts, possibly from her forced eviction in 1867.[85] In response to excavations in Hayti, another free Black settlement founded when Alexandria was still part of Washington, DC, the program turned to oral history to fill in gaps in the archival and archaeological record.[86] The city's archaeology program also loaned stoneware made by free and enslaved laborers that it had unearthed at the excavation of a pottery factory to the Black History Center.[87] One of the most sensitive projects, however, involved the excavation of what was called the "Alexandria Slave Pen," a complex of buildings used for the domestic slave trade from the 1820s through the Civil War. The property had functioned as an apartment and office building, but current owners had hired archaeologists to excavate the site so that they could better understand its role in slave trading. Coordinating with city archaeologists and ASPBH, the final report provided one of the first thorough analyses of Alexandria's role in the domestic slave trade.[88]

A year after the Black History Resource Center opened, the Alexandria city government attempted to install its own Black history exhibit. The Washington Metropolitan Council of Governments, an extragovernmental organization that coordinated projects across the District of Columbia, Maryland, and Virginia, recommended to its members that they partner with the Afro-American Institute to create a photographic exhibit. The Afro-American Institute had already written a three-volume study on the region in the hope of protecting key sites from development. They believed that an exhibit would communicate to a broader audience the importance of Black history. Entitled *Black Historic Landmarks in the Metropolitan Washington Region*, the exhibit consisted of fifteen to eighteen panels that would be displayed in several locations in the region simultaneously.[89] Alexandria along with neighboring counties and the District of Columbia agreed to participate, with the understanding that the Afro-American Institute would install the exhibit a year later at city hall.[90] The District, however, reportedly struggled to pay for their portion of the project, and the quality of the panels did not meet the expectations of other participating jurisdictions. The exhibit never came to fruition, and in 1987 the Council of Governments sued the Afro-American Institute for breach of contract.[91]

The failure of *Black Historic Landmarks in the Metropolitan Washington Region* did not end city government's growing support for African American history, however. In response to criticisms tied to the closure of the Parker-Gray School, the city council put aside $300,000 from the sale of the site for the promotion of Black history, and it invited the public to propose how the money should be spent. Sharp divisions among Black residents quickly emerged, revealing conflicting funding priorities and concerns about who would control the monies. Frustrated by community infighting, Roger Anderson established a new organization, the Friends of Alexandria Black History, which focused on fundraising and volunteer recruitment. The Friends also hoped to develop new exhibits and programs, including a partnership with the Smithsonian's Anacostia Neighborhood Museum, an African American community museum in Washington, DC.[92]

During a public hearing, the city council approved the use of the funds for the Alexandria Black History Resource Center. To do that, it combined ideas proposed by representatives of Parker-Gray Alumni Association, ASPBH, and Friends of Alexandria Black History. First, it would use most of the $300,000 (from the sale of the Parker-Gray School site) to expand the Black History Center, almost tripling its size, so that it would have a designated museum space along with offices, storage rooms, and an auditorium. Second, the city would either donate or purchase furniture and equipment, which all groups agreed were desperately needed. Third, the city supported the idea of hiring a curator whose job it would be to develop the Black History Center's collections and programming and to work with community groups. Finally, at the suggestion of Roger Anderson, the city council agreed that Alexandria's Office of Historic Alexandria would manage the Center. By the end of 1987, the Center was officially part of city government with its own staff, budget, and space.[93]

Around the same time that the Black History Museum became part of the city's museum offerings, a massive redevelopment project provided another opportunity for a public-private partnership related to African American history. By the 1970s, with the collapse of the railroad industry, hundreds of acres of land had fallen into disuse. The Norfolk Southern Railway, once one of the largest railroad companies operating in Alexandria, partnered with a Washington-based redevelopment company and tore out its old tracks and buildings in order to construct a mixed-use development. On the edge of Norfolk Southern's property, there existed an abandoned cemetery, which city workers had mowed since the mid-1970s. Because of its proximity to the new mixed-use development site, any soil disturbance would potentially unearth human remains, which meant that city archaeologists needed to monitor the project. In 1985, Cressey reported that there were no definitive findings of human remains on the surface, but her archival research provided critical information about who had founded the cemetery. The Baptist Cemetery Association, an affiliate of the Silver-Leaf Society, had provided burial services for African Americans in the late nineteenth century. A year later, city workers found a headstone in a nearby wooded area, making it increasingly possible that burials existed at that location.[94]

For the next few years, the future of the cemetery remained uncertain. Initially, city leaders and Black activists discussed the possibility of removing any human remains so that Alexandria could build a homeless shelter or sell the land to fund Black historic preservation or a scholarship program.[95] In 1988, Colonel Bernard "Ben" Brenman recommended the establishment of a committee "charged with developing conclusions and recommendations which are of benefit to the City and to the Black Community." A Pennsylvania transplant who served in the US Army for thirty-three years, Brenman had moved to Alexandria in 1970 where he became involved with the Alexandria Archaeological Commission, which he later chaired. Brenman argued that the city should procure the cemetery, which was one of three known nineteenth-century Black cemeteries in Alexandria, so that it could protect it.[96] By summer 1988, a committee was formed, and the city attorney began the process of acquiring the property.

That same summer, a van knocked over Alexandria's Confederate memorial, an incident that began to change the conversation about race and memorialization. The United Daughters of the Confederacy had installed the statue *Appomattox* in 1889 and successfully lobbied the Virginia General Assembly to require legislative action if it was ever to be removed. City council member Nelson Greene had proposed its removal as early as 1979. He explained, "It's asinine for me as a black to pass by it every day when it represents a cause that was trying to keep me in bondage." White outrage, pivoting on the Lost Cause rhetoric, together with the need for legislation, shut down Greene's proposal.[97] The racial politics centering on Confederate memorialization, however, was slowly changing. After the 1988 accident, the city's mayor, Jim Moran, proposed a compromise. The statue, located in the middle of George Washington Parkway, had become a safety hazard, and Virginia's Department of Transportation suggested that it be relocated.[98] The city, however, could not move it—not even for safety reasons—without Richmond's approval. Lacking support from Richmond, Moran suggested instead that Alexandria establish a new memorial to recognize the contributions of its Black leaders.[99]

Members of the Ad Hoc Committee on a Memorial to Honor Black Leaders, many of whom already served on the committee developing plans for the Baptist cemetery, merged the two projects together. In a February 1989 report, the Black Baptist Cemetery Work Group recommended that the city preserve the cemetery and create a memorial park using acreage donated by Norfolk Southern: "Since the key feature is the historic Black Cemetery, it should be a park tied to Alexandria's Black Community. The area should be a historic park commemorating black heritage. The area should be called *Alexandria's Black Heritage Park*."[100]

After several construction delays, the Alexandria African American Heritage Park opened to the public in 1995. The cemetery remained intact, with interpretive elements that explained its significance and honored Black leaders. Jerome Meadows, a well-known African American sculptor who taught at

Howard University, installed several artworks to bridge the memorialization elements with the natural environment.[101]

While the Alexandria African American Heritage Park addressed residents' demands for recognition and preserved a forgotten burial ground, the rediscovery of another cemetery experienced a much more complicated response. By the 1980s, the Federal Highway Administration began to evaluate the structural integrity of the Woodrow Wilson Bridge, a bridge constructed in 1961 that connected Virginia to Maryland and the District of Columbia as part of the metropolitan area's beltway. Preservationist and archaeological groups worried about the impact of a new bridge on Jones Point, an adjacent park that possibly held evidence of pre–Civil War ropemaking and shipbuilding. It also was the site where Benjamin Banneker had laid the first boundary stone for the newly established District of Columbia in 1791. Historians, however, soon learned that there was another significant, although forgotten, site near Jones Point: a federally run cemetery for self-emancipated men, women, and children that operated from 1864 through 1869. At least 1,879 African Americans were buried there.[102]

A 1997 *Washington Post* exposé revealed that the Federal Highway Administration had done little research on the cemetery, which the new bridge's construction would impact. Adding to public anger was the fact that a gas station, office building, parking lot, and highway had been constructed on top of the cemetery. The site had been literally erased from city records, including maps, and rezoned for commercial use in the late 1940s.[103] Lillie Finklea and Louise Massoud established Friends of Freedmen's Cemetery, an interracial advocacy group focused on the preservation of the cemetery and the commemoration of those buried there. Finklea and Massoud's friendship and activism reflected changes in late twentieth century Alexandria. Both women had been born in Washington, DC, in the late 1930s and moved to northern Virginia as children with their families. They attended segregated schools. Finklea graduated from Parker-Gray High School. She took the civil service exam and found federal employment as a typist and later a computer programmer. Massoud graduated from a white-only high school in Arlington County, Virginia, and later from George Washington University. In the 1970s, she worked at the US International Communication Agency, today known as the US Information Agency.[104] The Friends of Freedmen's Cemetery's first event was a wreath-laying ceremony on Memorial Day in 1997. City council members, parishioners from local Black churches, members of ASPBH, and staff and supporters of the Black History Center attended.[105] After the event, Finklea and Massoud drafted a proclamation for the city council, which not only included the creation of a "Week of Remembrance for the Freedmen's Cemetery" but also a statement affirming that Alexandria's government recognized the historical significance of cemeteries and its responsibility to these places. They wrote, "Alexandria recognizes that cemeteries are an important part of American history and a priceless cultural legacy for future generations, and the City wishes to protect and preserve this burial ground and to reclaim the site as historical property above ground before it is lost permanently to further development of the land."[106] A year later, the Virginia General Assembly passed a similar resolution for Freedmen's Cemetery. In recognition of the cemetery's extraordinary historical significance, it resolved that commemoration should be observed by the entire state.[107]

For the next two years, the Friends, in collaboration with city officials, raised awareness about the cemetery and the people who were buried there. In 1999, archaeologists identified grave shafts on city property and began the process of delineating the cemetery's boundaries.[108] At the same time, the Friends successfully applied for a Virginia Humanities Grant to develop a brochure and website where they shared their research.[109] The Black History Center worked with the Friends to open an exhibit, *Roots to Remembrance*, about the history of the cemetery and plans for memorialization. It also helped the Friends do genealogical research, which they hoped would lead to finding descendants. A year later, Virginia's Department of Transportation and Historic Resources installed a highway marker at the Friends' request.[110] Finklea explained to a reporter why all this work was important: "'People in this city have paved over almost everything that is important to the black community. We have to hold on to what is left.'"[111]

In the meantime, city government became increasingly frustrated with the Federal Highway Administration's response to their concerns about the destruction of archaeological resources and the pollution of the Potomac River's watershed. It, along with several community organizations, sued the Federal Highway Administration in 1998.[112] The US District Court initially sided with Alexandria; however, in an appeal, the Federal Highway Administration successfully rolled back much of the previous decision, arguing that it had met federal metrics for evaluating the project's impact.[113] Outside of court, the Federal Highway Administration renegotiated its plans for the bridge, recognizing its effect on historical and environmental resources. As part of the 2002 updated Woodrow Wilson Bridge Settlement Agreement, the federal government agreed that it would support the memorialization of Freedmen's Cemetery, including land acquisitions, archaeological excavations, and a memorial park.[114]

Figure 5.3. The Contrabands and Freedmen Cemetery Memorial.
Photograph by author, 2024.

The opening of the Contrabands and Freedmen Cemetery Memorial (see fig. 5.3) in 2014 was the culmination of almost two decades of local and federal negotiations about Alexandria's Black past. Ironically, the federal government had originally established the cemetery during the Civil War, and 136 years later it now contributed to its memorialization, thanks to the lobbying efforts of the Friends of Freedmen's Cemetery and the Alexandria city government.[115] As in the past, Black Alexandrians had to navigate local and federal politics to preserve their history. In this instance, city government had become an ally in the process of addressing past and present wrongs.

CONCLUSION

By the time that *Remember the Titans* appeared in movie theaters in 2000, Alexandria provided several places where residents and visitors could learn about the city's Black past. The process of restoring Alexandria's Black history required reeducation and collaboration among Black and white residents along with local, regional, and federal partnerships. Black activists—Carlton Funn, Eudora Lyles, Roger Anderson, Annie B. Rose, Nelson Greene, and Lillie Finklea (to name a few)—provided their historical knowledge to rewrite Alexandria's history and make it a more inclusive one. They also deployed their social and political assets on the local and federal levels to make policy changes that led to the establishing of cemetery memorials and a museum. Washington-based organizations such as ASALH and the Afro-American Institute provided additional support. None of these changes, however, would have occurred without new forms of collaboration with white residents, politicians, and city staff, whose social and political beliefs had been incubated during and after the Civil Rights Movement. Many of these men and women, such as Pamela Cressey, Jim Moran, and Colonel Ben Brenman, had moved to Washington for employment and decided to make it their home. They too became conduits for a more inclusive Alexandria.

By the end of the twentieth century, a very different interpretation of Alexandria's past had emerged, laying the foundation for future historical, preservationist, and archaeological work. That work, however, has continued to be reactive and piecemeal, and the impact of gentrification remains unresolved. African Americans and other low- to moderate-income families still struggle to find affordable places to live not only in Alexandria but also in the entire Washington metropolitan area.

Epilogue

In summer 2022, I exchanged emails with Ira Robinson (1938–2024), the first African American elected to Alexandria's City Council since Reconstruction. Robinson, then a retired lawyer who lived in Southern California, had moved to Alexandria in 1967 after obtaining a job in the legal department at Atlantic Research Corporation (ARC). Located just outside Alexandria, ARC has since evolved into a government contractor, exploring new technologies in space communication, nuclear medicine, weapon systems, and electronics.[1] Robinson, who had passed the bar before graduating from law school, had a handful of job options in Richmond, Virginia, his hometown. He could work for his uncle, who was also a lawyer, or for the famous civil rights firm, Hill, Tucker, and Marsh, for which he had clerked. Northern Virginia, however, provided new opportunities and decent salaries. Unlike other industries, government contractors had begun to desegregate during World War II and provided careers for African American professionals. Robinson's brother, an engineer, had found employment at ARC in 1956.[2]

When asked about what life was like in Alexandria in the late 1960s and early 1970s, Robinson compared the past to the present. "Alexandria was definitely not as integrated a city as it is now—from a housing, schools, and public and private jobs standpoint. Communities were much more segregated, the schools were more segregated, and people of color in city jobs were few and far between." Some problems have persisted because housing—which largely remains predetermined by twentieth-century segregation—continues to inform where children go to school. "I'm not sure many of the schools, especially at the elementary level, are not still that way today—primarily because of housing patterns aided by the continuing absence of opportunities for people of color to achieve anything like middle class wealth."[3] The legacies of local and federal policies that discriminated against African Americans in the past still affect where families live and go to school. And today's extraordinarily high home prices have made Alexandria unaffordable for African American families. Many have chosen to live elsewhere.[4]

The contradictory role that the federal government has played in the lives of Black Alexandrians was also not lost on Robinson. "I believe race relations and progress in Alexandria were clearly helped by the fact that numbers of Alexandria residents of color held government jobs in DC that would almost certainly not have been available to them in Virginia." However, it would take more than federal employment to change the racial status quo. Robinson continued, "A number of such local residents of color like Ferdinand Day [Alexandria's first African American school board member] brought to the Alexandria community the job security, training, intellect and leadership ... needed to focus and maintain the government and community's focus on issues that would otherwise have gone unaddressed."[5] Real change required community and leadership. In his humbleness, Robinson had neglected to note that Alexandria was lucky to have him as a leader and the impact that he made too.

Proximity to Power is about expanding our understanding of the ways in which everyday people negotiated and leveraged local and federal power structures to make the world a better place for themselves, their families and friends, and their communities. In many ways, Alexandria provides an important case study of how Black residents used their location to change the racialized power dynamics operating within American society. For the majority of Americans, the federal government is a massive bureaucracy that remains disconnected from their everyday lives. That is not the case in Alexandria or the rest of the Washington metropolitan area, where federal workers, contractors, and military personnel are our friends, neighbors, and families.

By the late twentieth century, as the Washington metropolitan area became more interconnected, the lines between jurisdictions have become more blurred. Yet, each one has a unique history of its own. Alexandria is one of the oldest, dating its founding to 1749. It also has the distinction of being part of the District of Columbia before its retrocession in 1846. That relationship with the nation's capital, while legally severed, never disappeared. Even today, Alexandrians often associate themselves more with the Washington metropolitan area than with the rest of Virginia.

While this book is an intellectual pursuit, it is also a self-reflective act, giving myself and other scholars the opportunity to think about why we do what we do and whose shoulders we stand on. For over a decade, I have worked with residents and city staff in an attempt to make Alexandria's history more accessible and inclusive. Together, we have attended contentious meetings where emotions ranged from angry yelling to applause, from tears of joy to profound sadness. Together, we have sat in archives and libraries, surrounded by books and boxes, wondering what new nugget of past lives awaited us. And together, we have written new interpretations of the past via the generation of reports, signage, presentations, panels, and even walking trails.

But this book is also a beginning. Alexandria's rich, messy, diverse, and complicated history cannot be fully explored in one lifetime. Or in one book. Among many of my fellow academics, local history has remained on the sidelines of sweeping analyses of large-scale forces that make the world of the past and present. Yet it is through the local that we can see how those broader phenomena impact people and what responses they engender. Places like Alexandria matter and deserve academia's attention.

APPENDIX

Proposal for
Afro-American Studies Course
in Alexandria, Virginia [1969]

Title of Course:	Afro-American Studies
Departmental Area of Offering:	Social Studies
Student Grade Level:	11th and 12th Grade
Credit for the Course:	½ Unit for either 18 weeks, 1 Unit for the entire year.

Aims of the Course:
1. To help eliminate misconceptions that may cause prejudice.
2. To develop an understanding of the culture of citizens with an Afro-American background.
3. To develop an understanding of the background of certain social problems in America.
4. To develop an understanding of social changes in American life.
5. To recognize accomplishments and contributions made to American life by Afro-Americans.

Course Outline:

I. African Beginnings up to 1800
    A. Motives for African Historical Study
    B. African Culture
    C. Theories of African Progress
    D. The Slave Trade
    E. Contributions from Africa

II. Afro-American History 1800 to 1896
    A. Slavery in America Contrasted with Slavery Elsewhere.
        1. Slavery in Latin America
        2. Slavery in Europe
        3. Slavery in other places and times
    B. African Culture Lost
    C. Abolition Movement
    D. Free Negroes
    E. Theories on the reasons for Negroes being selected as slaves.

III. Afro-American Awakenings (1896–1954)
    A. Northward migration and urban conflicts.
    B. W. E. B. Du Bois and the Niagara Movement
    C. N.A.A.C.P., Urban League, and early battles for rights
    D. World War, Garveyism, and Negro Cultural Renaissance
    E. The New Deal and Afro-Americans
    F. Era of Change—Progress and [a]chievements during World War II and after

IV. Afro-American Activism (1954 to Present)
    A. Segregation—Southern and Northern Style
    B. Protest in U.S.A.
        1. Civil Rights Movement (legal battles, Negro revolution, Civil Rights Acts, violence and racial tensions)
        2. Negro militancy (unrest in the cities, black power and extremism)
    C. The Negro Today and His Culture (politics, continuing problems and other fields)
    D. The Negro Tomorrow

Statement of method for the course:

In presenting the course, Afro-American Studies, to pupils, every attempt will be made to use as broad a multi-media approach as possible.

Course resources:

At present the attached bibliographies of materials have been designated in the respective schools.

NOTES

ABBREVIATIONS

AARC	Alexandria Archives and Records Center, Alexandria, VA
ED	Enumeration District
KWBBL	Special Collections, Kate Waller Barrett Branch Library, Alexandria, VA
Murray Papers	Freeman H. M. Murray Papers, Howard University, Washington, DC
NARA-DC	National Archives and Records Administration, Washington, DC
NARA-MD	National Archives and Records Administration, College Park, MD
RG 105	RG 105: Records of the Bureau of Refugees, Freedmen, and Abandoned Lands, Virginia, 1865–72

INTRODUCTION

1. Lynnwood Campbell, interview by Molly Kerr, March 10, 2011, transcript, Alexandria Legacies-Living Legends, www.alexandriava.gov/uploadedFiles/historic/info/history /OralHistoryCampbellLynnwood.pdf; "Campbell, Lynnwood. Induction Year: 2011," Living Legends of Alexandria, accessed December 3, 2024, https://alexandrialegends.org/lynnwood -campbell.

2. Campbell, interview; "Campbell, Lynnwood. Induction Year: 2011."

3. *1900 US Census* (Population Schedule), Fairfax County, Virginia, ED 5, sheet 14A, Frank Gaskins head of household, line 42, digital image; and *1910 US Census* (Population Schedule), Alexandria City, Virginia, ED 22, sheet 22A, Frank Gaskins head of household, line 7, digital image, accessed June 9, 2024, https://ancestry.com.

4. "Elizabeth Campbell," *Virginia Death Records, 1912–2014*; "John Henry Campbell and Sydna Holmes," *Virginia, Select Marriages, 1785–1940*; and *1880 US Census* (Population Schedule), Fauquier County, Virginia, ED 40, sheet 21, John H. Campbell in the household of Lucinda Bradford, line 7, digital image, accessed January 2, 2020, https://ancestry.com.

5. Green, *Secret City*; Brown, *Free Negros in the District*; Harrold, *Subversives*.

6. Green, *Secret City*, 7–43; Brown, *Free Negros in the District*, 61–63.

7. Blomberg, *Formation of Free Black Communities*, 4–8; Walker et al., *Archaeological Evaluation*; Bernstein, *Life and Times of George Lewis Seaton*, 21.

8. Green, *Secret City*, 20–27, 58–60.

9. Rothman, *Ledger and the Chain*.

10. Crothers, "1846 Retrocession," 142–44.

11. Green, *Secret City*, 44.

12. Blomberg, *Formation of Free Black Communities*, 50; Vaughn, "Freedom Is Not Enough," 30.

13. Gillette, *Between Justice and Beauty*; Masur, *Example for All the Land*; Asch and Musgrove, *Chocolate City*.

14. Lechner, "Massive Resistance"; Lassiter and Lewis, *Moderates' Dilemma*; Lewis, *Massive Resistance*; Bonastia, *Southern Stalemate*.

15. Gatewood, *Aristocrats of Color*; Moore, *Leading the Race*; Ruble, *Washington's U Street*; Lindsey, *Colored No More*.

16. E. S. Yellin, *Racism in the Nation's Service*.

17. Dailey, *Before Jim Crow*.

18. J. D. Smith, *Managing White Supremacy*.

19. Here are some exceptions: J. D. Smith, "'When Reason Collides,'" 22–50; Perry, Reybold, and Waters, "'Everybody Was Looking,'" 719–41; Moon, "African American Housing Crisis," 28–68; Moon, "Alexandria YWCA," 59–92.

20. Moore, *Leading the Race*.

21. "Changes in Districts: New Scheme for Grouping Counties of Virginia," *Washington Post*, February 25, 1902; "For Crumpacker Resolution: Mass Meeting of Colored Men Urges Its Passage by Congress," *Washington Post*, May 13, 1902; "Protest against 'Jim Crow' Cars," *Suburban Citizen* (Washington, DC), May 17, 1902.

22. Perry, Reybold, and Waters, "'Everybody Was Looking,'" 719–41; Green, *Secret City*; Krislov, *Negro in Federal Employment*.

23. A. Melvin Miller, "Desegregating Alexandria, Virginia, One Step at a Time," interview by Lisa Youngentob, February 12, 2007, transcript, Alexandria Archaeology, VA, https://collections.digitalmaryland.org/digital/collection/saac/id/4250/rec/1; US Commission on Civil Rights, "Testimony of Marion I. Johnson, Vice President, Alexandria Council on Human Relations," in *Hearings before the United States Commission on Civil Rights*, 106–8; "Statement of A. Melvin Miller, President Durant Civic Association," June 5, 1962, City Council Dockets/ Minutes, box 44, AARC.

24. Friedman, *Covert Capital*.

25. Repak, *Waiting on Washington*; Price and Whitworth, "Soccer and Latino Cultural Space," 167–87.

26. Chacko, "Identity and Assimilation," 491–506.

27. Marling, *George Washington Slept Here*; Lindgren, *Preserving the Old Dominion*; Bruggeman, *Here, George Washington Was Born*.

28. Blight, *Race and Reunion*; Fahs and Waugh, *Memory of the Civil War*; Cook, *Troubled Commemoration*.

29. See examples at Alexandria's public library and city archives. Barnwell and Mullen, *City of Alexandria*.

30. Savage, *Standing Soldiers*; Dagbovie, *Early Black History Movement*; Burns, *From Storefront to Monument*; Wilson, *Negro Building*; Rogers, "Black Campus Movement," 21–40.

31. Elsa L. Walsh, "Razing an Old Church," *Washington Post*, November 27, 1980, VA1–2.

CHAPTER ONE

1. William Syphax was born around 1825 at Arlington House, then owned by George Washington Parke Custis. His mother, Maria, was Custis's daughter and a domestic servant to Martha Washington. Around 1826, Maria, along with her two children Elinor (b. 1823) and William, were manumitted and granted a tract of land adjacent to the plantation. William attended school either in Washington, DC, or in Alexandria. It is unclear when he moved to the District of Columbia; however, by 1851, he had received a federal appointment to the Department of the Interior as a copyist. Later, he worked as a messenger in the Department of Interior, eventually heading the office. Preston, "William Syphax," 448–76.

2. *Alexandria Gazette*, July 18, 1865.

3. Litwack, *Been in the Storm*; Foner, *Forever Free*; Butchart, *Schooling the Freed People*; Williams, *Help Me Find My People*; Downs, *Sick from Freedom*; Ayers, *Thin Light of Freedom*; Manning, *Troubled Refuge*; Hunter, *Bound in Wedlock*.

4. Cooling and Owen, *Mr. Lincoln's Forts*.

5. Vaughn, "Freedom Is Not Enough," 59; Qua. Gen. M. C. Meigs to Sec. of War Edwin M. Stanton, May 8, 1865, Registers and Letters Received by the Commissioner of the Bureau of Refugees, Freedmen, and Abandoned Lands, 1865–72, M752, roll 16, RG 105, NARA-DC.

6. "Alexandria," *National Republican* (Washington, DC), May 28, 1861; "Chronicles of the War," *National Anti-Slavery Standard* (New York and Philadelphia), June 1, 1861; "Miscellaneous Department," *National Anti-Slavery Standard* (New York and Philadelphia), July 27, 1861; "Bull Run and Manassas," *The Liberator* (Boston, MA), April 11, 1862.

7. Dols, "Conduct of Union Soldiers," 85–87.

8. Henry Whittington Diary, July 17, 1862, KWBBL.

9. "Brutal Conduct of our Soldiers," *National Republican* (Washington, DC), September 19, 1862; "Outrages on the Colored People," *National Republican* (Washington, DC), July 3, 1862.

10. "Robert H. Dogan," Deposition of John A. Seaton, January 23, 1867, *U.S. Southern Claims Commission Allowed Claims, 1871–1880*, accessed July 5, 2023, https://ancestry.com.

11. Green, *Secret City*, 17–24; Brown, *Free Negros in the District*, 59–60; Hurst, *Alexandria on the Potomac*, 40.

12. J. Jones, *Labor of Love*, 43–76; Schwalm, *A Hard Fight for We*, 103–4; Farmer-Kaiser, *Freedwomen and the Freedman's Bureau*, 35–40.

13. Butchart, "Freedmen's Teacher Project"; Butchart, *Schooling the Freed People*, 20–21; US Office of Education, *History of Schools*, 285–87; Julia A. Wilbur Diary, June 18, 1863. For more information on Wilbur, see Tarnapol Whitacre, *Civil Life*.

14. "Contrabands," *Alexandria Gazette*, September 18, 1862.

15. "Albert Webb," Deposition of Albert Webb, March 3, 1873, *U.S. Southern Commission Allowed Claims, 1871–1880*, accessed July 8, 2018, https://ancestry.com.

16. "Robert H. Dogan," Deposition of Charles W. Brown, January 27, 1873, *U.S. Southern Claims Commission Allowed Claims, 1871–1880*, accessed July 8, 2018, https://ancestry.com.

17. This text will use the term "refugee" instead of "contraband" to emphasize the dislocation caused by war and enslavement and to avoid the perpetuation of reinforcing notions of enslaved men and women as property. Wartman, "Contraband, Runaways, Freemen," 122–29.

18. "Gen. Butler Contraband of War. Part VI," *The Liberator* (Boston, MA), September 6, 1861.

19. Harriet Jacobs to William Lloyd Garrison, August 1862, in J. F. Yellin, *Harriet Jacobs Family Papers*, 2:399–407.

20. Samuel G. Howe to Charles Sumner, January 21, 1862, Howe Family Papers, Houghton Library, Harvard University, Cambridge, MA (emphasis in original).

21. J. R. Bigelow to A. F. I. Commission, May 8, 1863, James Morrison MacKaye Papers, Manuscript Division, Library of Congress; "African-American Civilians and Soldiers Treated," 10.

22. Harriet Jacobs to William Lloyd Garrison, August 1862, in J. F. Yellin, *Harriet Jacobs Family Papers*, 2:399–407.

23. Julia A. Wilbur Diary, November 6, 1862. See also R. Hayden et al., *Freedom*, ser. 1, vol. 2, 250–51.

24. Julia A. Wilbur Diary, November 8, 1862.

25. Harriet Jacobs to William Lloyd Garrison, August 1862, in J. F. Yellin, *Harriet Jacobs Family Papers*, 2:399–407.

26. Lewis McKenzie to Honorable E. M. Stanton, September 19, 1862, in R. Hayden et al., *Freedom*, ser. 1, vol. 2, 268.

27. *1860 US Census*, Alexandria, Virginia, page 114, Lewis McKenzie head of household, line 23, digital image; and 1860 US Slave Schedules, Alexandria, Virginia, page 5, Lewis McKenzie, lines 19–21, digital image, accessed September 18, 2023, https://ancestry.com; Henry Whittington Diary, November 22, 1861, KWBBL.

28. Cap. John C. Wyman to Brig. Gen. John P. Slough, October 21, 1862, box 22, entry 225, Consolidated Correspondence File, 1794–1915, Alexandria, Virginia, RG 92: Records of the Office of the Quartermaster General, NARA-DC; Cap. John C. Wyman to Brig. Gen. John P. Slough, November 24, 1862, in R. Hayden et al., *Freedom*, ser. 1, vol. 2, 277; "Recruiting for the Thirty-Third Regiment," *Worcester (MA) Daily Spy*, June 2, 1862; *Worcester (MA) Daily Spy*, October 15, 1862.

29. C. B. Ferguson to Col. D. H. Rucker, December 10, 1862; and Col. D. H. Rucker to Brig. Gen. M. C. Meigs, December 11, 1862, box 22, entry 225, Consolidated Correspondence File, 1794–1915, Alexandria, Virginia, RG 92: Records of the Office of the Quartermaster General, NARA-DC; "The District of Columbia," in R. Hayden et al., *Freedom*, ser. 1, vol. 2, 268–78.

30. "Transcription of the Proclamation."

31. Julia A. Wilbur Diary, December 31, 1862.

32. *Alexandria Gazette*, January 3, 1863.

33. Butchart, *Schooling the Freed People*, 38; Butchart, "Freedmen's Teacher Project."

34. US Office of Education, *History of Schools*, 289–91; Julia A. Wilbur Diary, December 29, 1863, January 9, 1864; Letter from Harriet Jacobs, quoted in "Report of Friends' Association

for the Aid and Elevation of Freedmen," May 23, 1864, in J. F. Yellin, *Harriet Jacobs Family Papers*, 2:574.

35. Arlington County (Va.) Chancery Causes, 1786–1927, George W. Parker v. Mary Jane Parker, index no. 1867-006, Virginia Chancery Database, Library of Virginia, accessed June 6, 2024, www.lva.virginia.gov/chancery/case_detail.asp?CFN=013-1867-006; US Office of Education, *History of Schools*, 286.

36. US Office of Education, *History of Schools*, 289–91.

37. US Office of Education, *History of Schools*, 287, 290–91.

38. J. G. C. Lee to Gen. D. H. Rucker, February 11, 1864, box 22, entry 225, Consolidated Correspondence File, 1794–1915, Alexandria, Virginia, RG 92: Records of the Office of the Quartermaster General, NARA-DC.

39. Colored Laborers Commissary Department to Col. Bell, August 3, 1863; Free Colored Laborers in the Subsistence Department [Commissary Department] to Col. Bell, August 16, 1863; and Colored Labours [Laborers] of Alexandria, VA Commissary Department to Sec. of War, August 31, 1863, box 22, entry 225, Consolidated Correspondence File, 1794–1915, Alexandria, Virginia, RG 92: Records of the Office of the Quartermaster General, NARA-DC.

40. Report of Persons and Articles Employed and Hired at Alexandria, VA, during the Months of January, February, March, April 1863 by Officers of Various Staff Department, Quartermaster US Army, ca. December 1865, Records of the Field Offices for the State of Virginia, M1913, roll 53, RG 105, NARA-DC; "African-American Civilians and Soldiers Treated," 1–9; Julia A. Wilbur Diary, July 13, 1864.

41. Julia A. Wilbur Diary, July 14, 1864.

42. Julia A. Wilbur Diary, April 17, 1863.

43. J. G. C. Lee to Brig. Gen. K. P. Slough, July 10, 1864, Letters Received March–October 1865, M-R, Registers and Letters Received by the Commissioner of the Bureau of Refugees, Freedmen, and Abandoned Lands, 1865–72, M752, roll 6, RG 105, NARA-DC.

44. Henry Whittington Diary, May 21, 1863, KWBBL.

45. Henry Whittington Diary, June 15, 1863, KWBBL.

46. Edwin Bentley to R. O. Abbott, November 14, 1864, box 22, entry 225, Consolidated Correspondence File, 1794–1915, Alexandria, Virginia, RG 92: Records of the Office of the Quartermaster General, NARA-DC.

47. Lawrence, "Organization of the Hospitals"; Miller, "Volunteers for Freedom," 1–14.

48. Julia A. Wilbur Diary, December 27–28, 1864; Miller, "Volunteers for Freedom," 9–11.

49. Julia A. Wilbur to Anna M. C. Barnes, November 20, 1863; and Julia A. Wilbur to Anna M. C. Barnes, February 17, 1863, in J. F. Yellin, *Harriet Jacobs Family Papers*, 2:252, 450; Samuel Shaw to Dr. J. R. Bigelow, June 14, 1863, box 35, entry PI-17 360-A, Colored Troops Division—Letters Received 1863–88, RG 94: Adjutant General's Office, 1780s–1917, NARA-DC.

50. Edward Smith to Edwin M. Stanton, April 3, 1864, box 35, entry PI-17 360-A, Colored Troops Division—Letters Received 1863–88, RG 94: Adjutant General's Office, 1780s–1917, NARA-DC.

51. O'Brien, "Reconstruction in Richmond," 259–81.

52. Julia A. Wilbur to Anna M. C. Barnes, February 17, 1863, in J. F. Yellin, *Harriet Jacobs Family Papers*, 2:451.

53. Julia A. Wilbur Diary, March 12, 1863.

54. Capt. William McLean Gwynne to Brig. Gen. John Potts Slough, October 1, 1863; and Julia A. Wilbur to Anna M. C. Barnes, October 2, 1863, in J. F. Yellin, *Harriet Jacobs Family Papers*, 2:503–4, 510–18.

55. Samuel May Jr. to the Editor of the *National Anti-Slavery Standard* (New York and Philadelphia), October 30, 1864, in J. F. Yellin, *Harriet Jacobs Family Papers*, 2:586–87 (emphasis in original); US Office of Education, *History of Schools*, 291.

56. *Report to the Executive Committee of New England Yearly Meeting of Friends*, November 10, 1864, in J. F. Yellin, *Harriet Jacobs Family Papers*, 2:589–91.

57. US Office of Education, *History of Schools*, 291; *Report to the Executive Committee of New England Yearly Meeting of Friends*, 589–91.

58. Blomberg, *Formation of Free Black Communities*, 322; McCord, *Across the Fence*, 26.

59. Kenzer, *Kinship and Neighborhood*; Kenzer, *Enterprising Southerners*; Penningroth, *Claims of Kinfolk*.

60. Jackson, *Free Negro Labor*, 138, 157.

61. Friends of the Freedmen's Cemetery, "Alexandria Real and Personal Property Taxes."

62. Deed V3-336 (1864), and Deed V3-552 (1864), Land Deed Office, Alexandria Courthouse; *1860 US Census*, Alexandria, Virginia, page 197, George Seaton head of household, line 25, accessed February 17, 2022, https://ancestry.com.

63. Deed W3-35 (1864), Land Deed Office, Alexandria Courthouse; Friends of the Freedmen's Cemetery, "Alexandria Real and Personal Property Taxes."

64. Deed W3-23 (1864), Land Deed Office, Alexandria Courthouse; Voting Viva Voce Database.

65. Deed W3-178 (1864), Land Deed Office, Alexandria Courthouse; "Sales under U.S. Direct Tax Law," *Alexandria Gazette*, April 14, 1864; Alexandria Archaeology, "Harriet Williams Independent Enslaved Woman"; Terrie, "Social History."

66. George W. Parker, Lewis Williams, Samson White, Charles Watson, Rev. Thomas Henry Marshall, and Richard H. Lyles to John P. Slough, April 28, 1865, box 1, E. 20153 Letters Received and E. 2055 Telegrams Received, 1862–65, Records of US Army Continental Commands, RG 393: Offices of Military Governors, Alexandria, 1862–65, NARA-DC.

67. *Address of Loyal Virginians to Their Friends in the North*, ca. 1865, Library of Congress, https://lccn.loc.gov/17003655.

68. Convention of the Colored People of Virginia, *Liberty, and Equality before the Law*. See also Reidy, "'Coming from the Shadow of the Past,'" 422.

69. James J. Ferree to John P. Slough, June 23, 1865, Henry E. Alvord, Report of Adjudication of Case before Civil Justice Beach at Alexandria, VA, July 19, 1865, Records of the Field Offices for the State of Virginia, M1913, roll 47, RG 105, NARA-DC.

70. Henry E. Alvord to O. O. Howard, July 20, 1865, Records of the Field Offices for the State of Virginia, M1913, roll 53, RG 105, NARA-DC.

71. O. Brown and T. S. Evans to Alvord, July 26, 1865, Records of the Field Offices for the State of Virginia, M1913, roll 53, RG 105, NARA-DC.

72. "The 'Riot' at Alexandria," *Alexandria Gazette*, December 29, 1865; Justice [pseud.], "The Christmas Fuss," *Alexandria Gazette*, December 30, 1865; "Military Commission," *Alexandria Gazette*, January 11, 1866; "The Military Commission," *Alexandria Gazette*, February 2, 1866; "Military Commission," *Alexandria Gazette*, February 19, 1866; *Alexandria Gazette*, March 2, 1866; "Echo of 50 Years Ago," *Alexandria Gazette*, April 11, 1916. W. E. B. Du Bois

states that fourteen men died in the violence on Christmas Day in Alexandria, but I have not been able to confirm that number. Du Bois, *Black Reconstruction*, 538.

73. Newton Whitton to William W. Rogers, n.d., Records of the Field Offices for the State of Virginia, M1913, roll 48, RG 105, NARA-DC.

74. [Advertisement], *National Republican* (Washington, DC), May 10, 1867.

75. W. W. Rogers to Maj. Lee, April 21, 1866, Records of the Field Offices for the State of Virginia, M1913, roll 53, RG 105, NARA-DC. S. P. Lee to W. W. Rogers, October 10, 1866; Lewis Heard, "List of Persons to be Transferred to Freedmen's Village from L'Ouverture Hospital," n.d.; and "List of Persons Transferred to Freedmen's Village," December 19, 1866, Records of the Field Offices for the State of Virginia, M1913, roll 43, RG 105, NARA-DC. S. P. Lee to O. Brown, October 16, 1867, Records of the Field Offices for the State of Virginia, M1913, roll 54, RG 105, NARA-DC. See also Downs, *Sick from Freedom*, 138.

76. Hugh Latham to S. P. Lee, September 27, 1866, Records of the Field Offices for the State of Virginia, M1913, roll 43, RG 105, NARA-DC.

77. 1860 US Slave Schedules, Alexandria, Virginia, page 4, lines 31–32, digital image, accessed September 18, 2023, https://ancestry.com; *Alexandria Gazette*, April 3, 1863; "Confiscation," *Alexandria Gazette*, July 25, 1863; "Coming Home," *Virginia State Journal*, May 15, 1865.

78. O. O. Howard to C. H. Howard, October 2, 1866, Records of the Field Offices for the State of Virginia, M1913, roll 43, RG 105, NARA-DC.

79. Hugh Latham to S. P. Lee, September 8, 1866; Hugh Latham to S. P. Lee, October 23, 1867, Records of the Field Offices for the State of Virginia, M1913, roll 43, RG 105, NARA-DC. Hugh Latham to S. P. Lee, December 5, 1867, Records of the Field Offices for the State of Virginia, M1913, roll 44, RG 105, NARA-DC. S. P. Lee to Hugh Latham, October 25, 1867; Hugh Latham to S. P. Lee, November 12, 1867; and Hugh Latham to S. P. Lee, December 16, 1867, Records of the Field Offices for the State of Virginia, M1913, roll 46, RG 105, NARA-DC.

80. VF Mayors–Berkley, William N–Appointment, April 11, 1868, box 240, Special Collections, KWBBL; "The Republicans of Alexandria in the Field," *Alexandria Gazette*, March 4, 1867.

81. *Alexandria Gazette*, February 21, 1866; *Alexandria Gazette*, February 3, 1866; William F. Spurgin to J. A. Bushong, October 18, 1865, Records of the Field Offices for the State of Virginia, M1913, roll 53, RG 105, NARA-DC.

82. S. P. Lee to Brig. Gen. [Oliver O. Howard?], February 8, 1866, Records of the Field Offices for the State of Virginia, M1913, roll 40, RG 105, NARA-DC; S. P. Lee to W. W. Rogers, October 10, 1866, Records of the Field Offices for the State of Virginia, M1913, roll 43, RG 105, NARA-DC.

83. L. M. E. Hicks to S. P. Lee, October 30, 1866, Records of the Field Offices for the State of Virginia, M1913, roll 43, RG 105, NARA-DC.

84. W. W. Rogers to S. P. Lee, July 10, 1866; A. P. Ketchum to S. P. Lee, July 14, 1866; W. W. Rogers to S. P. Lee, July 18, 1866; W. W. Rogers to S. P. Lee, July 21, 1866; and W. W. Rogers to S. P. Lee, July 25, 1866, Records of the Field Offices for the State of Virginia, M1913, roll 43, RG 105, NARA-DC.

85. S. P. Lee to W. W. Rogers, December 12, 1866, Records of the Field Offices for the State of Virginia, M1913, roll 43, RG 105, NARA-DC.

86. S. P. Lee to O. Brown, May 30, 1867, Records of the Field Offices for the State of Virginia, M1913, roll 43, RG 105, NARA-DC.

87. Elizabeth Weden, to James Pryor, January 18, 1867; and S. P. Lee to W. W. Rogers, March 12, 1867, Records of the Field Offices for the State of Virginia, M1913, roll 43, RG 105, NARA-DC; *1870 US Census* (Population Schedule), Alexandria, Virginia, Second Ward, James Pryor head of household, page 40, line 1, digital image, accessed March 1, 2022, https://ancestry.com.

88. W. W. Rogers to S. P. Lee, April 16, 1866, Records of the Field Offices for the State of Virginia, M1913, roll 48, RG 105, NARA-DC; S. L. Woodward to S. P. Lee, December 7, 1866, Records of the Field Offices for the State of Virginia, M1913, roll 43, RG 105, NARA-DC; "Affidavit of an Arkansas Freedman," "Freedmen's Bureau Superintendent for Alexandria and Fairfax Counties, Virginia, to the Freedmen's Bureau Assistant Commissioner for the District of Columbia," and "Freedmen's Bureau Superintendent of the District of Eastern Arkansas to the Headquarters of the Arkansas Freedmen's Bureau Assistant Commissioner," in R. Hayden et al., *Freedom*, ser. 3, vol. 2, 824–25, 866–68.

89. Henry E. Alvord to John Eaton Jr., December 14, 1865, Records of the Field Offices for the State of Virginia, M1913, roll 53, RG 105, NARA-DC.

90. S. P. Lee to W. W. Rogers, March 12, 1867, Records of the Field Offices for the State of Virginia, M1913, roll 43, RG 105, NARA-DC.

91. Henry E. Alvord to John Eaton Jr., December 15, 1865; Report of Persons and Articles Employed; and McGeo. [office of O. O. Howard] to S. P. Lee, April 11, 1866, Records of the Field Offices for the State of Virginia, M1913, roll 53, RG 105, NARA-DC.

92. *1870 US Census* (Population Schedule), Centre Township, Fauquier County, Virginia, page 5, Peter Grant in the household of Aaron Grant, line 34, digital image; "Aaron Grant," *Virginia Death Records, 1912–2014*, accessed September 20, 2023, https://ancestry.com.

93. *1870 US Census*, Jefferson Township, Alexandria County, Virginia, page 29, H. Fractious head of household, line 40, digital image; and "Hampshire Fractious," *Virginia Deaths and Burials Index*, accessed July 15, 2016, https://ancestry.com; Deed Book X-3-98 (1866); Land Deed Office, Alexandria Courthouse; Deed Book D-4-243 (1878), and 111-409 (1905), Land Deed Office, Arlington County Courthouse.

94. *1870 US Census*, Fourth Ward, Alexandria, Virginia, page 96, Strother Morton [*sic*] head of household, line 8, digital image, accessed February 26, 2022, https://ancestry.com; Alexandria City (Va.) Chancery Causes, 1859–1925, Strother Morten [*sic*] & Wife v. Charles P. Chapman, etc., index no. 1891-030, Virginia Chancery Database, Library of Virginia, accessed June 5, 2018, www.lva.virginia.gov/chancery/case_detail.asp?CFN=510-1891-030.

95. Alexandria City (Va.) Chancery Causes, 1859–1925, Catherine Hansberry (Hansborough) v. George L. Seaton, index no. 1871-004, Virginia Chancery Database, Library of Virginia, accessed June 5, 2018, www.lva.virginia.gov/chancery/case_detail.asp?CFN=510-1871-004.

96. Jemima Harris Affidavit, June 20, 1868, Records of the Field Offices for the State of Virginia, M1913, roll 45, RG 105, NARA-DC.

97. Evidence against John Hodgkins in Case Performed by Deputy Sheriff Rock Tried November 5, 1867, Records of the Field Offices for the State of Virginia, M1913, roll 55, RG 105, NARA-DC; Harriet Williams to Oliver Otis Howard [telegram], November 2, 1867, Records of the Field Offices for the State of Virginia, M1913, roll 44, RG 105, NARA-DC.

98. Eliphalet Whittlesey to S. P. Lee, November 4, 1867, Records of the Field Offices for the State of Virginia, M1913, roll 44, RG 105, NARA-DC.

99. Moore, *Leading the Race*, 68–84.

100. [Advertisement], *Alexandria Gazette*, December 4, 1866.

101. "Municipal Election," *Alexandria Gazette*, March 5, 1867; "Alexandria and Vicinity," *Evening Star* (Washington, DC), August 16, 1867; "Local News," *Alexandria Gazette*, January 24, 1867.

102. "First Ward Radicals," *Alexandria Gazette*, December 23, 1868; "First Ward Radicals," *Alexandria Gazette*, June 9, 1869.

103. National Freedman's Relief Association of the District of Columbia, *First Annual Report*.

104. "Report of the 'First National Freedmen's School,' Alexandria, Va., for June 1865," *National Freedmen* (New York), August 15, 1865; "New England: Report of the Teachers' Committee," *American Freedmen* 1, no. 2 (May 1866): 28–29; US Office of Education, *History of Schools*, 290; Butchart, *Schooling the Freed People*, 78–119; Butchart, "Freedmen's Teacher Project."

105. S. P. Lee to O. Brown, May 8, 1867, Records of the Field Offices for the State of Virginia, M1913, roll 46, RG 105, NARA-DC.

106. Deed Book Y3-110 (1867), Z3-72 (1867), and Z3-74 (1867), Land Deed Office, Alexandria Courthouse; "Our Work and Our Superintendent at Alexandria, VA," *American Freedman* 2, no. 5 (August 1867), 302; "School at Alexandria," in J. F. Yellin, *Harriet Jacobs Family Papers*, 2:638–39.

107. William Shields to S. P. Lee, November 1, 1866, Records of the Field Offices for the State of Virginia, M1913, roll 48, RG 105, NARA-DC; George Seaton to unknown, December 8, 1866, Records of the Field Offices for the State of Virginia, M1913, roll 46, RG 105, NARA-DC; John Kimball to S. P. Lee, October 31, 1866, Records of the Field Offices for the State of Virginia, M1913, roll 43, RG 105, NARA-DC.

108. S. P. Lee to O. Brown, May 8, 1867, Records of the Field Offices for the State of Virginia, M1913, roll 46, RG 105, NARA-DC; "List of Public Property Received, One Volume, February–October 1867," Records of the Field Offices for the State of Virginia, M1913, roll 53, RG 105, NARA-DC.

109. Deed Book A4-80 (1868), Land Deed Office, Alexandria Courthouse.

110. Vaughn, "Freedom Is Not Enough," 17–18.

111. Morton, *Negro in Virginia Politics*, 23–40.

112. "The Loyal League," *Alexandria Gazette*, March 2, 1867; "Negro Suffrage," *Alexandria Gazette*, March 4, 1867.

113. "Negro Suffrage," *Alexandria Gazette*, March 4, 1867; "Election Preliminaries," *Alexandria Gazette*, March 4, 1867, 3; "Colored Mass Meeting," *Alexandria Gazette*, March 4, 1867; "Municipal Election," *Alexandria Gazette*, March 5, 1867.

114. "The Election Here," and "Gov. Peirpoint," *Alexandria Gazette*, March 5, 1867.

115. "Election," *Alexandria Gazette*, October 2, 1867; "The Election," *Alexandria Gazette*, October 23, 1867, p. 2; "Election," *Alexandria Gazette*, October 23, 1867, p. 3.

116. "Meeting of the City Council," *Alexandria Gazette*, April 29, 1868; "City Council," *Alexandria Gazette*, June 10, 1868.

117. "Colored Jurors," *Alexandria Gazette*, May 4, 1868.

118. "The Virginia Election," *New York Herald*, July 8, 1869.

119. "The Election," *Alexandria Gazette*, May 27, 1870; *1860 US Census*, Tudor Hall, Prince William County, Virginia, page 57, Travers Pinn in household of Houson Pinn, line 10,

digital image; and "William C. Beckley," Deposition of Traverse B. Pinn, December 10, 1872, *U.S. Southern Claims Commission Allowed Claims, 1871–1880*, accessed July 8, 2023, https://ancestry.com.

120. Julia A. Wilbur Diary, June 21, 1866.

CHAPTER TWO

1. Mabs Kemp, "Moabs' Diary," *Afro-American* (Baltimore, MD), October 4, 1986.

2. "Virginia: Alexandria, Va.," *Afro-American* (Baltimore, MD), February 22, 1930; "Pearson All Stars Drop Doubleheader," *New Journal and Guide* (Norfolk, VA), June 17, 1939. See also "Benevolent Societies," in Finkelman, *Encyclopedia of African American History*, 1:166.

3. Asch and Musgrove, *Chocolate City*, 186–216; Shoenfeld and Cherkasky, "'A Strictly White Residential Section.'"

4. Gatewood, *Aristocrats of Color*; Moore, *Leading the Race*; Ruble, *Washington's U Street*; Lindsey, *Colored No More*.

5. Scott, *Capital Engineers*; Kohler, *Capital Transit*; Schrag, *Great Society Subway*, 14–27; Griffin, *One Hundred Fifty Years*.

6. "Alexandrians Win 8-Cent Fare Fight," *Washington Post*, May 18, 1930.

7. Railroad Company v. Brown. 84 US 445 (1873). See Masur, "Patronage and Protest."

8. "Opposed to Separate Cars," *Alexandria Gazette*, December 17, 1891; "To Make It a City," *Washington Post*, December 19, 1891; "Desire Equal Rights," *Washington Post*, January 2, 1892.

9. Freeman H. M. Murray Diary, January 12, 1892, box 3, folder 50, Murray Papers. Charles Bendheim, the son of German-Jewish immigrants, was active in local politics and was Alexandria's delegate to the General Assembly from 1891 to 1894. "Charles Bendheim Claimed by Death," *Evening Star* (Washington, DC), May 1, 1934; "From Alexandria," *Baltimore (MD) Sun*, December 29, 1901.

10. Wynes, *Race Relations in Virginia*, 69; Kelley, *Right to Ride*, 142–43; Harris, "Barbara E. Pope," 289–91.

11. "Alexandria News in Brief," *Washington Post*, March 4, 1900 (quote); "Against 'Jim Crow' Cars," *Evening Star* (Washington, DC), January 26, 1901; "Protest of Colored Citizens," *Evening Star* (Washington, DC), February 5, 1901; "Protest against 'Jim Crow' Cars," *Suburban Citizen* (Washington, DC), May 17, 1902; "Colored Lawyers to Organize," *Evening Star* (Washington, DC), September 30, 1906.

12. "A Jim Crow Car Row," *Alexandria Gazette*, December 14, 1900; "Affairs in Alexandria," *Evening Star* (Washington, DC), January 27, 1902; "Railway Sued for $20,000," *Evening Star* (Washington, DC), September 28, 1906.

13. "Didn't Want to Ride in the 'Jim Crow' Car," *Alexandria Gazette*, March 26, 1901.

14. Harris, "Barbara E. Pope," 289–91.

15. Commonwealth of Virginia, General Assembly, *Acts and Joint Resolutions of the General Assembly*, 957.

16. Cox, "Alexandria Union Station," 6; Tindall, "Beginnings of Street Railways," 46–47.

17. "Jim Crow Bill Defeated," *Richmond (VA) Planet*, March 15, 1902.

18. "Changes in Districts: New Scheme for Grouping Counties of Virginia," *Washington Post*, February 25, 1902; "Jim Crowism Rebuked," *Colored American* (Washington, DC), March 15, 1902.

19. Commonwealth of Virginia, General Assembly, *Acts and Joint Resolutions of the General Assembly*, 639–40; "Railway Company Put 'Jim Crow' Law into Effect," *Washington Times*, May 2, 1902.

20. "First Case," *Alexandria Gazette*, May 3, 1902; "Alexandria News in Brief," *Washington Post*, May 4, 1902.

21. "Alexandria News in Brief," *Washington Post*, May 9, 1902; "Sat in Negroes' Seat: Daughter of Robert E. Lee Arrested on Electric Car," *Washington Post*, June 14, 1902; "Noted Lawyer is Dead," *Washington Post*, June 15, 1902.

22. "Testing the Validity of the 'Jim Crow' Law," *Washington Times*, March 21, 1904; "Verdict for the Plaintiff," *Evening Star* (Washington, DC), March 24, 1904. See also Kelley, *Right to Ride*, 121–24.

23. "Jitney Bus to Run as Far as Muhall," *Washington Times*, April 2, 1915.

24. "Not Allowed on Jitneys," *Washington Post*, June 16, 1915; "The Classification of Jitneys," *Evening Star* (Washington, DC), June 16, 1915; "Pageant by Children," *Washington Post*, July 4, 1915.

25. "Huge Area Opened to D.C. by Busses," *Evening Star* (Washington, DC), October 23, 1927.

26. *Code of Virginia as Amended*, 1043–44.

27. "VA. Jim Crow Law Jails N. Jersey Couple, Babe," *Afro-American* (Baltimore, MD), July 25, 1931.

28. "Man Facing Trial for Bus Assault," *Washington Post*, March 6, 1933.

29. Kincholow v. Peoples Rapid Transit Co. (1936), 88 F .2d 764; "Jailed Because She Failed to Move Back in Bus," *New Journal and Guide* (Norfolk, VA), March 14, 1936; "Write of Certiorari Denied Mrs. Kinchlow," *New Journal and Guide* (Norfolk, VA), June 5, 1937; "Echoes of a 5-Year-Old Bus Case Heard," *New Journal and Guide* (Norfolk, VA), October 30, 1937.

30. Anderson, *Education of Blacks*.

31. "City School Board," *Alexandria Gazette*, May 27, 1871; "School Examination," *Alexandria Gazette*, June 24, 1871; "City School Board," *Alexandria Gazette*, August 26, 1871.

32. "Our Public Schools," *Alexandria Gazette*, April 10, 1876; "City School Board," *Alexandria Gazette*, July 22, 1876.

33. "Industrial Schools," *American Freedmen* 2, no. 5 (May 1866), 148; "City School Board," *Alexandria Gazette*, May 27, 1871; "City School Board," *Alexandria Gazette*, July 29, 1871.

34. Trevilian Moncure, "School Progress," 42–49.

35. *Catalogue of the Officers and Students of Howard*, 10, 13, 16.

36. Lamb, *Howard University Medical Department*, 196; Freeman H. M. Murray Diary, March 9, 1885, and August 15, 1886, Murray Papers; *Directory of Deceased American Physicians, 1804–1929*, "William Henry Madella," accessed June 13, 2019, https://ancestry.com.

37. Lamb, *Howard University*, 139, 175–76, 220.

38. J. C. Smith, *Emancipation*, 227; Woods, "Alfred William Harris."

39. Gilmore, *Gender and Jim Crow*; Lindsey, *Colored No More*; Hunter, *Bound in Wedlock*.

40. Entry for October 26, 1883, Alexandria School Board Minute Book, 1871–92; Alexandria City Public Schools Archives; *Catalogue of Officers and Students from March 1881 to March*

1882, 11; *1860 US Census*, Alexandria, Virginia, page 263, Richard Lyles head of household, line 20, digital image; *1870 US Census*, Alexandria, Virginia, Ward 4, page 82, Rosier Lyles in household of Richard H. Lyles, line 5, digital image; and "Rozier D. Lyles," *Virginia Death Records, 1912–2014*, accessed June 13, 2019, https://ancestry.com.

41. "City School Board," *Alexandria Gazette*, August 26, 1871; "Local Brevities," *Alexandria Gazette*, May 24, 1909; *Catalogue of Officers and Students from March 1887 to March 1888*, 12; *Catalogue of Howard University for 1909–1910*, 190.

42. US Office of Education, *History of Schools*, 285–86; Florence B. Freedmen, "Introduction," in O'Conner, *Myrtilla Miner*, i–vi; Morrow, *Persons of Color*.

43. *Catalogue of the Officers and Students of Howard*, 79; *Catalogue of the Hampton Normal and Agricultural Institute*, 15; "City School Board," *Alexandria Gazette*, January 26, 1884; Freeman H. M. Murray Diary, September 28, 1886, Murray Papers.

44. "City School Board," *Alexandria Gazette*, August 2, 1889, 2; *Catalogue of Officers and Students from March 1887 to March 1888*, 6; "School Board," *Alexandria Gazette*, August 21, 1895, 3. *1900 US Census*, Washington, DC, ED 34, sheet 9B, Louisa Cabiness in the household of George Cabiness, line 78, digital image; *1910 US Census*, Washington, DC, ED 49, sheet 5B, Louisa Cabiness in household of George Cabiness, line 54, digital image; and "Louisa Tancil," *Virginia Death Records, 1912–2014*, accessed June 13, 2019, https://ancestry.com.

45. "City School Board," *Alexandria Gazette*, September 30, 1882.

46. "Public School Items," *Alexandria Gazette*, October 14, 1892; Norman Pinn, "A Card," *Alexandria Gazette*, October 15, 1892; "Local Brevities," *Alexandria Gazette*, October 15, 1892.

47. "The Washington Schools," *Alexandria Gazette*, September 23, 1899.

48. Charles "Buster" K. Williams, interview by Mitch Weinschenk, February 5, 1999, transcript, Office of Historic Alexandria, https://media.alexandriava.gov/docs-archives/historic/info/history/oralhistorywilliamsbuster.pdf; Elsie Thomas, interview by Donise Stevens, December 15, 2006, transcript, Office of Historic Alexandria, https://media.alexandriava.gov/docs-archives/historic/info/history/oralhistorythomaselsie2006.pdf.

49. "Trouble in the County," *Alexandria Gazette*, September 30, 1912.

50. "Alexandria News in Brief," *Washington Post*, November 11, 1901; "Alexandria News in Brief," *Washington Post*, January 4, 1902; "Schools for Alexandria will Open their Session on September 11," *Alexandria Gazette*, August 26, 1911.

51. "Snowden School Carpenter Shop," *Alexandria Gazette*, February 9, 1909; J. F. Parker and R. D. Lyles, "Snowden School Carpenter Shop," *Alexandria Gazette*, June 8, 1909; "Public Schools," *Alexandria Gazette*, June 16, 1909.

52. "School House Burns," *Alexandria Gazette*, March 27, 1916; "Enforced Vacation," *Alexandria Gazette*, March 28, 1916.

53. Superintendent Register, April 4, 1916, Alexandria City Public School Archives, Alexandria, VA; "Will Resume Studies," *Alexandria Gazette*, April 8, 1916.

54. "Urge City Council to Build New School," *Washington Herald*, February 3, 1917.

55. "Want New School Building," *Alexandria Gazette*, February 20, 1919.

56. L. Griffin Brooks and R. D. Lyles, "Parker-Gray School," *Alexandria Gazette*, May 4, 1921.

57. L. Griffin Brooks and R. D. Lyles, "New Colored School," *Alexandria Gazette*, May 27, 1920; Brooks and Lyles, "The Colored School," *Alexandria Gazette*, June 10, 1920; Brooks and Lyles, "Need $400 More," *Alexandria Gazette*, September 1, 1920; Brooks and Lyles,

"Parker-Gray School," *Alexandria Gazette*, May 4, 1921; "School Drive Ends," *Alexandria Gazette*, June 2, 1921.

58. "Board of Education Votes Ban on Non-Resident Pupils Here," *Alexandria Gazette*, April 22, 1926; "Non-resident Fees in Schools Urged," *Evening Star* (Washington, DC), February 22, 1928; "94,000 Predicted November Total," *Evening Star* (Washington, DC), September 8, 1935, sec. 6, 1; *Minutes of the Board of Education of the District of Columbia*, vol. 21, January 21, 1931; February 18, 1931; May 17, 1933; and November 4, 1936, District of Columbia Public School Archives.

59. Ballou v. Kemp. 92 F. 2d 556 (DC Cir. 1937); "Nearby Pupils Heighten Problem of Crowded Schools," *Evening Star* (Washington, DC), September 12, 1937.

60. "Crowdedness in Parker-Gray School Relieved," *New Journal and Guide* (Norfolk, VA), February 17, 1934; "Night Classes Started," *New Journal and Guide* (Norfolk, VA), January 20, 1934; "To Convert Factory into Colored School," *New Journal and Guide* (Norfolk, VA), February 24, 1934; "Schools $60,000 Loan Approved," *Alexandria Gazette*, August 28, 1934.

61. "Alexandria PTA Launches Drive to Have Parker-Gray High Accredited by State," *New Journal and Guide* (Norfolk, VA), May 16, 1936; Julius Newman, "In and Around Alexandria," *Chicago Defender*, October 28, 1939.

62. "Wesley D. Elam," *World War I Registration Cards, 1917–1918*, accessed September 25, 2023, https://ancestry.com; *Hill's Alexandria (Virginia) City Directory* (Richmond, VA: Hill Directory Co., 1928), 167.

63. Margo, *Race and Schooling*, 52–67; Wallenstein, *Blue Laws*, 89–92.

64. *Official Register of the United States*, 1:1210.

65. "Equal Salaries for All Teachers Being Sought," *New Journal and Guide* (Norfolk, VA), November 5, 1938; Newman, "In and Around Alexandria," *Chicago Defender*, October 28, 1939.

66. Alexandria School Board Minutes, December 11, 1940, Wesley D. Elam, Personnel Files (microfilm), Alexandria City Public Schools Archive.

67. Doyle, *New Men*.

68. E. S. Yellin, *Racism in the Nation's Service*.

69. Perry, Reybold, and Waters, "'Everybody Was Looking,'" 719–41.

70. E. S. Yellin, *Racism in the Nation's Service*, 3–4; Masur, "Patronage and Protest," 1055–57.

71. "Robert H. Dogan," Deposition of John A. Seaton, January 27, 1873, *U.S. Southern Claims Commission Allowed Claims, 1871–1880*, accessed July 5, 2023, https://ancestry.com; *Executive Documents Printed by the Order of the House of Representatives*, 18.

72. "William C. Beckley," Deposition of Traverse B. Pinn, December 10, 1872, *U.S. Southern Claims Commission Allowed Claims, 1871–1880*, accessed July 8, 2023, https://ancestry.com.

73. "Robert D. Ruffin," *Disallowed and Barred Claims, U.S. Southern Claims Commission, 1871–1880*, accessed July 5, 2023, https://ancestry.com; "Local Brevities," *Alexandria Gazette*, February 20, 1874; *Boyd's Business Directory of the Cities of Alexandria, Georgetown, and Washington* (Washington, DC: William H. Boyd, 1875), 41.

74. William Mahone to Col. D. A. Windsor, March 29, 1882, box 179, William Mahone Papers, David M. Rubenstein Rare Book and Manuscript Library, Duke University, Durham, NC. *1880 US Census*, Washington, DC, ED 5, page 3, Douglass Syphax head of household, line 32, digital image; and *1880 US Census*, Alexandria, Virginia, ED 3, page 18, David Windsor head of household, line 41 digital image, accessed March 15, 2022, https://ancestry.com.

75. [Note on envelope], R. G. Cunningham to William Mahone, April 3, 1882, box 179; William Mahone Papers; *1880 US Census*, Washington District, Alexandria County, Virginia, ED 8, page 15, R. G. Cunningham head of household, line 5, digital image, accessed June 11, 2024, https://ancestry.com.

76. "Virginia Appointments," *Alexandria Gazette*, June 6, 1873; "Civil Rights in Virginia," *New National Era* (Washington, DC), June 25, 1874.

77. Dailey, *Before Jim Crow*, 51–67.

78. "From Washington," *Alexandria Gazette*, May 23, 1885; "From Washington," *Alexandria Gazette*, October 18, 1893; *Official Register of the United States, Containing a List of Officers and Employés in the Civil, Military, and Naval Service of the First of July 1883*, vol. 2, 733.

79. George L. Preston to William Mahone, May 13, 1881; Preston to Mahone, July 22, 1881; box 30, William Mahone Papers.

80. Rubio, *There's Always Work*, 28; Perry, Reybold, and Waters, "'Everybody Was Looking,'" 720; Moore, *Leading the Race*, 26–27; E. S. Yellin, *Racism in the Nation's Service*, 1–7.

81. Freeman H. M. Murray Diary, January 17, 1884, box 3, folder 40, Murray Papers.

82. Freeman H. M. Murray Diary September 8, 1884, box 3, folder 41, Murray Papers.

83. Freeman H. M. Murray Diary, December 30, 1884, box 3, folder 41, March 26, 1885, April 2, 1885, box 3, folder 42, Murray Papers.

84. Freeman H. M. Murray Diary, February 14–28, 1887, box 3, folder 45, Murray Papers.

85. A. Jones, *African American Civil Rights*, 34; Ashton, "Du Bois's *Horizon*," 3–23.

86. Asch and Musgrove, *Chocolate City*, 192–200; Gillette, *Between Justice and Beauty*, 88–108; Ruble, *Washington's U Street*, 47–88.

87. Griffin, *One Hundred Fifty Years*, 128–32.

88. Virginia Post Roads, 1913–16, boxes 106–7, General Correspondence, 1893–1916, RG 30: Office of Public Records, NARA-MD.

89. "Joseph H. Cranford, Paving Firm Head, Dies of Pneumonia," *Evening Star* (Washington, DC), February 7, 1941.

90. "Alexandria, Virginia," *World War I Draft Registration Cards, 1917–1918*, accessed March 15, 2022, https://ancestry.com.

91. "Begin to Build Camp Humphreys, New Army Post," *Washington Times*, January 31, 1918; "Alexandria City and Suburbs," *Alexandria Gazette*, March 13, 1918.

92. "Lease Shipyard Site," *Alexandria Gazette*, December 21, 1917; "Building the Ships," *Alexandria Gazette*, June 12, 1918. See also Crampton, *Supplemental Report*, 4–6.

93. *Richmond's Directory of Alexandria, VA* (Washington, DC: W. L. Richmond, 1906), 234; "Fell through Window," *Alexandria Gazette*, October 4, 1912; "Lorenzo Chase" and "Lee Hollin," *World War I Draft Cards, 1917–1918*, accessed July 21, 2019, https://ancestry.com; *1900 US Census*, Alexandria, Virginia, Ward 1, ED 91, sheet 13B, Lorenzo Chase in household of Frank Chase, line 70, digital image; and *1910 US Census*, Alexandria, Virginia, Ward 1, ED 2, sheet 3B, Lorenzo Chase in household of Laura Chase, line 82, digital image, accessed March 15, 2022, https://ancestry.com.

94. "Charles Breisford" and "Samuel Jones," *World War I Draft Cards, 1917–1918*; and *1930 US Census*, Alexandria, Virginia, ED 101-8, sheet 15A, Samuel Jones head of household, line 40, digital image, accessed July 21, 2019, https://ancestry.com.

95. "Requests Negroes to Remain South," *Alexandria Gazette*, May 30, 1917.

96. "Negros Lured North," *Alexandria Gazette*, August 28, 1916; "Big Plants Lack Labor," *Washington Post*, November 13, 1916; "Requests Negroes to Remain South," *Alexandria Gazette*, May 30, 1917; "An Ordinance to Regulate the Employment of Persons for Service or Labor Outside of the State of Virginia," *Alexandria Gazette*, May 30, 1917.

97. "Public Is Invited to Naval Station," *Evening Star* (Washington, DC), October 22, 1931.

98. *Alexandria's City Directory* (Richmond: Hill Directory Co., Inc., 1923), 292; *1930 US Census*, Alexandria, Virginia, ED 105-8, sheet 15A, George E. Parker head of household, line 29, digital image, accessed March 17, 2022, https://ancestry.com.

99. Ziparo, *This Grand Experiment*.

100. Andrews, *My Studio Window*, 400–416.

101. *1910 US Census*, Alexandria, Virginia, Ward 3, ED 8, sheet 11B, Julia Washington in Andrew J. Washington household, line 54, digital image; and *1930 US Census*, Alexandria, Virginia, Ward 3, ED 101-6, sheet 24B, Julia Washington in Andrew J. Washington household, line 97, digital image, accessed June 9, 2024, https://ancestry.com.

102. *Boyd's Directory of the District of Columbia 1920* (Washington, DC: R. L. Polk & Co., 1920), 344; *1930 US Census*, Alexandria, Virginia, ED 101-11, sheet 15B, Carrie Jackson in Wickleff Jackson household, line 97, digital image; and "Carrie Jackson," *Virginia Select Marriages 1785–1940*, accessed September 27, 2023, https://ancestry.com.

103. *Hill's Alexandria (Virginia) City Directory* (1928), 204; *1920 US Census*, York Pennsylvania, Ward 1, ED 124, sheet 3B, Ethel [Hackley] Bond in the Harry Bond household, line 83, digital image; *1930 US Census*, Alexandria, Virginia, ED 101-7, sheet 2B, Ethel Hackley in Russell Hackley Household, line 93, digital image; and *1950 US Census*, Washington, DC, ED 1-677, sheet 74, Ethel V. B. Hackley in Russell Hackley Household, line 4, digital image, accessed June 11, 2024, https://ancestry.com.

104. "Night Classes Started," *New Journal and Guide* (Norfolk, VA), January 20, 1934.

105. Battery Cove, SP-21, Project Reports on Civilian Conservation Corps Projects in State and Local Parks, 1933–37, box 137, entry 95, RG 79: Records of the National Park Service, NARA-MD.

106. Clarence R. Johnson, [memorandum], November 18, 1940, box 12, folder: Alexandria, VA, Records of the Inter Group Relations Branch, 1936–63, RG 196: Records of the Public Housing Administration, NARA-MD.

107. *Alexandria Virginia Directory* (Alexandria, VA: Hill Directory Co., 1919), 162; *Hill's Alexandria (Virginia) City Directory* (Richmond, VA: Hill Directory Co., 1947), 100; *1920 US Census*, Alexandria, Virginia, ED 4, sheet 11B, Jesse Carter in the Belle Carter household, line 57, digital image; *1930 US Census*, Alexandria, Virginia, ED 101-8, sheet 14B, Jesse Carter in Beatrice Carter Household, line 83, digital image; *1940 US Census*, Alexandria, Virginia, ED 101-10, sheet 61B, Jessie Carter Head of Household, line 72, digital image; and "Jesse Harrison Carter," *World War II Draft Cards, 1940–1947*, accessed June 11, 2024, https://ancestry.com.

108. *Hill's Alexandria (Virginia) City Directory* (Richmond, VA: Hill Directory Co., 1954), 131; *1930 US Census*, Alexandria, Virginia, ED 101-10, sheet 12B, Lawrence Day in the Robert Day household, line 75, digital image; *1940 US Census*, Alexandria, Virginia, ED 101-2, sheet 4B, Lawrence Day head of household, line 41, digital image; and "Lawrence Dunbar Day," *World War II Draft Cards, 1940–1947*, accessed June 11, 2024, https://ancestry.com.

109. Sherman, "'Teachings at Hampton Institute.'"

110. Mitchell-Powell, *Public in Name Only*.

111. Murray, *Negro Handbook*, 45–46; Seehorn Brandt, "Alexandria, Virginia, Library," 25–26.

112. Smith, *Managing White Supremacy*, 260–61.

113. New Negro Alliance v. Sanitary Grocery Co., 303 U.S. 552 (1938).

114. Mitchell-Powell, *Public in Name Only*, 40.

CHAPTER THREE

1. Special Rezoning Meeting Verbatim Transcript, October 10, 1967, Docket Minutes, City Council, September 12, 1967–November 14, 1967, AARC.

2. Special Rezoning Meeting Verbatim Transcript, October 10, 1967.

3. Jackson, *Crabgrass Frontier*; Cohen, *Consumers' Republic*; Hayden, *Building Suburbia*.

4. Teaford, *Rough Road to Renaissance*; Delaney, *Race, Place, and the Law*; Freund, *Colored Property*; Brooks and Rose, *Saving the Neighborhood*; Rothstein, *Color of Law*; Shoenfeld and Cherkasky, "'Strictly White Residential Section'"; Santucci, "Documenting Racially Restrictive Covenants."

5. Hirsch, *Making the Second Ghetto*; Sugrue, *Origins of the Urban Crisis*; Bayor, *Twentieth-Century Atlanta*; Hirsch, "Containment on the Home Front"; Ferguson, *Black Politics*; Connolly, *World More Concrete*.

6. Smith, *Managing White Supremacy*, 250–84.

7. Ferguson, *Black Politics*, 262–66; Wiese, *Places of Their Own*, 209–54.

8. "Real Estate Gossip," *Evening Star* (Washington, DC), June 27, 1908.

9. Freund, *Colored Property*, 50.

10. McCord, *Across the Fence*; Cressey, "The Alexandria, Virginia City-Site."

11. "Real Estate Gossip," *Evening Star* (Washington, DC), June 27, 1909; "Alexandria's Progress," *Alexandria Gazette*, October 27, 1911; "Bankers Please Cause before Alderman," *Alexandria Gazette*, June 28, 1911; "Extends City Limits," *Washington Post*, March 12, 1915; Deed Book 119-490 (1909), Land Deed Office, Arlington County Courthouse; Deed Book 65-449 (1912), Land Deed Office, Alexandria City Courthouse.

12. Alexandria Annexation Collection, 1929–30, Loudoun County Courthouse, Leesburg, VA.

13. City Council Minutes, June 20, 1929, AARC.

14. City Council Minutes, October 18, 1923, and November 2, 1923, AARC. See also *Proposed Comprehensive Plan for Alexandria*, 18.

15. "Root Will Assist Alexandria Zoning," *Evening Star* (Washington, DC), November 16, 1930; Howard M. Baggett, "Alexandria Zoning Plan is Outlined," *Evening Star* (Washington, DC), December 7, 1930.

16. The State of Virginia passed legislation allowing for municipalities to create zoning ordinances in 1927. Va. Code §28800-2880ll (1930).

17. West Bros Brick Co. v. Alexandria. 169 Va. 271 (September 23, 1937).

18. Deed 152-272 (1939), Land Deed Office, Alexandria City Courthouse.

19. Rak, "History of Zoning"; *City of Alexandria Map*.

20. "City Plan of Alexandria," 1935, Davis Ruffner Files, Fairfax County Historic Records Center, City of Fairfax, VA.

21. "Crowdedness in Parker-Gray School Relieved," *New Journal and Guide* (Norfolk, VA), February 17, 1934; "Night Classes Started," *New Journal and Guide* (Norfolk, VA), January 20, 1934; "To Convert Factory into Colored School," *New Journal and Guide* (Norfolk, VA), February 24, 1934; "Schools $60,000 Loan Approved," *Alexandria Gazette*, August 28, 1934.

22. Teaford, *Rough Road to Renaissance*; Delaney, *Race, Place, and the Law*; Freund, *Colored Property*; Brooks and Rose, *Saving the Neighborhood*; Rothstein, *Color of Law*; Shoenfeld and Cherkasky, "'Strictly White Residential Section'"; Santucci, "Documenting Racially Restrictive Covenants."

23. Lingeman, *Don't You Know*; Ferguson, *Black Politics*; Reft, "Suburb and the Sword."

24. Rothstein, *Color of Law*, 63–67.

25. Housing Market Analysis, Washington, DC, July 1937, Federal Housing Administration Division of Economics and Statistics, August 5, 1937, 19–26, box 17, RG 31: Records of the Federal Housing Administration, NARA-MD.

26. "Restrictive Covenants Which Meet the Objectives as Set Forth on Page 8 of Circulate #5, Subdivision Standards," June 1, 1937, Braddock Heights folder, Davis-Ruffner Files, AARC.

27. Deed Book 153-178 (1939); Land Deed Office, Alexandria City Courthouse.

28. "Root Will Assist Alexandria Zoning," *Evening Star* (Washington, DC), November 16, 1930; Howard M. Baggett, "Alexandria Zoning Plan is Outlined," *Evening Star* (Washington, DC), December 7, 1930.

29. Logan, *Historic Capital*, 7–8.

30. "FHA Funds Aid Restoration of Gadsby Tavern," *Washington Post*, October 31, 1934.

31. "Ancient Home in Alexandria Is Remodeled," *Washington Post*, June 30, 1935.

32. Ferguson, *Black Politics*, 166–67.

33. Harper, *Real Property Survey*, 49, 73.

34. Harper, *Real Property Survey*, 89–111.

35. Ferguson, *Black Politics*, 172.

36. *Alexandria, Va. City Directory* (Richmond, VA: Hill Directory Co., Inc. 1920), 295; *1930 US Census*, Alexandria, Virginia, ED 101-6, sheet 12A, Hannah Nelson head of household, line 24, digital image, accessed July 31, 2023, https://ancestry.com.

37. Henry P. Thomas to Carl Budwesky, March 25, 1939, Regular Meeting, March 28, 1939, City Council Proceedings, AARC.

38. Lynn W. Ellis to Mayor and City Council, March 24, 1939, Regular Meeting, March 28, 1939, City Council Proceedings, AARC.

39. City Council Minutes, Regular Meeting, March 28, 1939, City Council Proceedings, AARC; *1930 US Census*, Alexandria, Virginia, ED 101-6, sheet 18B, Lynn Ellis head of household, line 88, digital image, accessed July 31, 2023, https://ancestry.com.

40. City Council Minutes, Regular Meeting, June 20 and 27, 1939, City Council Proceedings, AARC.

41. "Alexandria City Council to Meet Tonight," *Washington Post*, September 12, 1939; "USHA to Give $900,000 to Alexandria," *Washington Post*, October 29, 1939.

42. "240 Dwellings are Condemned by Alexandria Authorities," *Washington Post*, March 17, 1941; Building Permits, February 24, 1941, AARC.

43. "Alexandria Finds Housing Shortage," *Washington Post*, July 16, 1941.

44. "Only 4 Homes Await War Workers," *Washington Post*, June 11, 1943.

45. "Housing Developments in Washington Area," *Washington Post*, October 25, 1942.

46. Reft, "Suburb and the Sword."

47. "Trailer Row May Go Higher," *Alexandria Gazette*, June 12, 1943; "Condemn Trailer Camp Land," *Alexandria Gazette*, June 15, 1943; "51 Alexandria Negro Families to Be Moved," *Washington Post*, July 30, 1944.

48. City Council Minutes, Regular Meeting, May 11, 1943, City Council Proceedings, AARC.

49. City Council Minutes, Regular Meeting, June 15, 1943, City Council Proceedings, AARC.

50. Sipe and Snyder, *Documentary Study*.

51. City Council Minutes, Regular Meeting, June 8, 1954, AARC.

52. Fenwick, *Urban Restoration*, 48–49; Smith, "Beginnings of Historic Preservation," 1–34.

53. Ron Shaffer, "Shirlington Center: New Spark Needed," *Washington Post*, February 13, 1975.

54. "Accessibility Big Factor in Area's 'Success Story,'" *Washington Post*, October 13, 1949.

55. Fenwick, *Urban Restoration*, 34.

56. *Prince Street Shopping Center*.

57. City Council Minutes, Special Session, June 21, 1954, City Council Proceedings, AARC.

58. "Tuskegee Head Talks to 5,000 at Howard U.," *Washington Post*, June 11, 1938; "Integration by September Pushed in Alexandria," *Washington Post*, July 21, 1955; *1950 US Census*, Washington, DC, ED 1-1073, sheet 2, Edwin C. Brown head of household, line 21, digital image, accessed July 28, 2023, https://ancestry.com.

59. City Council Minutes, Special Session, June 21, 1954, City Council Proceedings, AARC.

60. City Council Minutes, Regular Meeting, November 22, 1955, City Council Proceedings, AARC.

61. Foard and Fefferman, "Federal Urban Renewal Legislation."

62. *Code of the City of Alexandria*, 415–20.

63. *Report of Alexandria Community Development Committee*.

64. Julia A. Wilbur to Anna M. C. Barnes, November 20, 1863, in J. F. Yellin, *Harriet Jacobs Family Papers*, 2:523–32; "Sugar War," *Alexandria Gazette*, May 9, 1876; "Mail Robbery," *Alexandria Gazette*, September 13, 1877.

65. Community Development Committee, *Report of Alexandria Community Development Committee*, n.p.; City Planning Department, *A Look at Our City . . . Alexandria, Virginia: Report One of the Land Use and Economic Base Survey* (Alexandria, VA: City Planning Department, September 1956), 84, box 19JJJ, City Planning Department, Alexandria City Records, Special Collections, KWBBL.

66. Victoria Stone, "Plans Revealed for Alexandria Urban Renewal," *Washington Post*, July 20, 1960; Everard Munsey, "Gentler Renewal Plan Wins Alexandria Over," *Washington Post*, February 21, 1961, A3; Fenwick, *Urban Restoration*, 52–58.

67. Gail Bensinger, "Suit Filed to Block Old Town Razings," *Washington Post*, December 16, 1967, B1; "Alexandria Approves Renewal," *Washington Post*, July 30, 1969, C5; McCloskey, "Urban Renewal and Historic Preservation," 63.

68. "Redeveloping History," *Washington Post*, January 31, 1962; *Gadsby Commercial Urban Renewal Project*, 17–19.

69. *Report of Alexandria Community Development Committee*.

70. "Report on Minority Group Considerations," n.d., box 297, Gadsby Residential Urban Renewal Project, 1962–65, KWBBL.

71. Kermit Sloan to Denis Cahill, April 9, 1954, Book 6: Materials on Centennial Commemoration, including Fort Ward; Dorothy Starr Civil War Research Library, Fort Ward Park and Museum, Alexandria, VA.

72. *Report of Alexandria Community Development Committee*; "Alexandria Ask Federal Aid for Park," *Washington Post*, July 31, 1962; "Ritual Plans Are Complete at Fort," *Alexandria Gazette*, May 28, 1964; Fort Ward Publicity, 1961–83 Scrapbook; E. H. Wiecking, President, "Notes for Statement to Alexandria Planning Commission," April 1, 1954; Dorothy Starr Civil War Research Library, Fort Ward Park and Museum, Alexandria, VA.

73. *Neighborhood Analysis*, 48–49.

74. Maydell Casey Belk, interview by Patricia Knock et al., June 6, 1994, transcript, Alexandria Archaeology, https://media.alexandriava.gov/docs-archives/historic/info/history/oralhistorybelkmaydellcasey.pdf.

75. *Report of Alexandria Community Development Committee*.

76. "Alexandria Picks Site for School," *Washington Post*, September 26, 1960.

77. "New School to Honor Williams," *Washington Post*, May 22, 1964.

78. Howard, "Historical Study of the Desegregation," 172–73.

79. 282 F. 2d 473 (4th Cir. 1960); "Alexandria Votes Local Pupil Plan," *Washington Post*, April 8, 1965.

80. Reed, *Building the Federal Schoolhouse*, 31–96.

81. "History of Public Housing for Negroes," 1954, box 1, Records of the Intergroup Relations Branch, 1936–63, RG 196: Records of the Public Housing Administration, NARA-MD; Pritchett, *Robert Clifton Weaver*, 55–59.

82. *Catalogue of Officers and Students from March 1883 to March 1884*; *1940 US Census*, Alexandria, Virginia, ED 101-11, sheet 13B, Samuel W. Madden head of household, line 76, digital image, accessed August 3, 2023, https://ancestry.com; "History," Hopkins House, accessed August 3, 2023, www.hopkinshouse.org/about/history.

83. "Studies: History of Public Housing for Negroes," 1954, box 1; Samuel Madden to Dr. Frank Horne, November 8, 1940; Clarence R. Johnson, Memorandum, November 18, 1940; Clarence R. Johnson, Memorandum, March 31, 1941; Clarence R. Johnson to Dr. Frank S. Horne, n.d.; box 12, Records of the Intergroup Relations Branch, 1936–63, RG 196: Records of the Public Housing Administration, NARA-MD.

84. Frank S. Horne to W. F. Wright, March 17, 1941; Frank S. Horne to W. F. Wright, January 18, 1941, box 12, Records of the Intergroup Relations Branch, 1936–63, RG 196: Records of the Public Housing Administration, NARA-MD.

85. HM [probably Henry Lee Moon] to Frank S. Horne, May 27, 1941, box 12, Records of the Intergroup Relations Branch, 1936–63, RG 196: Records of the Public Housing Administration, NARA-MD.

86. Robert Taylor, "Eminent Domain Law Comes under Fire of Property Owners," *The Courier* (Pittsburgh, PA), January 19, 1952, box 02120703, William C. Cleveland (Vice Mayoral) Papers, AARC.

87. Armistead L. Boothe to William S. Banks, November 30, 1964; and William S. Banks to Claude Wolford, April 19, 1965, Dorothy Starr Civil War Research Library, Fort Ward Park and Museum, Alexandria, VA. See also Smith, "'When Reason Collides with Prejudice:'" 5–46.

88. "Canine Corps in Alexandria to be Enlarged," *Washington Post,* January 15, 1960.

89. "Marion Irvin Johnson," *World War II Draft Cards, 1940–1947;* and "Marion Irvin Johnson," *Virginia Marriage Records, 1936–2014,* accessed July 28, 2023, https://ancestry.com.

90. "Neighbors Back Plea of Mudtown," *Washington Post,* November 23, 1960; "Compromise on Mudtown Is Proposed," *Washington Post,* November 16, 1960.

91. Schwab, "Patterns of Relocation and Adjustment."

92. US Commission on Civil Rights, "Testimony of Marion I. Johnson, Vice President, Alexandria Council on Human Relations," in *Hearings before the United States Commission on Civil Rights,* 106.

93. US Commission on Civil Rights, "Testimony of Marion I. Johnson," 108.

94. "Statement of A. Melvin Miller, President Durant Civic Association," June 5, 1962, Dockets/Minutes, City Council, March 27–June 19, 1962, box 44, AARC.

95. "Housing Plan for Negroes Is Approved," *Washington Post,* September 8, 1962.

96. "Human Rights Code of the City of Alexandria Virginia (Sec. 18A-1)," in *Code of the City of Alexandria.*

97. "Alexandria Lifts All Public Racial Bars," *Washington Post,* May 23, 1963; Leonard S. Brown, "Alexandria Desegregates City Jobs, Public Places," *Washington Afro-American,* June 18, 1963, accessed on December 20, 2011, www.afro.com.

98. Robert I. Terrell to Frank E. Mann, May 23, 1963, box 47, City Council Proceedings, AARC; *Hill's Alexandria (Virginia) City Directory* (Richmond, VA: Hill Directory Co., 1959), 642.

99. "Alexandria Council Gets $27,000,000 Apartment Project," *Evening Star* (Washington, DC), October 25, 1941; William J. Raspberry, "Parkfairfax Opens Doors to Negroes," *Washington Post,* August 12, 1963.

100. Taylor, *Race for Profit,* 68–76.

101. Dorothy Gilliam, "Urban League Hits Housing in D.C., Alexandria," *Washington Post,* August 7, 1964.

102. Walter B. Douglas, "Alexandria's Housing Plan Hits Barrier," *Washington Post,* January 10, 1964.

103. Maurine McLaughlin, "Alexandria to Dedicate 90-Unit Housing Project," *Washington Post,* June 25, 1967.

104. "ACCESS Pickets Apartments in Drive for Desegregation," *Washington Post,* December 4, 1967; Peter A. Jay, "Beltway March Swings into Md. Gains Support," *Washington Post,* June 10, 1966; Gail Bensinger, "25 March to Protest Negro Housing in Virginia," *Washington Post,* October 8, 1966; Bensinger, "ACCESS March in Virginia Will Highlight Negro Housing," *Washington Post,* September 29, 1966; "Numerous Fairfax Residents Back Open Occupancy Law," *Northern Virginia Sun* (Arlington County), May 1, 1968.

105. "Racial Bias Charged to Apartments," *Northern Virginia Sun* (Arlington County), October 21, 1967; "30 Groups to Ask County Board for Local Open Housing Ordinance," *Northern Virginia Sun* (Arlington County), January 15, 1968; "Numerous Fairfax Residents Back Open Occupancy Law," *Northern Virginia Sun* (Arlington County), May 1, 1968.

106. Planning Commission Minutes, June 5, 1962, October 29, 1963, and August 4, 1964; "Rezoning Requests," October 6, 1964, Planning Commission Reports, July 1964 to October 1964, AARC.

107. "NCHA Votes to Integrate 2 More Units," *Washington Post*, July 3, 1953; "FHA Steps Up Efforts to House Minorities," *Washington Post*, March 25, 1956; George Wilson, "Open Occupancy Policy Proves Trick for D.C.," *Evening Star* (Washington, DC), February 8, 1961.

108. "Housing Issues Aired by Forum of Alexandrians," *Northern Virginia Sun* (Arlington County), September 29, 1961.

109. Staff Report on Open Housing, 1967, City Council Proceedings, AARC.

110. Staff Report on Open Housing, 1967.

111. "Housing Tour," *Bulletin*, November 1961; and Sally Tongren, "Development of Human Resources," *Bulletin*, December 1967, League of Women Voters Records, box 238b, Special Collections, KWBBL.

112. Virginia did not pass Fair or Open Housing legislation until forced to meet federal guidelines. "Overview of Virginia Fair Housing Law and Fair Housing Office," Virginia Department of Professional and Occupational Regulation, accessed March 14, 2012, www.dpor.virginia.gov/dporweb/fho_overview.cfm#Fair%20Housing%20Law.

113. Brian Patrick Larkin, "Forty-Year 'First Step.'"

114. Maurine McLaughlin, "Open-Housing Law Adopted by Alexandria Council, 5 to 1," *Washington Post*, February 26, 1969.

115. Maurine McLaughlin, "The City Still Faces South a Century after the Civil War," *Washington Post*, June 26, 1969.

CHAPTER FOUR

1. Special Meeting, October 20, 1969, City Clerk, Docket Minutes, AARC; "Church Calendar," *Northern Virginia Sun* (Arlington County), January 18, 1969; Maurine McLaughlin, "Alexandria Has 6th Night of Disorder," *Washington Post*, June 4, 1970.

2. Ira Robinson, email to author, June 6, 2022; October 24, 2022.

3. Special Meeting, October 20, 1969, City Clerk, Docket Minutes, AARC.

4. Taylor, *Race for Profit*, 5. See also Gill, "Moving to Integration?"; Tuck, *Beyond Atlanta*, 192–243; Minchin and Salmond, *After the Dream*, 128–205.

5. Friedman, *Covert Capital*; Repak, *Waiting on Washington*; Gjelten, *Nation of Nations*.

6. Schaller, *Reckoning with Reagan*; Johnson, *Sleepwalking through History*.

7. Clavel, *Activists in City Hall*; Winnick, "Triumph of Housing Allowance Programs."

8. Head, "Reagan, Nuclear Weapons," 81–100; Evangelista, *Innovation and Arms Race*.

9. Griffis, *Listing of Virginia's Prime Defense Contractors*.

10. Committee on Banking, Finance, and Urban Affairs, *Housing Needs of Hispanics*.

11. Eric Tang explores a similar case study in the Bronx. Tang, *Unsettled*.

12. Tuck, "African American Protest," 119–34; Nesbitt, *Race for Sanctions*; von Hoffman, *House by House*.

13. Will Book 7-126 (1854), Arlington County Courthouse; "Auction Sales," *Alexandria Gazette*, April 30, 1860; [Announcements], *Alexandria Gazette*, April 25, 1866; "Local News," *Alexandria Gazette*, October 13, 1866; "Auction Sales," *Alexandria Gazette*, November 8, 1895.

14. "Railroads," *Alexandria Gazette*, April 6, 1900.

15. *Town of Potomac.*

16. *1870 US Census*, Jefferson Township, Alexandria County, Virginia, pages 29–30, H. Fractious in James Hilton household, line 40, digital image, accessed July 15, 2016, https://ancestry.com; Deed Book A-4-243 (1870), D-4-243 (1878), and 111-409 (1905), Land Deed Office, Arlington County Courthouse.

17. Article of Agreement between Thornton Hyatt and S. P. Lee, March 1, 1866, Records of the Field Offices for the State of Virginia, M1913, roll 53, RG 105, NARA-DC; "Local Brevities," *Alexandria Gazette*, April 9, 1896.

18. *1930 US Census*, Alexandria, Virginia, ED 101-1, sheet 1A, lines 1–11, 24–50, sheet 1B, lines 51–62, digital image, accessed July 15, 2016, https://ancestry.com; Sunnyside Subdivision, Davis-Ruffner Title Company Papers, AARC.

19. Alexandria Deed Book 139-104 (1937), 139-344 (1937), 139-422 (1937), Land Deed Office, Alexandria Courthouse; "Hechinger Project Head Since 1938," *Washington Post*, June 27, 1966; [Advertisement], *Washington Post*, March 5, 1939; "Beverly Plaza Park-and-Shop Center Liked," *Washington Post*, January 30, 1938.

20. Conrad P. Harness, "Alexandria, Nearby Md. Units Set," *Washington Post*, July 20, 1947; "'Arlandria' Shopping Center Opens Friday in Virginia," *Washington Post*, November 9, 1947; "Arlandria to Celebrate on Monday," *Washington Post*, October 22, 1950.

21. Mary Battiata, "Flood Waters Down, Property Values Up," *Washington Post*, November 16, 1981.

22. Maurine McLaughlin, "The City Still Faces South a Century after the Civil War," *Washington Post*, June 26, 1969.

23. Moon, "African American Housing Crisis."

24. "Know Your City . . . a Little Better," *Bulletin*, February 1969, 3, League of Women Voters Records, box 238B, file 4; Special Collections, KWBBL.

25. "Minor Burglaries Reported in City; Four Are Arrested," *Alexandria Gazette*, April 6, 1968.

26. Sandee Toothman, "Clash in Arlandria Brings Arrest of 5," *Alexandria Gazette*, October 6, 1969; "Arlandria Negroes Protest Police Action," *Washington Post*, October 6, 1969; "Melee Shakes Alexandria," *Washington Post*, October 10, 1969.

27. Special Meeting, October 20, 1969; City Clerk, Docket Minutes, AARC; "Arlandria Negroes Protest Police Action," *Washington Post*, October 6, 1969; "Melee Shakes Alexandria," *Washington Post*, October 10, 1969; Sandee Toothman, "Columbus St. Market Hit by Fire Bomb," *Alexandria Gazette*, October 20, 1969; Sandee Toothman, "2 Nights of Fire Bombs Rock Area," *Alexandria Gazette*, October 20, 1969; "Police Continue Investigation of Fire Bombings; No Arrests," *Alexandria Journal*, October 20, 1969.

28. Michigan State University School of Police Administration and Public Safety, "Report of a Study of Police-Community Relations in Alexandria, Virginia," (December 1969), 1970 Michigan State Police/Community Relations Report File, Police Department Records, AARC.

29. Special Meeting, City Council, June 2, 1970, City Clerk, Docket Minutes, AARC.

30. Bryan Harrison, "$65,000 Harm to Home Listed; Occupants Safe," *Alexandria Gazette*, June 1, 1970, 1 and 12; Bryan Harrison, "Police Arrest Two in Night of Fire-Bombing," *Alexandria Gazette*, June 3, 1970; David Slack, "Modified Curfew Measure Enacted," *Alexandria Gazette*, June 3, 1970; "Bulletin," *Alexandria Gazette*, June 3 1970; E. J. Bachinski and Michael

Hodge, "Youth Slain, Disorder Hits Alexandria," *Washington Post*, May 30, 1970; Joseph D. Whitaker, "Alexandria Group Cools the Streets," *Washington Post*, September 21, 1971.

31. City Council Meeting, December 9, 1969, June 24, 1970, City Clerk, Docket Minutes, AARC.

32. Rome, *Bulldozer in the Countryside*, 3.

33. "Violent Storms," *Alexandria Gazette*, August 18, 1873; "Notes," *Alexandria Gazette*, June 3, 1889.

34. "Flood Report Lists Damage in Alexandria," *Washington Post*, September 7, 1963.

35. "Army Rejects Flood Aid in Four Mile Run Area," *Washington Post*, May 8, 1964.

36. Alexandria City Council Minutes, May 27, 1969, City Hall, Alexandria; Joanne Reckler, "4 Mile Run Plan Endorsed," *Washington Post*, May 30, 1969.

37. Committee on Public Works, *Highway Beautification*, 43.

38. Shabman and Damianos, *Land Prices*.

39. William Chapman, "New GI Bill of Rights is Signed by Johnson," *Washington Post*, March 4, 1966; "No Payoff Penalty on VA," *Washington Post*, September 21, 1968.

40. Taylor, *Race for Profit*; Bonastia; *Knocking on the Door*, 89–135.

41. *A Study of Mortgage Recordings in Alexandria City, Virginia from Sept. 1, 1971 through Aug. 31, 1972* (Washington, DC: Rufus S. Lusk and Son, n.d.), Rufus S. Lusk and Son Papers, George Washington University, Washington, DC.

42. *Northern Virginia Real Estate Guide* (Washington, DC: Rufus S. Lusk & Son, 1969); *Northern Virginia Real Estate Guide* (Washington, DC: Rufus S. Lusk & Son, 1970); *Northern Virginia Real Estate Guide* (Washington, DC: Rufus S. Lusk & Son, 1971); *Northern Virginia Real Estate Guide* (Washington, DC: Rufus S. Lusk & Son, 1972), Rufus S. Lusk and Son Papers, George Washington University, Washington, DC.

43. United States v. Mumford, 630 F.2d 1023 (1980); Jane Seaberry, "Bankrupt Firm's Chairman Is Fined," *Washington Post*, October 21, 1978; "Pair Convicted in Real Estate Fraud Case," *Washington Post*, January 18, 1979.

44. "Fairfax Flood Death Raises Toll to 15," *Washington Post*, June 27, 1972; Special Meeting, August 8, 1972, City Clerk, Docket Minutes, City Council, June 27, 1972–September 6, 1972, AARC.

45. US Army Corps of Engineers, *Four Mile Run Local Flood Protection*.

46. Correspondence-Four Mile Run, Frank Mann (Mayoral) Papers, 1976–79, AARC.

47. Robert F. Levey, "50,000 Exiles in District Area Live with Their Laments and Hopes," *Washington Post*, August 15, 1971; Singer, "Metropolitan Washington," 19.

48. US Bureau of the Census, *U.S. Census of Population and Housing, Census Tracts Washington, D.C.-MD.-VA.*

49. "Luis Vidana," *Virginia Divorce Records, 1918–2014*, accessed September 9, 2023, https://ancestry.com; Committee of the Spanish-Speaking Community of Virginia, *1979 Survey*; Susan Jacoby, "Spanish Pupils Pose Problem," *Washington Post*, September 23, 1967.

50. Committee of the Spanish-Speaking Community of Virginia, *1979 Survey*.

51. Luis Vidaña to Russell E. Owens, November 2, 1977, Frank Mann (Mayoral) Papers, 1976–79, AARC.

52. Nancy Scannell, "Hispanics Seek to Expand Services," *Washington Post*, July 31, 1980.

53. *1978 Annual Report: City of Alexandria Virginia*, AARC; Tang, *Unsettled*, 54–55.

54. Bong Wright, "Welcome House of Alexandria"; Ronald D. White and Jane Freundel, "Indochinese Survivors of Boat Trip Get a Helping Hand," *Washington Post*, August 16, 1979; Kerry Dougherty, "Refugees Adjusting to a Land of Plenty," *Washington Post*, February 14, 1980.

55. Kim Cook, phone interview with author, October 26, 2015.

56. Finnan, Cooperstein, and Wright, *Southeast Asian Refugee Resettlement*, 119–33.

57. *Northern Virginia Real Estate Guide* (Washington, DC: Rufus S. Lusk & Son, 1969), 9379, 9591; "Gilbert L. Weeder" and "Robert M. Logan," *Virginia Marriage Records, 1936–2014*, accessed September 4, 2023, https://ancestry.com; "Gilbert L. Weeder," *Virginia Divorce Records, 1918–2014*, accessed September 4, 2023, https://ancestry.com.

58. Data collected from *Virginia Marriage Records, 1936–2014*, accessed September 18, 2016, https://ancestry.com.

59. "Youth from Kenya Missing in D.C.," *Washington Post*, September 15, 1979.

60. Rhoda Worku, interview by Krystyn R. Moon, May 20, 2015, transcript, Immigrant Alexandria: Past, Present, and Future Project, Office of Historic Alexandria, www.alexandriava .gov/uploadedFiles/historic/info/Immigration/WorkuRhoda1.pdf; "Ethiopian, 28, Shot to Death," *Washington Post*, October 21, 1982; Scott Woehr, phone conversation with the author, August 26, 2016.

61. *The City of Alexandria Annual Report 1986*, AARC.

62. Kim McGuire and Mary Jordan, "Justice Dept. Probes Reports of Racial Tension in Arlandria," *Washington Post*, June 27, 1986; Mary Jordan, "Arlandria Tenants' Frustrations Erupt," *Washington Post*, June 24, 1986.

63. Mary Jordan, "Arlandria's Hispanics Must Move; Redeveloped Area to Lure Professionals," *Washington Post*, June 16, 1986.

64. Repak, *Waiting on Washington*.

65. "Popular Education Process/*Proceso de Educación Popular*," July 12, 1987, United Tenants and Workers Archives, Alexandria, VA.

66. *City of Alexandria 1980 Annual Report*, AARC.

67. Glass, *Introduction to London*; Nelson, *Gentrification and Distressed Cities*.

68. Teaford, *Rough Road to Renaissance*, 249–50; Jossart-Marcetti, *$16 Taco*, 155–59.

69. *1977 Annual Report: City of Alexandria, Virginia*; *City of Alexandria 1980 Annual Report*; *City of Alexandria Annual Report: 1981*; *The City of Alexandria Annual Report: 1982*; and *City of Alexandria 1984 Annual Report*, all in AARC.

70. *The City of Alexandria: Annual Report 1983*; *The City of Alexandria 1984 Annual Report*; and *The City of Alexandria Annual Report: 1985*, all in AARC.

71. Mary Jordan, "Arlandria Developers' Dream, Tenants' Nightmare," *Washington Post*, July 23, 1985; *The City of Alexandria Annual Report: 1985*, AARC.

72. Memorandum, Lionel R. Hope and Carlyle C. Ring Jr. to Mayor and City Council, City Clerk, Docket Minutes, City Council, October 28–November 15, 1986, AARC.

73. Mary Jordan, "Tenant Group Gets $16,000 in Alexandria; Organization's Flier Angers Mayor Moran," *Washington Post*, March 12, 1986; Mary Jordan, "Apartment Purchase Plan Stirs Controversy," *Washington Post*, June 11, 1986; "Magda Alicia Lopez Mijangos," *Virginia Marriage Records, 1936–2014*, accessed September 6, 2023, https://ancestry.com.

74. "Around the Region," *Washington Post*, June 4, 1986; "Around the Region," *Washington Post*, August 22, 1986.

75. Kim McGuire, "Keeping Sunnyside Up Is Goal of Residents," *Washington Post*, June 26, 1986.

76. "Arlandria Inner Group 1986 File," Citizen Assistance, Subject Files, January 1986, AARC.

77. *1940 US Census*, Alexandria, Virginia, ED 101-10, sheet 17B, Jacob T. Hughes head of household, line 68, digital image; and "Jacob T. Hughes," *World War II Registration Card*, accessed September 6, 2023, https://ancestry.com; Sipe and Snyder, *Documentary Study*, 200, 318; *Hill's Alexandria (Virginia) City Directory* (Richmond, VA: Hill Directory Co., 1957), 299.

78. Jon Liss, interview by John Reibling, April 14, 2015, transcript, Immigrant Alexandria: Past, Present, and Future Project, Office of Historic Alexandria, www.alexandriava.gov /uploadedFiles/historic/info/Immigration/LissJon.pdf.

79. "Jacob T. Hughes," *Virginia Death Records, 1912–2014*, accessed September 6, 2023, https://ancestry.com.

80. Virginia Mansfield, "Tenants, Officials Upset by Rent Rise," *Washington Post*, October 9, 1986; Ed Miller, "Tenants: Moving Money Won't Help," *Alexandria Packet*, November 20, 1986; Tony Wassell, "Protests Don't Halt Arlandria Plan," *Alexandria Gazette*, November 17, 1986.

81. "Alexandria Council Approves Relocation Plan for Tenants," *Washington Post*, September 25, 1986.

82. Memorandum, City Manager to Mayor and City Council, Feb 20, 1987, City Clerk, Docket Minutes, City Council, February 27, 1987, AARC.

83. Mary Jordan, "Builder Wins to Move 1,500 Tenants," *Washington Post*, November 16, 1986; Carlyle Murphy, "Alexandria to Buy Low-Income Units," *Washington Post*, November 25, 1986. See reports on the Arlandria Emergency Relocation Fund, City Clerk, Docket Minutes, City Council, February 24, 1987, AARC.

84. Memorandum, Patricia Ticer to Mayor and City Council, September 1, 1987; "Virginia Housing Partnership Fund," August 4, 1987, City Clerk, Docket Minutes, City Council, September 8, 1987; AARC.

85. Mary Jordan, "Alexandria Plan Aims to Add Low-Cost Rental; Parking Rules for Renovations Stiffened," *Washington Post*, January 25, 1987.

86. Public Hearing, November 15, 1986, City Clerk, Docket Minutes, City Council, October 28–November. 15, 1986, AARC.

87. Clavel, *Activists in City Hall*, 50–51.

88. Lawrence (Larry) "Harbottle" Kamakawiwoole, interview by Gary T. Kubota, 2015–16, transcript, Kokua Hawaii Oral History Project, https://scholarspace.manoa.hawaii.edu /server/api/core/bitstreams/9ec80c4e-2c49-4b86-abab-8f4203402439/content.

89. Lawrence Kamakawiwoʻole [Arlandria Community Campaign to Save Our Homes], "Testimony on the Bruce Street Group Apartments Conversion Assistance Plan before the Alexandria City Council," September 13, 1986, City Clerk—Docket Minutes—City Council—July 17–September 13, 1986, AARC.

90. Special Meeting, September 13, 1986, City Clerk, Docket Minutes, City Council, July 17–September 13, 1986, AARC.

91. Carlyle Murphy, "Housing Protests Angers Alexandria Officials," *Washington Post*, February 24, 1986.

92. Mary Jordan, "Alexandria Tenant Move Protested," *Washington Post*, September 24, 1986; "Va. Evictions Protested," *Washington Post*, March 24, 1987.

93. Liss, interview; Sandra Evans, "Alexandria Tenants Protest," *Washington Post*, February 22, 1987; Carlyle Murphy, "Housing Protests Angers Alexandria Officials," *Washington Post*, February 24, 1987.

94. *Rental Housing Affordability*, 2–3.

95. *Rental Housing Affordability*, 24–25.

96. *Rental Housing Affordability*, 117–22.

97. *Rental Housing Affordability*, 16–24, 25–28.

98. Brown v. Artery Organization Inc. 654 F. Suppl. 1106 (D.D.C., 1987).

99. Mary Jordan, "Apartment Purchase Plan Stirs Controversy," *Washington Post*, June 11, 1986.

100. Nancy Lewis, Mary Jordan, "Judge Gives Reprieve to Arlandria Tenants," *Washington Post*, February 25, 1987; Nancy Lewis, "Judge Orders Evictions Barred in Arlandria," *Washington Post*, March 20, 1987; "136 Tenants Ask to Become Plaintiffs," *Washington Post*, April 3, 1987.

101. *City of Alexandria Annual Report: 1987*, AARC.

102. "About Us," Community Lodgings, accessed September 6, 2016, www.community lodgings.org/about-us.

103. Liss, interview.

104. Kim Cook, interview by author, October 26, 2015.

105. Chacko, "Ethiopian Ethos."

106. Stephanie Griffith, "Tensions Plagues Neighborhood as Melting Pot Boils Over," *Washington Post*, November 12, 1990; Carlyle Murphy, "Alexandria Apartment Firebomb Injures 3," *Washington Post*, September 16, 1986. See also Repak, *Waiting on Washington*.

107. Robert F. Howe, "Arlandria: A Neighborhood That's Happily in Transition," *Washington Post*, October 14, 1989.

108. Stephanie Griffith, "Tensions Plagues Neighborhood as Melting Pot Boils Over," *Washington Post*, November 12, 1990.

CHAPTER FIVE

1. Paul Bradley, "Glory Days; Alexandria Remembers Championship Season," *Richmond (VA) Times-Dispatch*, September 28, 2000, accessed May 30, 2022, LexisNexis.com.

2. Hazel Rigby, "Remember the Titans' Reality," *Washington Post*, October 7, 2000.

3. Jennifer Frey, "A Winning Team," *Washington Post*, September 26, 2000.

4. Patrick Welsh, "At T. C. Williams, Separate Fields of Play," *Washington Post*, October 22, 2000.

5. Lindgren, *Preserving the Old Dominion*; Marling, *George Washington Slept Here*; Bruggeman, *Here, George Washington was Born*; Logan, *Historic Capital*.

6. Wiggins, *O Freedom!*; Laurie F. Maffly-Kipp, "Redeeming Southern Memory: The Negro Race History, 1874–1915," in Brundage, *Where These Memories Grow*, 169–90; Dagbovie, "'Most Honorable Mention'"; Fleming, "Impact of Social Movements."

7. Woodson, *Mid-Education of the American Negro*.

8. Meier and Rudwick, *Black History and the Historical Profession*; Goggin, *Carter G. Woodson*; Dagbovie, *Early Black History Movement*.

9. Rogers, "Black Campus Movement"; Wei, *Asian American Movement*; Rhea, *Race Pride*, 94–121; Gordon, *Spirit of 1976*; Burns, *From Storefront to Monument*; Kytle and Roberts, *Denmark Vesey's Garden*; Wilson, *Negro Building*.

10. Gastner, "Valuing 'Others,'" 34.

11. Savage, *Standing Soldiers, Kneeling Slaves*; Blight, *Race and Reunion*; Alderman and Dwyer, "Putting Memory in Its Place"; Fletcher, "Founding Baltimore's Mount Auburn Cemetery and Its Importance to Understanding African American Burial Rights," in Amanik and Fletcher, *Till Death Do Us Part*, 129–56; Jeffrey E. Smith, "Till Death Keeps Us Apart: Segregated Cemeteries and Social Values in St. Louis, Missouri," in Amanik and Fletcher, *Till Death Do Us Part*, 157–82.

12. *Archaeology at Alexandria Freedmen's Cemetery* (brochure).

13. There are several entries in Murray's diaries about attending lectures and debates. Freeman H. M. Murray Diary, March 5, 1884; March 26, 1884; August 20, 1884, box 3, folder 40; and December 22, 1885; January 12, 1886, box 3, folder 43, Freeman H. M. Murray Papers, Howard University. See also Dagbovie, "'Most Honorable Mention,'" 301.

14. Penn, *Afro-American Press and its Editors*, 150–54.

15. This organization was also called the Frederick Douglass Club and the Frederick Douglass Literary Association. "The Frederick Douglass Club," *The Leader* (Alexandria, VA), December 8, 1888; *The Leader* (Alexandria, VA), February 16, 1889; "Alexandria, Va. Department," *The Leader* (Alexandria, VA), December 14, 1889; "Emancipation Celebration in Alexandria," *Washington Post*, December 28, 1889.

16. "Virginia: Alexandria, Va.," *Afro-American* (Baltimore, MD), February 22, 1930; "Alexandria," *Afro-American* (Baltimore, MD), February 21, 1931.

17. "New Curriculum Studied by Virginia's Teachers," *New Journal and Guide* (Norfolk, VA), November 13, 1937; "School News," 7.

18. "Dr. Luther Jackson Talks in Alexandria," *New Journal and Guide* (Norfolk, VA), July 13, 1946.

19. Borome, "Additional Light on Frederick Douglass."

20. "Biographical Sketch: Judge Joseph C. Waddy."

21. "Constance Winsor McLaughlin Green," 89.

22. Green, *Washington: Village and Capital, 1800–1878*. An earlier essay by Oscar Sherwin briefly mentioned Alexandria's role in the internal slave trade. Sherwin, "Trading in Negroes."

23. Lofton, Review of *Washington, Village and Capital, 1800–1878*, by Constance McLaughlin Green.

24. Constance McLaughlin Green later published *The Secret City: A History of Race Relations in the Nation's Capital*, which explicitly looks at the history of Washington's race relations, including the early republican and antebellum periods during which Alexandria was part of the District of Columbia. Green, *Secret City*. For other scholars inspired by Green's research, see Brown, *Free Negroes in the District*; Harrold, *Subversives*; Crothers, "1846 Retrocession of Alexandria," 141–68; Asch and Musgrove, *Chocolate City*.

25. "Teacher Unit Lists Goals for Negroes," *Evening Star* (Washington, DC), October 30, 1963.

26. Dean, "'Who Controls the Past Controls the Future,'" 321–31.

27. Dagbovie, "'Most Honorable Mention,'" 295–324; Givens, *Fugitive Pedagogy*.

28. Carlton Allyn Funn obituary, Legacy.com, accessed September 9, 2023, www.legacy
.com/funeral-homes/obituaries/name/carlton-funn-obituary?pid=159873889&v=batesvi
lle&view=guestbook.

29. Joan Matthews, "Virginia News Section," *Washington Informer*, August 14, 1980; Jay
Mathews, "A Life Aimed at Making Education Come Alive: Carlton Funn Pioneered Teaching
of Black History," *Washington Post*, February 15, 2001.

30. "Citizens Wishing to Address the School Board," Alexandria City Public School Minutes, March 19, 1969, Alexandria City Public School Archives.

31. "Alexandria Cites Ferdinand T. Day," *Department of State Newsletter*, no. 129 (January
1972): 56; Jeanne Theismann, "Alexandria Civil Rights Pioneer Ferdinand Day Dies," *Alexandria Gazette Packet*, January 8, 2015, www.connectionnewspapers.com/news/2015/jan/08
/civil-rights-pioneer-ferdinand-day-dies.

32. "Instruction," Alexandria City Public School Minutes, April 16, 1969, Alexandria City
Public School Archives; Maurice McLaughlin, "Alexandria Black Study Sit-In Ends," *Washington Post*, April 17, 1969.

33. Alexandria City Public School Minutes, June 18, 1969, Alexandria City Public School
Archives.

34. Julie Parker, "14-Year Collection Aids Black Studies," n.d.; "Integrated Team will Con-
duct Summer Black Studies Course," n.d.; "Pilot Black Studies Course Draws Enthusiastic
Response," July 10, 1969; "Summer Black Studies Course Fizzles for Lack of Students," n.d.;
Afro-American Scrapbook, Carlton A. Funn Collection, Alexandria Black History Museum,
Alexandria, VA.

35. Carlton A. Funn, "The Collection Has Been Displayed at the Following Places," n.d.,
box 199701002, Office of Historic Alexandria Papers, AARC.

36. "Black History, Culture Discussed for Police," n.d., clipping; and John B. Holihan,
Chief of Police to Carlton A. Funn, September 29, 1970, box 199701002, Office of Historic
Alexandria Papers, AARC.

37. Jacobson, *Roots Too*.

38. Hazel Garland, "Funn Exhibit to Highlight Pittsburgh's Black History Week," *New
Pittsburgh (PA) Courier*, February 9, 1974.

39. "Achievements, Contributions of Minorities on Display," *New Pittsburgh (PA) Courier*,
December 11, 1976.

40. Afro-American Bicentennial Corporation, *Afro-American History and the National
Park Service*.

41. Sprinkle, *Heritage Conservation in the United States*, 29, 128–29.

42. D. Listokin, B. Listokin, and Lahr, "Contributions of Historic Preservation."

43. McCloskey, "Urban Renewal and Historic Preservation"; Smith, "Saga of Saving and
Reconstructing Ramsay House"; Smith, "Beginnings of Historic Preservation."

44. *Russell Wright Report*.

45. *Alexandria, Virginia HUD Model Neighborhood Grant Application*, Part II (Alexandria,
VA: City Clerk's Office, 1967), 1–2.

46. Planning Commission Minutes, December 12, 1973, AARC; Robert Taylor, "New
Project to Uproot 65 Families," *The Courier* (Pittsburgh, PA), January 19, 1952, William C.

Cleveland (Vice Mayoral) Papers, 1989–2002, AARC; Eudora Lyles, interview by unknown person, November 18, 1999, transcript, Oral History Interviews with Alexandria Seniors, 1998–99, Office of Historic Alexandria Papers, AARC. For a more thorough discussion on the creation of the Parker-Gray Historic District, see Miliaras, "Parker-Gray District."

47. Hammer, Siler, George Associates, *NEA Study Report to the City of Alexandria, Virginia*, December 31, 1975, box 199200101, Department of Planning and Zoning, AARC.

48. Lawrence Jointer to Clifford H. Rausch Jr., August 5, 1974; and Clifford H. Rausch Jr. to Lawrence Jointer, September 16, 1974, box 199200101, Department of Planning and Zoning, AARC (emphasis in original).

49. Hammer, Siler, George Associates, *NEA Study Report to the City of Alexandria*.

50. Hammer, Siler, George Associates, *NEA Study Report to the City of Alexandria*.

51. Blackshear Res. Org. v. Housing Auth. of City of Austin. 347 F. Supp. 1138 (W.D. Tex. 1972); Otero v. New York City Housing Authority. 484 F.2d 1122. (US App. 1973); Crow v. Brown. 332 F. Supp. 382 (N.D. Ga. 1971).

52. Memo, J. Howard Middleton Jr. and Burton B. Hanbury Jr. to Douglas Harman, May 13, 1976, box 199200101, Department of Planning and Zoning, AARC.

53. Patricia Camp, "Residents Oppose Plan for House Sales in Old Town Area," *Washington Post*, July 15, 1976.

54. "Low-Income Housing to Blend with Historic," *Washington Post*, September 13, 1975.

55. "Alexandria Votes New Housing Plan," *Washington Post*, September 14, 1972; Doug Brown, "Alexandria Clears Renewal for Dip," *Washington Post*, January 24, 1975; "After 8 Years, 1st Phase of the Dip Renewal to Open," *Washington Post*, September 1, 1976.

56. "Alexandria Approves 'Dip' Plan," *Washington Post*, June 3, 1970.

57. Wallace, Cain, and Rowe, *I Once was Young*; "Alfred Street Baptist Church," 2003, National Register of Historic Places and National Historic Landmarks Program Records, 2013–17, RG 79: Records of the National Park Service, NARA-MD.

58. Alice Digilio, "Alfred Street Church's age is less than 100," *Washington Post*, February 17, 1977; Patricia Camp Washington, "Alexandria to Demolish Old Buildings," *Washington Post*, March 23, 1977.

59. "Petition and Documented Evidence to Prevent the Demolition of the Old Alfred Street Baptist Church," n.d., box 199001004, Office of Housing Papers, AARC.

60. "Roger C. Anderson," *World War II Draft Cards, 1940–1947*, accessed September 12, 2023, https://ancestry.com; "Roger C. Anderson," Find a Grave, accessed September 12, 2023, www.findagrave.com/memorial/287041/roger-c-anderson; *Hill's Alexandria City Directory* (1959), 21.

61. Afro-American Institute for Historic Preservation and Community Development, "Alfred Street Baptist Church," in *A Study of Historic Sites*, 86–94.

62. Madeleine Lewis, "Getting Digs In," *Washington Post*, June 26, 1979; Suzanne Corber, "Digging Deep into the Past," *Washington Post*, November 3, 1978; Cressey, "An Enduring Afro-American Neighborhood," 10.

63. Roger Davis, "Alexandria City Council Hearing," November 18, 1980, Alfred Street Baptist Church, 1977–80, box 199001004, Office of Housing Papers, AARC.

64. Memorandum, Suzanne Schell et al. to Douglas Harman, November 11, 1980, box 199001004, Office of Housing Papers, AARC.

65. "Nelson Greene Sr.," Living Legends of Alexandria, accessed September 12, 2023, https://alexandrialegends.org/nelson-greene-sr.

66. City Council Meeting Transcript, December 12, 1980, box 199001004, Office of Housing Papers, AARC.

67. Virginia Mansfield, "Alexandria Church Lets out its Seams," Washington Post, April 27, 1989.

68. Stephen J. Lynton, "Metro Extension Opens with Flourish," Washington Post, December 18, 1983.

69. Miliaras, "Parker-Gray District," 6; Michael Martinez, "Growing Alexandria Old Town Could Uproot Black Community," Washington Post, December 26, 1983; Petition, Northwest Old Town Citizens Association, January 30, 1984, Parker-Gray Historic District Papers, Special Collections, KWBBL.

70. Barbara J. Walker to Charles E. Beatley, Mayor, April 6, 1984, Parker-Gray Historic District Papers, Special Collections, KWBBL.

71. Eudora Lyles, Roger Anderson, and John Stanton to Mayor and City Council, June 4, 1984; and Sixteenth Census Tract Crisis Committee to Mayor and City Council, June 14, 1984, Inner City Civic Association Memo, ca. June 17–23, 1984, Parker-Gray Historic District Papers, Special Collections, KWBBL.

72. Michael Martinez, "Residents Submit Preservation Plan," Washington Post, June 17, 1984; Leslie Marshall and Leah Y. Latimer, "State Taking Over Sheriff Probe," Washington Post, June 27, 1984.

73. Robert L. Crabill to Eudora Lyles, August 10, 1984; Robert L. Crabill to Eudora Lyles, September 4, 1984, Parker-Gray Historic District Papers, Special Collections, KWBBL.

74. US Department of Housing and Urban Development, "Final Investigative Report."

75. Carlyle Murphy, "HUD Raps Parker-Gray Decision," Washington Post, January 15, 1988; Carlyle Murphy, "Alexandria Dispute Unresolved," Washington Post, January 12, 1988.

76. Mary Jordan, "Alexandria Blacks File Complaint," Washington Post, July 6, 1985; Mary Jordan, "HUD Clears Alexandria in Housing Bias Complaint," Washington Post, January 8, 1986; Mary Jordan, "Alexandria Threatening Black Area," Washington Post, November 3, 1986; Murphy, "HUD Raps Parker-Gray Decision."

77. Dwyer and Alderman, Civil Rights Memorials; Burns, From Storefront to Monument; Fleming, "Impact of Social Movements," 44–73; Kytle and Roberts, Denmark Vesey's Garden; R. Smith, "Philip N. J. Wythe's Headstone"; Leib, "Tale of Two Civil War Statues"; Wessler, "Developers Found Graves in the Virginia Woods."

78. [Welcome letter], James E. Henson Sr., August 5, 1976, in Memories of Parker-Gray School 1920–65 Program, box 02120604, Frank Mann (Mayoral) Papers, 1976–79, AARC; Cliff Jones, "In Nineteenth-Century Alexandria Black Businessmen Played a Role," Alexandria Gazette Packet, July 16, 1998.

79. Planning Commission Minutes, March 1, 1977, AARC.

80. "Museum Resources of Alexandria," April 1979, box 02120604, Frank Mann (Mayoral) Papers, 1976–79, AARC; H. Bradford Fish, "Ex-Slave Market for Sale Again in Expanding Old Town Alexandria," Washington Post, November 8, 1979; Memorandum, Douglas Harman to Mayor and City Council, November 13, 1980, box 199001004, Office of Housing Papers, AARC.

Notes to Chapter Five

81. Mary Battiata, "Parker-Gray Name Saved," *Washington Post*, December 9, 1981; Michel Marriott, "Black Heritage in Alexandria: Groups Work to Organize City Black," *Washington Post*, January 5, 1983.

82. Burns, *From Storefront to Monument*, 4.

83. Michel Marriott, "Black Heritage in Alexandria: Groups Work to Organize City Black," *Washington Post*, January 5, 1983; Virginia Mansfield, "Alexandria Remembers 'Miss Annie,'" *Washington Post*, May 11, 1989.

84. Deetz, *In Small Things Forgotten*, 187–211.

85. Terrie, "Social History of the 500 Block."

86. "Alexandria Afro-American Neighborhood Archaeology Project," ca. 1981, box 02060401, Office of Historic Alexandria Papers, AARC.

87. "Loaned for Exhibit at Opening of the Alexandria Society for Preservation of Black Heritage," June 23, 1983, box 3, Alexandria Archaeology Papers, AARC.

88. Artemel, Crowell, and Parker, *Alexandria Slave Pen*.

89. Afro-American Institute for Historic Preservation and Community Development, *Study of Historic Sites*; "Black Historic Sites in the Metropolitan-Washington Region," n.d., box 200702102, Office of Historic Alexandria Papers, AARC.

90. Walter A. Scheiber to Charles E. Beatley, December 14, 1983, box 200702102, Office of Historic Alexandria Papers, AARC.

91. *Metropolitan Washington Council of Governments vs. The Afro-American Institute*, 1987, box 200702102, Office of Historic Alexandria Papers, AARC.

92. Memo and Supporting Documents, Vola Lawson to Mayor and City Council, February 13, 1987, Docket Minutes, February 4–March 10, 1987, box 02120504, City Clerk Department, AARC.

93. Memo and Supporting Documents, Lawson to Mayor and City Council, February 13, 1987.

94. Anderson, *African American Heritage Park*.

95. Norman Gomlak, "City, Blacks Seek to Save Graveyard," *Alexandria Journal*, August 3, 1988.

96. Ben Brenman to Lionel Hope March 3, 1988, Alexandria Archaeological Commission Files, Alexandria Archaeology; *1950 US Census*, Maple Shade, Burlington County, New Jersey, ED 3-70, sheet 34, Bernard Brenman head of household, line 1, digital image, accessed September 13, 2023, https://ancestry.com; House Joint Resolution No. 383, February 19, 1998, accessed September 13, 2023, https://lis.virginia.gov/cgi-bin/legp604.exe?981+ful+HJ383ER+pdf.

97. "Confederate Soldier 1979," box 19961301, Charles E. Beatley (Mayoral) Papers, 1979–84, AARC.

98. In June 2020, the United Daughters of the Confederacy obtained a permit to remove *Appomattox* to an undisclosed location. Mary Jordan, "Wreck Toppled Old Town Bone of Contention," *Washington Post*, August 21, 1988; Kent Jenkins Jr., "Toppling of Alexandria Confederate Memorial Reopens Old Wounds," *Washington Post*, August 23, 1988; Carlyle Murphy, "Alexandria to Restore its Confederate Statue," *Washington Post*, October 12, 1988.

99. Memorandum, James Moran to City Council, October 7, 1988, box 200702102, Office of Historic Alexandria Papers, AARC.

100. Black Baptist Cemetery Work Group, "Report of the Black Baptist Cemetery Work Group," February 1, 1989, Alexandria Archaeological Commission Files, Alexandria Archaeology (emphasis in original).

101. Sandra Evans, "Park Pays Homage to Alexandria's Past: Area's African American History is Memorialized at a New Nine-Acre Heritage Center," *Washington Post*, July 6, 1995.

102. Pippenger, *Alexandria, Virginia Death Records*; T. Michael Miller, "Historical News Flash: Freedmen and Contraband Burial Ground Identified in Alexandria, Virginia," January 11, 1991, box 02160402, Alexandria Archaeology Papers, AARC.

103. *Woodrow Wilson Bridge Improvement Study*; Alice Reid, "Cemetery Prompts Questions on Bridge," *Washington Post*, January 30, 1997.

104. Obituary for Lillie Finklea, Phillip Bell Sr. and Winona Morrissette-Johnson, P.A. Funeral Services, accessed September 30, 2023, www.bmjfuneralservice.com/obituaries/Lillie -Finklea/#!/Obituary; "Lillie Finklea," US High School Yearbooks, 1900–2016, accessed September 30, 2023, https://ancestry.com; *Telephone Directory for the Department of State . . .* (Washington, DC: Government Printing Office, Fall 1979), 146.

105. Friends of Freedmen's Cemetery Incorporation Papers, 1997; and "Freedmen's Cemetery Wreath Laying," *Points of Interest*, n.d., both in box 02160402, Alexandria Archaeology Papers, AARC; [Newspaper clippings], box 02120703, William C. Cleveland (Vice Mayoral) Papers, AARC.

106. Memorandum, Lillie Finklea and Louise Massoud to City Clerk and Clerk Council, May 29, 1997, box 02120703, William C. Cleveland (Vice Mayoral) Papers, AARC.

107. Senate Joint Resolution No. 59, accessed October 8, 2022, https://lis.virginia.gov/cgi -bin/legp604.exe?981+ful+SJ59ER+pdf; Susan Clarke Schaar to Vola Lawson, April 7, 1998, box 02120703, William C. Cleveland (Vice Mayoral) Papers, AARC.

108. Slaughter, Miller, and Janowitz, *Archaeological Investigations*.

109. *Freedmen's Cemetery* (brochure). See also The Friends of Freedmen's Cemetery website, accessed October 10, 2022, www.freedmenscemetery.org/index.shtml.

110. Roots of Remembrance Press Release, April 14, 1999; and "Roots to Remembrance: An Exhibit," *Alexandria Gazette Packet*, July 1, 1999, both in box 02160402, Alexandria Archaeology Papers, AARC; "Contrabands and Freedmen Cemetery," National Register of Historic Places Registration form, listed on August 15, 2015, Virginia Department of Historic Resources, www.dhr.virginia.gov/wp-content/uploads/2018/04/100-1021-1085_Contrabands_and _Freedmen_Cemetery_2012_NRHP_FINAL.pdf.

111. Stephen Hein, "Reviving Lost History," *Alexandria Journal*, box 02160402, Alexandria Archaeology Papers, AARC.

112. Mike Allen, "Alexandria Votes to File Suit, Seeking Smaller Replacement," *Washington Post*, January 28, 1998; Toni Locy, "Opponents See 12-Lane Path to Destruction," *Washington Post*, April 26, 1998.

113. City of Alexandria v. Slater 46F. Suppl.2d 35 (D.D.C. 1999); City of Alexandria v. Slater, 1998 F.3d 862 (A.D.C. 1999).

114. Memo, Richard J. Baier to Mayor and City Council, November 12, 2002, box 02120703, William C. Cleveland (Vice Mayoral) Papers, AARC.

115. Trischmann, *"Faithful Contrabands."*

1. "Atlantic Research Forms Division Here for Ordnance Work," *Washington Post*, February 23, 1966; "ARC Officials Expect Year of Records," *Washington Post*, July 2, 1966.

2. Ira Robinson, email to author, June 6, 2022; October 24, 2022.

3. Ira Robinson, email to author, June 6, 2022.

4. Mary Ann Barton, "Alexandria: One of the Best Places to Live, Also One of the Most Expensive," *Patch*, October 12, 2015, accessed September 27, 2022, https://patch.com/virginia /delray; Jeff Clabaugh, "Alexandria's Housing Market Now More Expensive Than Arlington," *WTOP News*, November 25, 2019, accessed September 27, 2022, https://wtop.com. See Wiese, *Places of Their Own*, 255–92.

5. Ira Robinson, email to author, June 6, 2022.

BIBLIOGRAPHY

PRIMARY SOURCES

Manuscript and Archival Collections

Alexandria, VA
    Alexandria Archaeology
        Alexandria Archaeological Commission Files
    Alexandria Archives and Records Center
        Alexandria Archaeology Papers
        Alexandria City Council, Dockets and Minutes
        Building Permits
        Charles E. Beatley Jr. (Mayoral) Papers, 1979–84
        Citizen Assistance—Subject Files
        City of Alexandria Annual Reports
        Davis-Ruffner Files
        Department of Planning and Zoning Papers
        Frank Mann (Mayoral) Papers, 1976–79
        Office of Historic Alexandria Papers
        Office of Housing Papers
        Planning Commission Minutes
        Police Department Records
        William C. Cleveland (Vice Mayoral) Papers, 1989–2002
    Alexandria Black History Museum
        Carlton A. Funn Collection
    Alexandria City Public Schools Archives
    Alexandria Courthouse
        Land Deed Office

Fort Ward Park and Museum, Dorothy Starr Civil War Research Library
Fort Ward Park and Museum Archive
Kate Waller Barrett Branch Library, Special Collections
Alexandria Redevelopment and Housing Authority Papers
City Planning Department, Alexandria City Records
Gadsby Residential Urban Renewal Project, 1962–65 Papers
Henry Whittington Diary, 1861–65
Historic Alexandria Foundation Papers
League of Women Voters Records
Parker-Gray Historic District Papers
Vertical Files—Mayors
Office of Historic Alexandria
Alexandria Legacies-Living Legends Oral History Project
Immigrant Alexandria: Past, Present, and Future Oral History Project
Office of Real Estate Assessment
Real Estate Assessments
United Tenants and Workers Archives
Arlington County, VA
Arlington County Courthouse
Land Deed Office
Will Books
Cambridge, MA
Harvard University, Houghton Library
Howe Family Papers
College Park, MD
National Archives and Records Administration
RG 30: Office of Public Records
RG 31: Records of the Federal Housing Administration
RG 79: Records of the National Park Service
RG 196: Records of the Public Housing Administration
Durham, NC
David M. Rubenstein Rare Book and Manuscript Library, Duke University
William Mahone Papers
Fairfax, VA
Fairfax County Circuit Court Historic Records Center
Davis-Ruffner Files
Land Deed Office
Leesburg, VA
Loudoun County Courthouse
Alexandria Annexation Collection, 1929–30
Richmond, VA
Library of Virginia
Virginia Memory: Chancery Records Index
Washington, DC
Charles Sumner School Museum and Archives

District of Columbia Public School Archives
George Washington University
    Rufus S. Lusk and Son Papers
Howard University
    Freeman H. M. Murray Papers
Library of Congress, Manuscript Division
    James Morrison MacKaye Papers
National Archives and Records Administration
    RG 92: Records of the Office of the Quartermaster General
    RG 94: Adjutant General's Office, 1780s–1917
    RG 105: Records of the Bureau of Refugees, Freedmen,
        and Abandoned Lands, Virginia, 1865–72
    RG 217: Southern Claims Commission Records
    RG 393: Offices of Military Governors, Alexandria, 1862–65

Online Databases

1850–1950 U.S. Censuses. https://ancestry.com
U.S. City Directories, 1822–1995. https://ancestry.com
U.S. High School Yearbooks, 1900–2016. https://ancestry.com
U.S. Southern Claims Commission Allowed Claims, 1871–1880. https://ancestry.com
Virginia Birth Registers, 1912–2015. https://ancestry.com
Virginia Death Records, 1912–2014. https://ancestry.com
Virginia Deaths and Burials Index, 1853–1917. https://ancestry.com
Virginia Divorce Records, 1918–2014. https://ancestry.com
Virginia Select Marriages, 1785–1940. https://ancestry.com
Voting Viva Voce. Institute for Advanced Technology in the Humanities,
    University of Virginia. 2025. https://sociallogic.iath.virginia.edu
World War I Draft Cards, 1917–1918. https://ancestry.com
World War II Draft Cards, 1940–1947. https://ancestry.com

Newspapers and Periodicals

Afro-American (Baltimore, MD)
Alexandria Gazette
Alexandria Journal
American Freedmen (New York)
Baltimore (MD) Sun
Chicago Defender
Colored American (Washington, DC)
The Courier (Pittsburgh, PA)
Evening Star (Washington, DC)
The Leader (Alexandria, VA)

The Liberator (Boston, MA)
National Anti-Slavery Standard
    (New York and Philadelphia)
National Freedmen (New York)
National Republican (Washington, DC)
New Journal and Guide (Norfolk, VA)
New National Era (Washington, DC)
New Pittsburgh (PA) Courier
Northern Virginia Sun
    (Arlington County)

Richmond (VA) Planet
Richmond (VA) Times-Dispatch
Suburban Citizen (Washington, DC)
Washington Afro-American

Washington Informer
Washington Post
Washington Times
Worcester (MA) Daily Spy

Published Primary Sources

Address of Loyal Virginians to Their Friends in the North. Alexandria, VA, June 30, 1865.

Advisory Council on Historic Preservation. *The Contribution of Historic Preservation to Urban Revitalization.* Washington, DC: Government Printing Office, 1979.

Afro-American Bicentennial Corporation. *Afro-American History and the National Park Service.* Washington, DC: US Department of the Interior, 1972.

Afro-American Institute for Historic Preservation and Community Development. *A Study of Historic Sites in the Metropolitan Washington Regions of Northern Virginia and Southern Maryland.* Washington, DC: The Institute, 1978.

"Alexandria, Virginia Part II." Alexandria, VA: City Clerk's Office, 1967.

Anderson, Adrian D. *The African American Heritage Park, Alexandria, Virginia.* Minneapolis: Tellus Consultants, 1992.

Andrews, Marietta Minnigerode. *My Studio Window: Sketches of the Pageant of Washington Life.* New York: E. P. Dutton, 1928.

Archaeology at Alexandria Freedmen's Cemetery: A Memorial in Progress (brochure). Accessed August 8, 2022. https://media.alexandriava.gov/docs-archives/historic/info/archaeology /contrabandscemeteryarchaeologybrochure.pdf.

Artemel, Janice G., Elizabeth A. Crowell, and Jeff Parker. *The Alexandria Slave Pen: The Archaeology of Urban Captivity.* Washington, DC: Engineering-Science, 1987.

Ballou v. Kemp. 92 F. 2d 556 (DC Cir. 1937).

Barnwell, Eugene L., and Margaret Mullen, comp. *City of Alexandria, Virginia: Home Town of George Washington and Robert E. Lee.* Alexandria, VA: City of Alexandria, 1960.

"Biographical Sketch: Judge Joseph C. Waddy." *Negro History Bulletin* 26, no. 3 (December 1962): 110, 129.

Blackshear Res. Org. v. Housing Auth. of City of Austin, 347 F. Supp. 1138 (W.D. Tex. 1972).

Bong Wright, Jackie. "The Welcome House of Alexandria: An Experiment in Refugee Resettlement." Unpublished manuscript. December 2015.

Borome, Joseph A. "Additional Light on Frederick Douglass." *Journal of Negro History* 38, no. 2 (April 1953): 216–24.

Brown v. Artery Organization Inc. 654 F. Supp. 1106 (D.D.C., 1987).

Catalogue of Howard University for 1909–1910. Washington, DC: Howard University, 1910.

Catalogue of Officers and Students from March 1881 to March 1882. Washington, DC: Herbert A. Gibbs Printer, 1882.

Catalogue of Officers and Students from March 1883 to March 1884. Washington, DC: Johnson and Blackwell Printer, 1884.

Catalogue of Officers and Students from March 1887 to March 1888. Washington, DC: R. Beresford Printer, 1888.

Catalogue of the Hampton Normal and Agricultural Institute, Hampton, Virginia, 1872–73. Hampton, VA: Normal School Press, 1873.

Catalogue of the Officers and Students of Howard University for the Years 1868–1869. Washington, DC: Judd and Detweiler Printers, 1869.

City of Alexandria Map. 1934. Geography and Map Division, Library of Congress, Washington, DC.

City of Alexandria v. Slater. 46F. Suppl.2d 35 (D.D.C. 1999).

City of Alexandria v. Slater. 1998 F.3d 862 (A.D.C. 1999).

Code of the City of Alexandria, Virginia. Charlottesville, VA: Michie City Publications, 1963.

Code of Virginia as Amended to Adjournment of General Assembly. Charlottesville, VA: Michie Company, 1930.

Committee of the Spanish-Speaking Community of Virginia. *1979 Survey of the Spanish-Speaking Community of the State of Virginia: Technical Documentation: Analysis and General Recommendations.* Annandale, VA: The Committee, 1979.

Committee on Banking, Finance, and Urban Affairs. *Housing Needs of Hispanics: Hearing before the Subcommittee on Housing and Community Development of the Committee on Banking, Finance and Urban Affairs.* House of Representatives. Ninety-Ninth Congress. First Session. September 18, 1985, serial no. 99-38. Washington, DC: Government Printing Office, 1985.

Committee on Public Works. *Highway Beautification. Hearings before the Subcommittee on Public Works.* US Senate. Ninety-First Congress. First Session. June 17–18, 1969, serial no. 91-14. Washington, DC: Government Printing Office, 1969.

Commonwealth of Virginia, General Assembly. *Acts and Joint Resolutions of the General Assembly of the Commonwealth of Virginia during the Session of 1893–1894.* Richmond, VA: J. H. O'Bannon, Superintendent of Public Printing, 1894.

———. *Acts and Joint Resolutions of the General Assembly of the State of Virginia during the Session of 1901–1902.* Richmond, VA: J. H. O'Bannon, Superintendent of Public Printing, 1902.

Community Lodgings. Accessed September 6, 2016. www.communitylodgings.org.

"Constance Winsor McLaughlin Green." In *The Pulitzer Prize Archive: A History and Anthology of Award-Winning Materials in Journalism, Letters, and Arts.* Part F: *Documentation.* Edited by Heinz-Dietrich Fischer. Vol. 16. Munich: K. G. Saur, 2002.

Convention of the Colored People of Virginia. *Liberty, and Equality before the Law: Proceedings of the Convention of the Colored People of VA, Held in the City of Alexandria, Aug. 2, 3, 4, 5, 1865.* Alexandria, VA: Cowing and Gillis, 1865.

Cressey, Pamela J. "An Enduring Afro-American Neighborhood: An Archaeological Perspective from Alexandria, Virginia." *Black Heritage* 20, no. 1 (September–October 1980): 1–10.

Crow v. Brown. 332 F. Supp. 382 (N.D. Ga. 1971).

Executive Documents Printed by the Order of the House of Representatives during the Second Session of the Forty-First Congress, 1869–70. Vol. 7, no. 188. Washington, DC: Government Printing Office, 1870.

Freedmen's Cemetery (brochure). 2000. www.freedmenscemetery.org/brochure/brochure.pdf.

Friends of the Freedmen's Cemetery. "Alexandria Real and Personal Property Taxes Paid by African Americans, 1865." Transcript. Accessed August 2017. www.freedmenscemetery .org/resources/documents/1865taxes.shtml.

Gadsby Commercial Urban Renewal Project Phase No. 1, Alexandria, Virginia. Alexandria, VA: Office of Urban Renewal, 1963.

Griffis, Robert J. *Listing of Virginia's Prime Defense Contractors Ranked by Contract Amount: 1991.* Richmond, VA: Virginia Employment Commission in Conjunction with the Inter-Agency Task Force on Defense Conversion and Economic Adjustment, 1993.

Harper, Ellen R. *Real Property Survey and Low-Income Housing Area Survey, Alexandria, Virginia.* 2 vols. Alexandria, VA: Works Projects Administration, 1939.

Harris, Harrison L. *Harris' Masonic Text-Book: A Concise Historical Sketch of Masonry.* Petersburg, VA: The Masonic Visitor Company, 1902.

Hayden, René, Anthony E. Kaye, Kate Masur, Steven F. Miller, Susan E. O'Donovan, and Leslie S. Rowland, eds. *Freedom: A Documentary History of Emancipation, 1861–1867.* Series 1, Vol. 2: *The Wartime Genesis of Free Labor: The Upper South.* Chapel Hill: University of North Carolina Press, 2013.

Hayden, René, Anthony E. Kaye, Kate Masur, Steven F. Miller, Susan E. O'Donovan, Leslie S. Rowland, and Stephen A. West, eds. *Freedom: A Documentary History of Emancipation, 1861–1867.* Series 3, Vol. 2: *Land and Labor, 1866–1867.* Chapel Hill: University of North Carolina Press, 2013.

Hearings before the United States Commission on Civil Rights: Housing in Washington. Washington, DC: Government Printing Office, 1962.

Hill v. School Board. 282 F. 2d 473 (4th Cir. 1960).

"History." Hopkins House. Accessed September 26, 2023. www.hopkinshouse.org/about /history.

Kincholow v. Peoples Rapid Transit Co. 88 F. 2d 764 (DC Cir. 1936).

Lamb, Daniel Smith, comp. and ed. *Howard University Medical Department, Washington D.C.: A Historical Biographical, and Statistical Souvenir.* Washington, DC: R. Beresford, 1900.

Lofton, Williston H. Review of *Washington, Village and Capital, 1800–1878,* by Constance McLaughlin Green. *Journal of Negro History* 48, no. 3 (July 1963): 225–26.

The Mudtown Project: Urban Renewal Goes to Work . . . to Improve Our City. Alexandria, VA: Office of Urban Renewal, 1963.

Murray, Florence. *The Negro Handbook.* New York: Wendell Malliet, 1942.

National Freedman's Relief Association of the District of Columbia. *First Annual Report.* Washington, DC: M'Gill and Witherow, 1863.

Neighborhood Analysis: Alexandria, Virginia. Alexandria, VA: Urban Renewal Office, 1966.

New Negro Alliance v. Sanitary Grocery Co., 303 U.S. 552 (1938).

Northern Virginia Real Estate Guide. Washington, DC: Rufus S. Lusk and Son, 1971.

O'Conner, Ellen M. *Myrtilla Miner: A Memoir.* New York: Arno Press, 1969.

Official Register of the United States, Containing a List of Officers and Employees in the Civil, Military, and Naval Service. Vol. 1. Washington, DC: Government Printing Office, 1905.

Official Register of the United States, Containing a List of Officers and Employés in the Civil, Military, and Naval Service of the First of July 1883. 2 vols. Washington, DC: Government Printing Office, 1884.

Otero v. New York City Housing Authority. 484 F.2d 1122. (US App. 1973).

Penn, Irvine Garland. *The Afro-American Press and Its Editors.* Springfield, MA: Willey, 1891.

Pippenger, Wesley E. *Alexandria, Virginia Death Records, 1863–1868 (The Gladwin Record) and 1869–1896.* Westminster, MD: Fine Line Publications, 1995.

Bibliography

Prince Street Shopping Center. Alexandria, VA: Alexandria Redevelopment and Housing Authority 1953.

Proposed Comprehensive Plan for Alexandria, Virginia, 1970–1980. Alexandria, VA: Planning Advisory Committee, January 1972.

Railroad Company v. Brown. 84 US 445 (1873).

Rental Housing Affordability for Low-And Moderate-Income People. Hearing before the Subcommittee on Housing and Community Development of the Committee on Banking, Finance and Urban Affairs. House of Representatives. First Session. February 24, 1987. Serial No. 100-4. Washington, DC: US Government Printing Office, 1987.

Report of Alexandria Community Development Committee. Alexandria, VA: Newell-Cole, 1958.

Report to the Executive Committee of New England Yearly Meeting of Friends upon the Conditions and Needs of the Freed People of Color in Washington and Virginia. New Bedford, MA: E. Anthony and Sons, 1864. https://archive.org/details/reporttoexecutivoosoci/page/n1/mode/2up.

The Russell Wright Report. Alexandria, VA: Department of Planning and Regional Affairs, 1970.

"School News." *Negro History Bulletin* 1, no. 5 (February 1938): 7.

Senate Joint Resolution No. 59. Accessed October 8, 2022. https://lis.virginia.gov/cgi-bin/legp604.exe?981+ful+SJ59ER+pdf.

Shabman, Leonard A., and Demetrios Damianos. *Land Prices in Flood Hazard Areas: Applying Methods of Land Value Analysis.* Blacksburg, VA: Virginia Water Resources Center, Virginia Institute and State University, 1976.

Sherwin, Oscar. "Trading in Negroes." *Negro History Bulletin* 8, no. 7 (April 1945): 160–64.

Slaughter, Bernard W., George L. Miller, and Meta Janowitz. *Archaeological Investigations to Define the Boundaries of Freedmen's Cemetery (44AX0179), within the Property Owned by the Virginia Department of Transportation.* Alexandria, VA: The Potomac Crossing Consultants, 2001.

Supplement Report: U.S. Army Reserve Training Headquarters: Survey and Evaluation. Baltimore, MD: US Department of Transportation Federal Highway Administration, Office of Planning and Program Development, 1996.

Telephone Directory for the Department of State. Washington, DC: Government Printing Office, Fall 1979.

Terrie, Philip. "A Social History of the 500 Block, King Street in Alexandria, Virginia." Alexandria, VA: Alexandria Archaeological Research Center, 1979.

Thomas, Reverend William N. "A Study and History of the Zion Baptist Church Alexandria, Virginia." Alexandria, VA: Alexandria Archaeology, n.d.

The Town of Potomac: 1924 Year Book and Directory. Arlington County, VA, 1924.

"Transcription of the Proclamation." National Archives Online Exhibits. Accessed February 22, 2022. www.archives.gov/exhibits/featured-documents/emancipation-proclamation/transcript.html.

United States v. Mumford, 630 F.2d 1023 (1980).

US Army Corps of Engineers, *Four Mile Run Local Flood Protection, Alexandria/Arlington Counties: Environmental Impact Statement, 1971.* Accessed July 6, 2022. https://catalog.hathitrust.org/Record/100938072.

US Bureau of the Census. *U.S. Census of Population and Housing, Census Tracts Washington, D.C.-MD.-VA.* Washington, DC: Government Printing Office, 1962.

US Department of Housing and Urban Development. "Final Investigative Report: 16th Census Tract Crisis Committee vs. City of Alexandria 03-85-0305-1." Washington, DC: HUD, 1986.

US Office of Education. *History of Schools for the Colored Population*. 1871. Reprint, New York: Arno Press, 1969.

Va. Code §28800-288oll (1930).

Vautier, John D. *History of the 88th Pennsylvania Volunteers in the War for the Union, 1861–1865*. Philadelphia: J. B. Lippincott, 1894.

West Bros Brick Co. v. Alexandria. 169 Va. 271 (1937).

Wilbur, Julia A. Diary, 1862–1865. Transcript. Office of Historic Alexandria. Accessed August 15, 2017. www.alexandriava.gov/uploadedFiles/historic/info/civilwar /JuliaWilburDiary1860to1866.pdf.

Woodrow Wilson Bridge Improvement Study, I-95 to MD Route 210, Alexandria County and Fairfax County (VA), Prince George's County (MD), DC: Environmental Impact Statement. Supplemental Draft Environmental Impact Statement, Section 4(f) Evaluation (January 1996), 3–82. https://catalog.hathitrust.org/Record/100980210.

Yellin, Jean Fagan, ed. *The Harriet Jacobs Family Papers*. 2 vols. Chapel Hill: University of North Carolina Press, 2008.

SECONDARY SOURCES

"African-American Civilians and Soldiers Treated at Claremont Smallpox Hospital, Fairfax County, Virginia, 1862–1865." Friends of Freedmen's Cemetery. Accessed April 15, 2013. www.freedmenscemetery.org/resources/documents/claremont.pdf.

Alderman, Derek H., and Owen J. Dwyer. "Putting Memory in Its Place: The Politics of Commemoration in the American South." In *WorldMinds: Geographical Perspectives on 100 Problems*, edited by Donald G. Janelle, Barney Warf, and Kathy Hansen, 55–60. Dordrecht, Netherlands: Springer, 2004.

Alexandria Archaeology. "Harriet Williams Independent Enslaved Woman (112–114 South St. Asaph Street)." Accessed July 19, 2017. www.alexandriava.gov/uploadedFiles/historic /info/archaeology/500BlockKingHarrietWilliams.pdf.

Amanik, Allan, and Kami Fletcher, eds. *Till Death Do Us Part: American Ethnic Cemeteries as Borders Uncrossed*. Oxford: University Press of Mississippi 2020.

Anderson, James D. *The Education of Blacks in the South, 1860–1935*. Chapel Hill: University of North Carolina Press, 1988.

Ashton, Susanna. "Du Bois's *Horizon*: Documenting Movements of the Color Line." *MELUS* 26, no. 4 (Winter 2001): 3–23.

Ayers, Edward. *The Thin Light of Freedom: The Civil War and Emancipation in the Heart of America*. New York: W. W. Norton, 2017.

Batts Morrow, Diane. *Persons of Color and Religious at the Same Time: The Oblate Sisters of Providence 1828–1860*. Chapel Hill: University of North Carolina Press, 2002.

Bayor, Ronald H. *Race and the Shaping of Twentieth-Century Atlanta*. Chapel Hill: University of North Carolina Press, 1996.

Bibliography

Bernstein, Peter. *The Life and Times of George Lewis Seaton*. Alexandria, VA: Alexandria Archaeology Publications, 2003.

Blight, David W. *Race and Reunion: The Civil War in American Memory*. Cambridge, MA: The Belknap Press of Harvard University Press, 2001.

Blomberg, Belinda. *The Formation of Free Black Communities in Nineteenth Century Alexandria, Virginia*. Alexandria, VA: Alexandria Archaeology Publications, 1989.

———. "Free Black Adaptive Responses to the Antebellum Urban Environment: Neighborhood Formation and Socioeconomic Stratification in Alexandria, Virginia, 1790–1850." PhD diss., American University, 1988.

Bonastia, Christopher. *Knocking on the Door: The Federal Government's Attempt to Desegregate the Suburbs*. Princeton, NJ: Princeton University Press, 2006.

———. *Southern Stalemate: Five Years without Public Education in Prince Edward County, Virginia*. Chicago: University of Chicago Press, 2012.

Bromberg, Francine, and Pamela Cressey. "Digging the Past for Fifty Years: A Model for Community Archaeology." 45th Annual Society for Historical Archaeology Conference, Baltimore, MD, January 6, 2012.

Brooks, Richard R. W., and Carol M. Rose. *Saving the Neighborhood: Racially Restrictive Covenants, Law, and Social Norms*. Cambridge, MA: Harvard University Press, 2013.

Brown, Letitia Woods. *Free Negroes in the District of Columbia, 1790–1846*. New York: Oxford University Press, 1972.

Bruggeman, Seth C. *Here, George Washington Was Born: Memory, Material Culture, and the Public History of a National Monument*. Athens: University of Georgia Press, 2008.

Brundage, W. Fitzhugh, ed. *Where These Memories Grow: History, Memory, and Southern Identity*. Chapel Hill: University of North Carolina Press, 2000.

Burns, Andrea A. *From Storefront to Monument: Tracing the Public History of the Black Museum Movement*. Amherst: University of Massachusetts Press, 2013.

Butchart, Ronald E. "Freedmen's Teacher Project." Version 1. Harvard Dataverse. May 6, 2022. https://doi.org/10.7910/DVN/0HBDZD.

———. *Schooling the Freed People: Teaching, Learning, and the Struggle for Black Freedom, 1861–1876*. Chapel Hill: University of North Carolina Press, 2012.

Chacko, Elizabeth. "Ethiopian Ethos and the Creation of Ethnic Places in the Washington Metropolitan Area." *Journal of Cultural Geography* 20, no. 2 (2003): 21–42.

———. "Identity and Assimilation among Young Ethiopian Immigrants in Metropolitan Washington." *Geographical Review* 93, no. 4 (October 2003): 491–506.

Clavel, Pierre. *Activists in City Hall: The Progressive Response to the Reagan Era in Boston and Chicago*. Ithaca, NY: Cornell University Press, 2010.

Cohen, Lizabeth. *A Consumers' Republic: The Politics of Mass Consumption in Postwar America*. New York: Vintage, 2003.

Connolly, N. D. B. *A World More Concrete: Real Estate and the Remaking of Jim Crow South Florida*. Chicago: University of Chicago Press, 2014.

Cook, Robert J. *Troubled Commemoration: The American Civil War Centennial, 1861–1865*. Baton Rouge: Louisiana State University Press, 2007.

Cooling, Benjamin Franklin, III, and Walton H. Owen II. *Mr. Lincoln's Forts: A Guide to the Civil War Defenses of Washington*. Lanham, MD: Scarecrow Press, 2009.

Cox, Al. "The Alexandria Union Station." *Historic Alexandria Quarterly* 1, no. 1 (Winter 1996): 1–11.

Crampton, Alice C. *Supplemental Report: U.S. Army Reserve Training Headquarters: Survey and Evaluation.* Fairfax, VA: Parsons Engineering Science, March 1996.

Cressey, Pamela J. "The Alexandria, Virginia City-Site: Archaeology in an Afro-American Neighborhood, 1830–1910." PhD diss., University of Iowa, 1985.

Crothers, A. Glenn. "The 1846 Retrocession of Alexandria: Protecting Slavery and the Slave Trade in the District of Columbia." In *In the Shadow of Freedom: The Politics of Slavery in the National Capital,* edited by Paul Finkelman and Donald R. Kennon, 142–44. Athens: Ohio University Press, 2011.

————. *Quakers Living in the Lion's Mouth: The Society of Friends in Northern Virginia, 1730–1865.* Gainesville: University Press of Florida, 2012.

Dagbovie, Pero Gagloe. *The Early Black History Movement: Carter G. Woodson and Lorenzo Johnston Greene.* Champaign: University of Illinois Press, 2007.

————. "'Most Honorable Mention . . . Belongs to Washington, DC': The Carter G. Woodson Home and the Early Black History Movement in the Nation's Capital." *Journal of African American History* 96, no. 3 (Summer 2011): 295–324.

Dailey, Jane. *Before Jim Crow: The Politics of Race in Postemancipation Virginia.* Chapel Hill: University of North Carolina Press, 2000.

Dean, Adam Wesley. "'Who Controls the Past Controls the Future': The Virginia History Textbook Controversy." *Virginia Magazine of History and Biography* 117, no. 4 (2009): 321–31.

Deetz, James. *In Small Things Forgotten: An Archaeology of Early American Life.* New York: Anchor, 2010.

Delaney, David. *Race, Place, and the Law, 1836–1948.* Austin: University of Texas Press, 1998.

Denning, Michael. *The Cultural Front: The Laboring of American Culture in the Twentieth Century.* New York: Verso, 1997.

Dols, Jonathan R. "The Conduct of Union Soldiers toward Civilians in Alexandria, Virginia, and New Orleans, Louisiana." Master's thesis, Wake Forest University, 1995.

Downs, Jim. *Sick from Freedom: African-American Illness and Suffering during the Civil War and Reconstruction.* New York: Oxford University Press, 2015.

Doyle, Don H. *New Men, New Cities, New South: Atlanta, Nashville, Charleston, Mobile, 1860–1910.* Chapel Hill: University of North Carolina Press, 1990.

Du Bois, W. E. B. *Black Reconstruction; An Essay toward a History of the Part Which Black Folk Played in the Attempt to Reconstruct Democracy in America, 1860–1880.* New York: Harcourt, Brace, 1935.

Dwyer, Owen J., and Derek H. Alderman. *Civil Rights Memorials and the Geography of Memory.* Chicago: Center for American Places at Columbia College, 2008.

Evangelista, Matthew. *Innovation and the Arms Race: How the United States and the Soviet Union Develop New Military Technologies.* Ithaca, NY: Cornell University Press, 1988.

Fahs, Alice, and Joan Waugh, eds. *The Memory of the Civil War in American Culture.* Chapel Hill: University of North Carolina Press, 2004.

Farmer-Kaiser, Mary. *Freedwomen and the Freedman's Bureau: Race, Gender, and Public Policy in the Age of Emancipation.* New York: Fordham University Press, 2010.

Fenwick, Patricia Miles. "Urban Restoration in Old Town, Alexandria, Virginia." Master's thesis, Kent State University, 1969.

Ferguson, Karen J. *Black Politics in New Deal Atlanta*. Chapel Hill: University of North Carolina Press, 2002.

Finkelman, Paul, ed. *Encyclopedia of African American History, 1896 to the Present*. 5 vols. New York: Oxford University Press, 2009.

Finnan, Christine R., Rhonda Ann Cooperstein, and Anne R. Wright. *Southeast Asian Refugee Resettlement at the Local Level: The Role of the Ethnic Community and the Nature of Refugee Impact*. Menlo Park, CA: SRI International, November 1983.

Fleming, John E. "The Impact of Social Movements on the Development of African American Museums." *Public Historian* 40, no. 3 (August 2018): 44–73.

Foard, Ashley A., and Hilbert Fefferman. "Federal Urban Renewal Legislation." In *Urban Renewal: The Record and the Controversy*, edited by James Q. Wilson, 93–99. Cambridge, MA: Harvard University Press, 1966.

Foner, Eric. *Forever Free: The Story of Emancipation and Reconstruction*. New York: Vintage, 2006.

Freund, D. M. P. *Colored Property: State Policy and White Racial Politics in Suburban America*. Chicago: University of Chicago Press, 2008.

Friedman, Andrew. *Covert Capital: Landscapes of Denial and the Making of U.S. Empire in the Suburbs of Northern Virginia*. Berkeley: University of California Press, 2013.

Gastner, Mary Katherine. "Valuing 'Others': Free African American Neighborhoods in Antebellum Alexandria." Master's thesis, University of Maryland, 2011.

Gatewood, Willard B. *Aristocrats of Color: The Black Elite, 1880–1920*. Bloomington: Indiana University Press, 1990.

Gill, Andrea M. K. "Moving to Integration? The Origins of Chicago's Gautreaux Program and the Limits of Voucher-Based Housing Mobility." *Journal of Urban History* 38, no. 4 (July 2012): 662–86.

Gillette, Howard, Jr. *Between Justice and Beauty: Race, Planning, and the Failure of Urban Policy in Washington, D.C.* Baltimore, MD: Johns Hopkins University Press, 1995.

Gilmore, Glenda Elizabeth. *Gender and Jim Crow: Women and the Politics of White Supremacy in North Carolina 1896–1920*. Chapel Hill: University of North Carolina Press, 1996.

Givens, Jarvis R. *Fugitive Pedagogy: Carter G. Woodson and the Art of Black Teaching*. Cambridge, MA: Harvard University Press, 2021.

Gjelten, Tom. *A Nation of Nations: A Great American Immigration Story*. New York: Simon and Schuster, 2015.

Glass, Ruth. *Introduction to London: Aspects of Change*. London: Centre for Urban Studies, 1964.

Goggin, Jacqueline Anne. *Carter G. Woodson: A Life in Black History*. Baton Rouge: Louisiana State University Press, 1997.

Gordon, Colin. *Patchwork Apartheid: Private Restriction, Racial Segregation, and Urban Inequality*. New York: Russell Sage Foundation, 2023.

Gordon, Tammy S. *The Spirit of 1976: Commerce, Community, and the Politics of Commemoration*. Amherst: University of Massachusetts Press, 2013.

Green, Constance McLaughlin. *The Secret City: A History of Race Relations in the Nation's Capital*. Princeton, NJ: Princeton University Press, 1967.

———. *Washington: Village and Capital, 1800–1878*. Princeton, NJ: Princeton University Press, 1962.

Griffin, William E., Jr. *One Hundred Fifty Years of History along the Richmond, Fredericksburg and Potomac Railroad*. Richmond, VA: Whittet and Shepperson, 1984.

Hanna, Stephen P. "Placing the Enslaved at Oak Alley Plantation: Narratives, Spatial Contexts, and the Limits of Surrogation." *Journal of Heritage Tourism* 11, no. 3 (2015): 219–34.

Harris, Jennifer. "Barbara E. Pope 1854–1908." *Legacy: A Journal of American Women Writers* 32, no. 2 (2015): 281–97.

Harrold, Stanley. *Subversives: Antislavery Community in Washington, D.C., 1828–1865*. Baton Rouge: Louisiana State University Press, 2003.

Hayden, Dolores. *Building Suburbia: Green Fields and Urban Growth, 1820–1900*. New York: Vintage, 2004.

Hayes, Lawrence J. W. "Negro Federal Government Worker: A Study in His Classification Status in the District of Columbia." Master's thesis, Howard University, 1941.

Head, Simon. "Reagan, Nuclear Weapons, and the End of the Cold War." In *Ronald Reagan and the 1980s: Perceptions, Policies, Legacies*, edited by Cheryl Hudson and Gareth Davies, 81–100. New York: Palgrave, 2008.

Hickin, Patricia. "Gentle Agitator: Samuel M. Janney and the Anti-slavery Movement in Virginia, 1842–1851." *Journal of Southern History* 37 (May 1971): 168–72.

Hirsch, Arnold R. "Containment on the Home Front: Race and Federal Housing Policy from the New Deal to the Cold War." *Journal of Urban History* 26 (2000): 158–89.

———. *Making the Second Ghetto: Race and Housing in Chicago, 1940–1960*. Chicago: University of Chicago Press, 1983.

Holloway, Pippa. *Sexuality, Politics, and Social Control in Virginia, 1920–1945*. Chapel Hill: University of North Carolina Press, 2006.

Howard, Mark. "An Historical Study of the Desegregation of the Alexandria, Virginia, City Public Schools, 1954–1973." PhD diss., George Washington University, 1976.

Hume, Ivor Noël. *Martin's Hundred*. New York: Alfred A. Knopf, 1982.

Hunter, Tera W. *Bound in Wedlock: Slave and Free Black Marriage in the Nineteenth Century*. Cambridge, MA: Harvard University Press, 2017.

Hurst, Harold W. *Alexandria on the Potomac: The Portrait of an Antebellum Community*. Lanham, MD: University Press of America, 1991.

Jackson, Kenneth T. *Crabgrass Frontier: The Suburbanization of the United States*. New York: Oxford University Press, 1987.

Jackson, Luther Porter. *Free Negro Labor and Property Holding in Virginia, 1830–1860*. 1942. New York: Atheneum, 1969.

———. *Negro Office Holders in Virginia, 1865–1895*. Norfolk, VA: Guide Quality Press. 1946.

Jacobson, Mathew Frye. *Roots Too: White Ethnic Revival in Post–Civil Rights America*. Cambridge, MA: Harvard University Press, 2008.

Joassart-Marcelli, Pascale. *The $16 Taco: Contested Geographies of Food, Ethnicity, and Gentrification*. Seattle: University of Washington Press, 2021.

Johnson, Haynes. *Sleepwalking through History: America in the Reagan Years*. New York: W. W. Norton, 2003.

Johnson, Walter. *Soul by Soul: Life inside the Antebellum Slave Market*. Cambridge, MA: Harvard University Press, 1999.

Jones, Angela. *African American Civil Rights: Early Activism and the Niagara Movement*. New York: Praeger, 2011.

Jones, Jacqueline. *Labor of Love, Labor of Sorrow: Black Women, Work, and the Family from Slavery to the Present.* New York: Basic Books, 1985.

Kenzer, Robert C. *Enterprising Southerners: Black Economic Success in North Carolina, 1865–1915.* Charlottesville: University of Virginia Press, 1997.

———. *Kinship and Neighborhood in a Southern Community: Orange County, North Carolina, 1849–1881.* Knoxville: University of Tennessee Press, 1987.

Knack, Ruth, and Israel Stollam. "The Real Story Behind the Standard Planning and Zoning Acts of the 1920s." *Land Use Law* 48, no. 2 (February 1996): 3–9.

Kohler, Peter C. *Capital Transit: Washington's Street Cars: The Final Era 1933–1962.* Colesville, MD: National Capital Trolley Museum 2001.

Krislov, Samuel. *The Negro in Federal Employment: The Quest for Equal Opportunity.* Minneapolis: University of Minnesota Press, 1967.

Kytle, Ethan J., and Blain Roberts. *Denmark Vesey's Garden: Slavery and Memory in the Cradle of the Confederacy.* New York: The New Press, 2018.

Larkin, Brian Patrick. "Notes: The Forty-Year 'First Step': The Fair Housing Act as an Incomplete Tool for Suburban Integration." *Columbia Law Review* 107 (2007): 1621–24.

Lassiter, Matthew, and Andrew B. Lewis, eds. *The Moderates' Dilemma: Massive Resistance to School Desegregation in Virginia.* Charlottesville: University of Virginia Press, 1998.

Lawrence, Susan C. "Organization of the Hospitals in the Department of Washington." Civil War Washington. Accessed on July 8, 2018. http://civilwardc.org/introductions/other/hospitals.php.

Lechner, Ira M. "Massive Resistance: Virginia's Great Leap Backward." *Virginia Quarterly Review* 74 (Autumn 1998): 631–40.

Leib, Jonathan I. "A Tale of Two Civil War Statues: Teaching the Geographies of Memory and Heritage in Norfolk, Virginia." *Southeastern Geographer* 52, no. 4 (2012): 398–412.

Lewis, George. *Massive Resistance: The White Response to the Civil Rights Movement.* 2nd ed. Lanham, MD: Rowman and Littlefield, 2006.

Lieb, Emily. "The 'Baltimore Idea' and the Cities It Built." *Southern Cultures* 25, no. 2 (Summer 2019): 104–19.

Lightner, David L. *Slavery and the Commerce Power: How the Struggle against the Interstate Slave Trade Led to the Civil War.* New Haven, CT: Yale University Press, 2006.

Lindgren, James M. *Preserving the Old Dominion: Historic Preservation and Virginia Traditionalism.* Charlottesville: University of Virginia Press, 1993.

Lindsey, Treva. *Colored No More: Reinventing Black Womanhood in Washington, D.C.* Champaign: University of Illinois Press, 2017.

Lingeman, Richard R. *Don't You Know There's a War On? The American Home Front, 1941–1945.* Ann Arbor: University of Michigan Press, 1970.

Listokin, David C., Barbara Listokin, and Michael L. Lahr. "The Contributions of Historic Preservation to Housing and Economic Development." *Housing Policy Debate* 9, no. 3 (January 1998): 431–78.

Litwack, Leon F. *Been in the Storm So Long: The Aftermath of Slavery.* New York: Vintage, 1980.

Logan, Cameron. *Historic Capital: Preservation, Race, and Real Estate in Washington, D.C.* Minneapolis: University of Minnesota Press, 2017.

Manning, Chanda. *Troubled Refuge: Struggling for Freedom in the Civil War.* New York: Vintage, 2017.

Margo, Robert A. *Race and Schooling in the South, 1880–1950: An Economic History.* Chicago: University of Chicago Press, 1990.

Marling, Karal Ann. *George Washington Slept Here: Colonial Revivals and American Culture, 1876–1986.* Cambridge, MA: Harvard University Press, 1988.

Masur, Kate. *An Example for All the Land: Emancipation and the Struggle over Equality in Washington D.C.* Chapel Hill: University of North Carolina Press, 2010.

———. "Patronage and Protest in Kate Brown's Washington." *Journal of American History* 99, no. 4 (March 2013): 1047–71.

McCloskey, Patricia Ellen. "Urban Renewal and Historic Preservation: A Case Study of Alexandria, Virginia." Master's thesis, George Washington University, 1999.

McCord, T. B. *Across the Fence, but a World Apart: The Coleman Site, 1776–1907.* Alexandria, VA: Alexandria Urban Archaeological Program, 1985.

McQueeney, Kevin G. "More Than Recreation: Black Parks and Playgrounds in Jim Crow New Orleans." *Louisiana History* 60, no. 4 (Fall 2019): 437–78.

Meier, August, and Elliott Rudwick. *Black History and the Historical Profession, 1915–1980.* Champaign: University of Illinois Press, 1986.

———. "Negro Boycotts of Segregated Streetcars in Virginia, 1904–1907." *Virginia Magazine of History and Biography* 81, no. 4 (October 1973): 479–87.

Miliaras, Catherine K. "The Parker-Gray District: Examining a Local Historic District a Generation Later." *Alexandria Chronicle*, no. 1 (Spring 2015): 1–11.

Miller, Edward A., Jr. "Volunteers for Freedom: Black Civil War Soldiers in Alexandria National Cemetery, Part I." *Historic Alexandria Quarterly*, Fall 1998, 1–14.

Minchin, Timothy J., and John A. Salmond. *After the Dream: Black and White Southerners since 1965.* Lexington: University of Kentucky Press, 2011.

Mitchell-Powell, Brenda. *Public in Name Only: The 1939 Alexandria Library Sit-In Demonstration.* Amherst: University of Massachusetts Press, 2022.

Moon, Krystyn R. "The African American Housing Crisis in Alexandria, Virginia, 1930s–1960s." *Virginia Magazine of History and Biography* 124, no. 1 (2016): 28–68.

———. "The Alexandria YWCA, Race, and Urban (and Ethnic) Revival: The Scottish Christmas Walk, 1960s–1970s." *Journal of American Ethnic History* 35, no. 4 (Summer 2016): 59–92.

———. "Finding the Fort: African American History and Memory at Fort Ward Historic Park." Alexandria Archaeology, Office of Historic Alexandria, July 2014.

———. "Scottish White Ethnic Revivalism and Usable Pasts in Alexandria, Virginia." IEHS Online. Accessed December 31, 2019. https://iehs.org/krystyn-moon-scottish-white-alexandria.

Moore, Jacqueline M. *Leading the Race: The Transformation of the Black Elite in the Nation's Capital, 1880–1920.* Charlottesville: University Press of Virginia, 1999.

Morton, Richard Lee. *The Negro in Virginia Politics, 1865–1902.* Charlottesville: University of Virginia, 1919.

Murphy Kelley, Blair. *Right to Ride: Streetcar Boycotts and African American Citizenship in the Era of Plessy v. Ferguson.* Chapel Hill: University of North Carolina Press, 2010.

Myers Asch, Chris, and George Derek Musgrove. *Chocolate City: A History of Race and Democracy in the Nation's Capital* Chapel Hill: University of North Carolina Press, 2012.

Nelson, Kathryn P. *Gentrification and Distressed Cities: An Assessment of Trends in Intrametropolitan Migration.* Madison: University of Wisconsin Press, 1988.

Nesbitt, Francis Njubi. *Race for Sanctions: African Americans against Apartheid, 1946–1994.* Bloomington: Indiana University Press, 2004.

O'Brien, John T. "Reconstruction in Richmond: White Restoration and Black Protest, April–June 1865." *Virginia Magazine of History and Biography* 89, no. 3 (July 1981): 259–81.

O'Brien, William E. "State Parks and Jim Crow in the Decade before *Brown v. Board of Education*." *Geographical Review* 102, no. 2 (April 2012): 166–79.

Penningroth, Dylan C. *Claims of Kinfolk: African American Property and Community in the Nineteenth-Century South.* Chapel Hill: University of North Carolina Press, 2003.

Perry, Nancy, L. Earle Reybold, and Nigel Waters. "'Everybody Was Looking for a Good Government Job': Occupational Choice during Segregation in Arlington, Virginia." *Journal of Urban History* 40, no. 4 (2014): 719–41.

Pflugrad-Jackish, Ami. *Brothers of a Vow: Secret Fraternal Orders and the Transformation of White Male Culture in Antebellum Virginia.* Athens: University of Georgia Press, 2010.

Pope, Michael Lee. *Shotgun Justice: One Prosecutor's Crusade against Crime and Corruption in Alexandria and Arlington.* Charleston, SC: The History Press, 2012.

Preston, E. Delorus, Jr. "William Syphax, a Pioneer in Negro Education in the District of Columbia." *Journal of Negro History* 20, no. 4 (October 1935): 448–76.

Price, Marie, and Courtney Whitworth. "Soccer and Latino Cultural Space: Metropolitan Washington Fútbol Leagues." In *Hispanic Spaces, Latino Places: Community and Cultural Diversity in Contemporary America,* edited by Daniel D. Arreola, 167–87. Austin: University of Texas Press, 2004.

Price, Marie, and Elizabeth Chacko. "The Mixed Embeddedness of Ethnic Entrepreneurs in a New Immigrant Gateway." *Journal of Immigrant and Refugee Studies* 7 (2009): 328–46.

Prichard, Robert W., and Julia E. Randle. *Hail! Holy Hill! A Pictorial History of the Virginia Theological Seminary.* Brainerd, MN: RiverPlace Communication Arts, 2012.

Pritchett, Wendell E. *Robert Clifton Weaver and the American City: The Life and Times of an Urban Reformer.* Chicago: University of Chicago Press, 2008.

Rak, Jonathan. "A History of Zoning and Segregation in Virginia: Lessons for Today." Webinar. Center for Real Estate Entrepreneurship, George Mason University, April 29, 2021. www.youtube.com/watch?v=ongeywE-0B0.

Reed, Douglas S. *Building the Federal Schoolhouse: Localism and the American Education State.* New York: Oxford University Press, 2014.

Reft, Ryan. "The Suburb and the Sword: Wartime Housing, Integration, and Suburbanization in Alexandria, VA, 1942–1968." *Tropics of Meta: Historiography for the Masses* (blog), March 14, 2013. https://tropicsofmeta.wordpress.com/2013/03/14/the-suburb-and-the-sword-wartime-housing-integration-and-suburbanization-in-alexandria-va-1942-1968.

Reidy, Joseph P. "'Coming from the Shadow of the Past': The Transition from Slavery to Freedom at Freedmen's Village, 1863–1900." *Virginia Magazine of History and Biography* 95, no. 4 (October 1987): 403–28.

Repak, Terry A. *Waiting on Washington: Central American Workers in the Nation's Capital.* Philadelphia: Temple University Press, 1995.

Rhea, Joseph Tilden. *Race Pride and the American Identity.* Cambridge, MA: Harvard University Press, 1997.

Rice, Roger L. "Residential Segregation by Law, 1910–1917." *Journal of Southern History* 34, no. 2 (May 1968): 179–99.

Rogers, Ibram H. "The Black Campus Movement and the Institutionalization of Black Studies, 1965–1970." *Journal of African American Studies* 16, no. 1 (March 2021): 21–40.

Rome, Adam. *Bulldozer in the Countryside: Suburban Sprawl and the Rise of American Environmentalism*. New York: Cambridge University Press, 2001.

Rothman, Joshua D. *The Ledger and the Chain: How Domestic Slave Traders Shaped America*. New York: Basic Books, 2021.

Rothstein, Richard. *The Color of Law: A Forgotten History of How Our Government Segregated America*. New York: Liveright, 2017.

Rubio, Philip F. *There's Always Work at the Post Office: African American Postal Workers and the Fight for Jobs, Justice, and Equality*. Chapel Hill: University of North Carolina Press, 2010.

Ruble, Blair A. *Washington's U Street: A Biography*. Baltimore, MD: Johns Hopkins University Press, 2012.

Santucci, Larry. "Documenting Racially Restrictive Covenants in 20th Century Philadelphia." *Cityscape* 22, no. 3 (2020): 241–68.

Savage, Kirk. *Standing Soldiers, Kneeling Slaves: Race, War, and Monument in Nineteenth-Century America*. Princeton, NJ: Princeton University Press, 1997.

Schaller, Michael. *Reckoning with Reagan: America and Its President in the 1980s*. New York: Oxford University Press, 1994.

Schrag, Zachary M. *The Great Society Subway: A History of the Washington Metro*. Baltimore, MD: Johns Hopkins University Press, 2006.

Schwab, Rochelle H. "Patterns of Relocation and Adjustment from an Urban Renewal Area." Master's thesis, Howard University, 1969.

Schwalm, Leslie A. *A Hard Fight for We: Women's Transition from Slavery to Freedom in South Carolina*. Champaign: University of Illinois Press, 1997.

Scott, Pamela. *Capital Engineers: The U.S. Army Corps of Engineers in the Development of Washington, D.C., 1790–2004*. Alexandria, VA: US Army Corps of Engineers, Office of History, 2011.

Seehorn Brandt, Beverly. "The Alexandria, Virginia, Library: Its History, Present Facilities, and Future Program." PhD diss., Catholic University of America, 1950.

Sherman, Richard B. "The 'Teachings at Hampton Institute': Social Equality, Racial Integrity, and the Public Assemblages Act of 1926." *Virginia Magazine of History and Biography* 95, no. 3 (July 1987): 275–300.

Shoenfeld, Sarah Jane, and Mara Cherkasky. "'A Strictly White Residential Section': The Rise and Demise of Racially Restrictive Covenants in Bloomingdale." *Washington History* 29, no. 1 (Spring 2017): 24–41.

Simkins, Francis Butler. *Virginia: History, Government, Geography*. New York: Scribner, 1957.

Singer, Audrey. "Metropolitan Washington: A New Immigrant Gateway." In *Hispanic Migration and Urban Development: Studies from Washington, D.C.*, edited by Enrique S. Pumar, 3–24. Washington, DC: Emerald, 2013.

Sipe, Boyd, and Kimberly Snyder. *Documentary Study and Archaeological Resource Assessment for the James Bland Homes, City of Alexandria, Virginia*. Gainesville, VA: Thunderbird Archaeology, 2010.

Skowronek, Stephen. *Building a New American State: The Expansion of National Administrative Capacities, 1877–1920*. New York: Cambridge University Press, 1982.

Smith, J. Clay, Jr. *Emancipation: The Making of the Black Lawyer 1844–1944*. Philadelphia: University of Pennsylvania Press, 1993.

Smith, J. Douglas. *Managing White Supremacy: Race, Politics, and Citizenship in Jim Crow Virginia*. Chapel Hill: University of North Carolina Press, 2002.

———. "'When Reason Collides with Prejudice': Armistead Lloyd Boothe and the Politics of Moderation." In *The Moderates' Dilemma: Massive Resistance to School Desegregation in Virginia*, edited by Matthew Lassiter and Andrew B. Lewis, 22–50. Charlottesville: University of Virginia Press, 1998.

Smith, Peter H. "The Beginnings of Historic Preservation in Alexandria—Moving Toward the Creation of the Old and Historic District." *Alexandria Chronicle* 4 (Winter 1996): 1–34.

———. "The Saga of Saving and Reconstructing Ramsay House." *Alexandria Chronicle Commemorative Issue* 7 (Winter–Spring 1998–99): 2–33.

Smith, Ryan K. "Philip N. J. Wythe's Headstone." *Southern Cultures* 23, no. 3 (Fall 2017): 39–46.

Sprinkle, John H., Jr. *Heritage Conservation in the United States: Enhancing the Presence of the Past*. New York: Routledge, 2023.

St. Pierre, Maurice A. "Reaganomics and Its Implications for African-American Family Life." *Journal of Black Studies* 21, no. 3 (March 1991): 325–40.

Sugrue, Thomas J. *The Origins of the Urban Crisis: Race and Inequality in Postwar Detroit*. Chapel Hill: University of North Carolina Press, 1996.

Suydam, Marty. "From Trolley Park to Sewage Treatment: Luna Park." *Arlington Historical Magazine* 15, no. 4 (2016): 45–47.

Tang, Eric. *Unsettled: Cambodian Refugees in the NYC Hyperghetto*. Philadelphia: Temple University Press, 2015.

Tappey Squires, William Henry. *Unleashed at Long Last: Reconstruction in Virginia, April 9, 1865–January 26, 1870*. Portsmouth, VA: Printcraft Press, 1939.

Tarnapol Whitacre, Paula. *A Civil Life in an Uncivil Time: Julia Wilbur's Struggle for Purpose*. Lincoln: Potomac Books, 2017.

Taylor, Keeanga-Yamahtta. *Race for Profit: How Banks and the Real Estate Industry Undermined Black Homeownership*. Chapel Hill: University of North Carolina Press, 2019.

Teaford, Jon C. *The Rough Road to Renaissance: Urban Revitalization in America, 1940–1985*. Baltimore, MD: Johns Hopkins University Press, 1990.

Tindall, William. "Beginnings of Street Railways in the National Capital." *Records of the Columbia Historical Society* 21 (1918): 24–86.

Trevilian Moncure, Henry. "The School Progress and Social Adjustment of a Selected Group of Pupils Entering Alexandria, Virginia, High School in 1926." PhD diss., College of William and Mary, 1936.

Trischmann, Laura V. *"The Faithful Contrabands Will Be Justly Entitled to Their Share": A History of the Contrabands and Freedmen Cemetery in Alexandria, Virginia*. Washington, DC: EHT Traceries, September 2015.

Tuck, Stephen G. N. "African American Protest during the Reagan Years: Forging New Agendas, Defending Old Victories." In *Ronald Reagan and the 1980s: Perceptions, Policies, Legacies*, edited by Cheryl Hudson and Gareth Davies, 119–34. New York: Palgrave, 2008.

———. *Beyond Atlanta: The Struggle for Racial Equality in Georgia, 1940–1980*. Athens: University of Georgia Press, 2003.

Tyler-McGraw, Marie. *An African Republic: Black and White Virginians in the Making of Liberia.* Chapel Hill: University of North Carolina Press, 2007.

Vaughn, Curtis L. "Freedom Is Not Enough: African Americans in Antebellum Fairfax County." PhD diss., George Mason University, 2014.

von Hoffman, Alexander. *House by House, Block by Block: The Rebirth of America's Urban Neighborhoods.* New York: Oxford University Press, 2004.

Vose, Clement E. *Caucasians Only: The Supreme Court, the NAACP, and the Restrictive Covenant Cases.* Berkeley: University of California Press, 1959.

Walker, Mark K., Madelein Pappas, Jesse Daugherty, Christopher Martin, and Elizabeth A. Crowell. *Archaeological Evaluation of the Alfred Street Baptist Church (44X161) Alexandria, Virginia.* Washington, DC: Engineering Science, Chartered, December 1992.

Wallace, Alton S., Katherine E. Cain, and Carolyn C. Rowe. *I Once Was Young: History of the Alfred Street Baptist Church, 1803–2003.* Littleton, MA: Tapestry Press, 2003.

Wallenstein, Peter. *Blue Laws and Black Codes: Conflict, Courts, and Change in Twentieth-Century Virginia.* Charlottesville: University of Virginia Press, 2004.

———. *Race, Sex, and the Freedom to Marry: Loving v. Virginia.* Lawrence: University Press of Kansas, 2014.

Wartman, Michelle. "Contraband, Runaways, Freemen: New Definitions of Reconstruction Created by the Civil War." *International Social Science Review* 76, no. 3–4 (2001): 122–29.

Wei, William. *The Asian American Movement.* Philadelphia: Temple University Press, 1993.

Wessler, Seth Freed. "Developers Found Graves in the Virginia Woods." *ProPublica,* December 16, 2022. www.propublica.org/article/how-authorities-erased-historic-black-cemetery-virginia.

Wiese, Andrew. *Places of Their Own: African American Suburbanization in the Twentieth Century.* Chicago: University of Chicago Press, 2005.

Wiggins, William H., Jr. *O Freedom! Afro-American Emancipation Celebrations.* Knoxville: University of Tennessee Press, 1987.

Williams, Heather Andrea. *Help Me Find My People: The African American Search for Family Lost in Slavery.* Chapel Hill: University of North Carolina Press, 2012.

Wilson, Mabel O. *The Negro Building: Black Americans in the World of Fairs and Museums.* Berkeley: University of California Press, 2021.

Winnick, Louis. "The Triumph of Housing Allowance Programs: How a Fundamental Policy Conflict Was Resolved." *Cityscape: A Journal of Policy Development and Research* 1, no. 3 (September 1995): 95–121.

Wolcott, Victoria W. *Struggle over Segregated Recreation in America.* Philadelphia: University of Pennsylvania Press, 2014.

Woods, Michael J. "Alfred William Harris." In *Dictionary of the Library of Virginia.* Accessed June 8, 2024. http://mlkcommission.dls.virginia.gov/lincoln/pdfs/bios/harris_alfred_william.pdf.

Woodson, Carter G. *The Mis-education of the American Negro.* 1933. Reprint, Radford, VA: Wilder Publications, 2008.

Woodward, C. Vann. *The Strange Career of Jim Crow.* 1955. Reprint, New York: Oxford University Press, 2001.

Bibliography

Wynes, Charles E. *Race Relations in Virginia, 1870–1902.* Charlottesville: University of Virginia Press, 1961.

Yellin, Eric S. *Racism in the Nation's Service: Government Workers and the Color Line in Woodrow Wilson's America.* Chapel Hill: University of North Carolina Press, 2013.

Ziparo, Jessica. *This Grand Experiment: When Women Entered the Federal Workforce in Civil War–Era Washington, D.C.* Chapel Hill: University of North Carolina Press, 2017.

INDEX

Page numbers in italics refer to illustrations.

Greyhound Bus Company, 45
Groton Iron Works, 57–58
Gum Springs, VA, 85

Hackley, Ethel, 59
Haley, Alex, 118; *Roots*, 118
Hallowell School for Girls, 46, 49, 50
Hampton Institute, 48, 51
Hansberry, Catherine, 33
Harris, Alfred W., 47
Harris, Harrison L., 47
Harris, Jemima, 33
Hart–Cellar Act (1965), 92
Hawai'i, 111
Hayti, 4, 134
heritage tourism: Alexandria, 70–71, 76, 78, 124–25; Mount Vernon, 43, 57, 67–68
Hershaw, Lafayette M., 56
Historic Alexandria Foundation, 76
historic preservation, 124–32; Association for the Preservation of Virginia Antiquities, 125; Black vs. white, 9–10, 70–71 124–25; Board of Architectural Review, 74, 108, 125, 126; and gentrification, 9–10, 12, 107, 118, 125, 127, 131–32, 141; of housing, 116–17; Landmarks Society of Alexandria, 125; local legislation on, 131–32; Mount Vernon Ladies' Association, 9, 125; as neighborhood preservation, 127; Old and Historic District, 74, 125, 126, 127–28, 129, 131–32; Parker-Gray Special Historic Preservation District, 131–32; Society for the Restoration of Historic Alexandria, 125
Hollin, Lee, 57
Hopkins House, 59, 80
Horizon, The (periodical), 55
Horne, Frank, 80–81
housing: affordability of, 92–93; and annexation, 66–68, 73; civil rights activism and, 65, 71–72, 79–87; during Civil War, 20–21, 25–27; discrimination, 63–69, 71–72; and gentrification, 107–14; immigration and, 8–9, 11, 93,

103, 105–7, 109, 112–14; public housing, 71–72, 76–77, 81; racially restrictive covenants, 64, 67, 70; urban renewal, 73–79, 81–82; unsafe conditions in, 20, 31, 71, 74
Housing Act (1954), 75
Housing and Community Development Act (1974), 108
Howard, Oliver Otis, 30, 31, 34
Howard University, 47–48, 53–54, 59–60, 80, 120
Howe, Samuel G., 19
HUD, 8, 10, 65, 85, 92–93, 108, 112, 113, 125, 128–29, 131–32. *See also* Federal Housing Administration (FHA); HUD Act (1968)
HUD Act (1968), 91, 99, 129. *See also* HUD
Hughes, Jacob T., 109–10
Human Rights Ordinance (1963), 83–84
Hunnicutt, John W., 34
Hyatt, Thornton, 94

immigration, 8, 91–92, 103–6, 113–14; from Canada, 103; from Cuba, 103–4; from El Salvador, 9, 105, 106, 113; from Ethiopia and Eritrea, 9, 105–6, 113; and housing in Alexandria, 8–9, 11, 93, 103, 105–7, 109, 112–14; from Southeast Asia, 8, 104–5, 113
Indochinese Refugee Social Services, 104
industrialization, 8, 56–58, 59, 64, 68, 90, 92, 95, 143
in-migration, 2–3, 97, 104
Inner-City Civic Association, 126
Institute for Public Representation (Georgetown University), 111
integration, of schools. *See* desegregation, of schools

Jackson, Carrie, 59
Jackson, Lucinda, 30
Jackson, Luther Porter, 26, 120; *Free Negro Labor and Property Holdings in Virginia*, 120; *Negro Office Holders in Virginia*, 120
Jacobs, Harriet, 19–20, 21, 25–26

www.ingramcontent.com/pod-product-compliance
Lightning Source LLC
Chambersburg PA
CBHW030320270326
41926CB00010B/1440